PASADENA BEFORE THE ROSES

YVETTE J. SAAVEDRA

PASADENA BEFORE THE ROSES

Race, Identity, and Land Use in Southern California, 1771–1890

THE UNIVERSITY OF ARIZONA PRESS
TUCSON

The University of Arizona Press
www.uapress.arizona.edu

First paperback edition 2020

ISBN-13: 978-0-8165-3553-8 (cloth)
ISBN-13: 978-0-8165-4086-0 (paper)

Cover design by Carrie House, HOUSEdesign llc
Cover images: [*top*] Panoramic view of Mission Street and Orange Grove, ca. 1874, USC and California Historical Society; [*bottom*] Detail from *The Old Spanish and Mexican Ranchos of Los Angeles County* by Gerald Eddy, Courtesy of the Library of Congress, Geography and Map Division.

Publication of this book is made possible in part by the proceeds of a permanent endowment created with the assistance of a Challenge Grant from the National Endowment for the Humanities, a federal agency.

Library of Congress Cataloging-in-Publication Data
Names: Saavedra, Yvette J., author.
Title: Pasadena before the roses : race, identity, and land use in southern California, 1771–1890 / Yvette J. Saavedra.
Description: Tucson : The University of Arizona Press, 2018 | Includes bibliographical references and index.
Identifiers: LCCN 2018009205 | ISBN 9780816535538 (cloth : alk. paper)
Subjects: LCSH: Pasadena (Calif.)—History—19th century. | Pasadena (Calif.)—History—18th century.
Classification: LCC F869.P3 S23 2018 | DDC 979.4/93—dc23 LC record available at https://lccn.loc.gov/2018009205

Printed in the United States of America
⊗ This paper meets the requirements of ANSI/NISO Z39.48-1992 (Permanence of Paper).

CONTENTS

ILLUSTRATIONS

FIGURES

TABLES

ACKNOWLEDGMENTS

SO MANY WONDERFUL PEOPLE have accompanied me on the long and winding journey to completing this book. Both professionally and personally, I have had the backing of mentors, family, and friends who have guided and supported me in countless ways. I could not have completed this book or my PhD without them.

During my graduate study in borderlands history at the University of Texas at El Paso, Cheryl Martin, Jeffrey Shepherd, and Emma Pérez helped me develop my understanding of the past in a unique way. Their enthusiastic support of my creative interpretations and analysis, as well as their strength as scholars and professors, has greatly influenced the way I approach my scholarship and the profession. I offer a warm heartfelt thank-you to Deena González, professor, esteemed mentor, and trusted friend. Although I didn't know it then, my journey to the PhD began in her undergraduate Chicana/o history class so many years ago. Thank you for your invaluable support, guidance, and friendship throughout the years.

I would like to thank the archivists, librarians, and staff at the various repositories I used in putting this project together. I'd especially like to acknowledge those at the Huntington Library, the Bancroft Library, the Honnold-Mudd Library Special Collection in Claremont, the Los Angeles City Archives, Special Collections at the Pasadena City Library, the Santa Barbara Mission Archives, the California State Archives, the USC Libraries, the Seaver Center for Western History Research, and the California State Historical Society. I want to thank everyone from the University of Arizona Press, especially Kristen Buckles. Thank you for your help and support throughout the process; you helped make it a seamless and wonderful experience.

Throughout the years I have been fortunate enough to work with and learn from an amazing community of scholars. I especially thank Antonia Castañeda for her wonderful advice and help at the early stages of this project; her words were invaluable in my conceptualization of this work. I also thank the other scholars—Karen Davalos, Linda Heidenreich, Marne Campbell, Deena González, Annemarie Pérez, and Isabel Millán—who read this work in its different stages; their feedback along the way helped make it what it is today. To the women of MALCS (Mujeres Activas en Letras y Cambio Social), thank you for showing me the importance and value of the work we do as academics and women of color in the academy. I appreciate your guidance and help with my work but also admire you for your dedication to making a difference on a grander scale.

Thank you to my colleagues in the History Department and the College of Social and Behavioral Sciences at California State University San Bernardino. Your support has been crucial to finishing this project. From research funds and course releases to overall encouragement, you have provided much needed assistance. I truly am lucky to be in such a great department and institution.

Along this road, when I least expected it, I met my partner, Isabel Millán. Thank you for your unconditional love and support in all my endeavors—academic, professional, and otherwise. I thank you for patiently and critically listening to me talk about this work and encouraging me to just get it done. Thanks for your laughter and love, through the seemingly endless work sessions, the nerd weekends, and the stress; you have been my love, my colleague, and my best friend. I dedicate this book to my parents, Jorge and Leonor. Thank you for instilling in me a love of knowledge. Most of all, thank you for all your hard work; you provided me the opportunity to pursue my dreams, and for this I will be forever grateful. To Crystal, you inspire me in infinite ways; you may not know it, but you kept me going when I wanted to quit. Thanks to my friends Lamin Whittiker, Renee Valenuzuela, and Jose Guerra for your unwavering support. To my many other colleagues and friends—Manijeh Badiee, Annika Anderson, Liliana Gallegos, Cherstin Lyon, Marne Campbell, Karen Mary Davalos, and Jeff Shepherd—you all kept me sane through this process. To all of you, and the countless others who have made this book possible, thank you for helping me get here.

PASADENA BEFORE THE ROSES

INTRODUCTION

BEFORE THE ROSES

Every landscape is thus marked by and offers clues not just to its own history but also, and more profoundly, the layered accumulation of racial formations that are simultaneously local, national, and global.

LAURA BARRACLOUGH, *MAKING THE SAN FERNANDO VALLEY: RURAL LANDSCAPES, URBAN DEVELOPMENT, AND WHITE PRIVILEGE*

THE CITY OF PASADENA is world renowned for its annual Tournament of Roses Parade and Rose Bowl football game. On any given weekend, tourists and locals alike congregate along Colorado Boulevard in Old Town Pasadena to patronize the high-end shops, pubs, and gourmet restaurants. As they traverse the streets of Old Town, the building facades and alleyways transport them to turn-of-the-century Pasadena, a town that emerged out of a colossal land boom resulting from the railroad's inauguration into the region. Throughout the city, local establishments display countless photographs of orange groves, majestic landscapes, and harvest festivals—complete with pictures of men riding horses and ostriches—to tell the story of Pasadena's early American settlers. In 1873 pioneers from Indiana left the cold harsh Midwestern winters behind to establish an agricultural colony in Southern California. From 1873 to 1886 the Indiana Colony grew from a small colony into the city of Pasadena.

Framed in such a way, Pasadena's story is one of Anglo progress. These images and public displays produce a narrative that tether the modern city of Pasadena to its agricultural roots while simultaneously providing a story of transition or progression from uncivilized past to a civilized present.[1] This story represents the Indiana Colony as the beginning of the region's history, displacing the history of the Tongva Indians, Spanish missionaries and colonists, and Californios (Mexican rancheros) that came before the roses.

The story of Anglo progress in Pasadena is only one layer of a more complex regional history comprising Indigenous, Spanish, Californio, and American attempts to negotiate their landscapes, visions of land use, identities, status, and cultures during California's Mission, Rancho, and early American Periods. In this work, I conceptualize these negotiations within the theoretical frameworks of *competing visions* and *dynamic continuities*. Competing visions refer to the different ways that missionaries, rancheros, and American farmers perceived optimal land use and how these visions influenced their construction of sociocultural identities and hierarchies. I use dynamic continuity to refer to the commonalities that existed among attempts by missionaries, rancheros, and American farmers to maintain their positions of power in relationship to Indians and the landless classes.[2] These frameworks help explain the various contentious and complementary power relationships that emerged during the 120-year period during which San Gabriel Mission lands became Rancho San Pascual and subsequently Pasadena.

This book is a history of competing visions of land use and their effect on racial and cultural identity in Pasadena, California, from 1771 to 1890. By examining changing ideas about race, gender, culture, and land use in the San Gabriel region over 120 years, I explore how culturally subjective ideas about race and visions of optimal land use became tangible representations of Spanish, Californio, and American political projects of empire building, nation building, expansion, and conquest. I argue that racial and cultural attitudes about optimal land use defined regional inhabitants' social identities and determined social power dynamics that manifested themselves on the physical land through the mission, rancho, or homestead. A close look at the power dynamics in these relationships shows how optimal ideas of land use and improvement were the basis of Spanish, Californio, and American hegemony during their respective eras.

The establishment of the San Gabriel Mission among the Tongva people in 1771 changed Indigenous cultural practices and land use patterns. Missionaries' ideas about optimal land use affected how they sought to eradicate Indigenous culture and assimilate the Tongva into Christianity and Spanish culture. Because they considered farming and livestock grazing as indicative of a civilized society, Spanish missionaries imposed a labor regiment that required Indians to learn Spanish farming techniques and animal domestication as part of their "civilizing process."[3] The link between land and labor as an indication of civilization defined mission Indians based on their relationship to the land. Missionaries, and colonial society at large, referred to Indians as *gente sin razón* (people without reason) to distinguish them from Spanish missionaries and colonists, who were regarded as *gente de razón* (people of reason). As the mission grew in self-sufficiency and wealth, missionaries' vision of land use changed to one in which agricultural production and cattle grazing were ways of making profit. Indian labor then came to represent the means of obtaining and maintaining economic stability rather than solely a means of Indians' religious conversion. The imposition of labor on mission Indians in combination with perceptions of them as gente sin razón further solidified their place at the bottom of the colonial hierarchy while ensuring the missionaries' agricultural visions for the mission landscape.

Through the end of the eighteenth and the beginning of the nineteenth century, the San Gabriel Mission grew in wealth and regional influence. Increased regional trade and a steadily growing civilian population made the mission the region's economic center. An emerging landed class resentful of missionaries' control of premium lands indicted the mission system as an archaic institution that hindered the region's economic development. Mexican independence and liberalism gave rise to calls for mission secularization and Indian emancipation.

In 1833, when the implementation of the federal Secularization Act opened mission lands to private colonization, San Gabriel's mission lands became Rancho San Pascual. Through the creation of a social network based on familial relations and cultural bonds, would-be oligarchs took advantage of secularization's distribution of mission lands to obtain large land grants, resulting in the emergence of a rancho system and Californio identity linked to land ownership. By the late 1830s and 1840s the California rancho and ranchero class had successfully replaced the mission and the Franciscans of the previous era. The changing landscape and the increased desire and competition for land prompted many landowners to use economic denouncement, a process by which petitioners might increase their land holdings by claiming that land was abandoned due to the owner's financial inability to develop it. Throughout California, economic denouncements caused land to change hands among an elite class of people who defined honor by their ability to keep their lands. Rancho San Pascual was not immune to this process, and in the 1830s it changed hands twice amid charges of physical and economic abandonment. By emphasizing a racialized vision of land use sustained through their classification as Spanish gente de razón and the display of material culture, Californios placed themselves at the top of California's socioeconomic structure and the landless classes at the bottom.[4]

As the rancho era progressed and the region expanded, wealthy Californios' social differentiation based on a classed system of shared identity as gente de razón facilitated Euro-American migrants' integration into elite circles during the 1830s. After the American Conquest of 1848 the social order changed and Euro-Americans were no longer minorities within a Californio system, but were steadily increasing their status within an emerging racial hierarchy fueled by the ideals of Manifest Destiny and progress.[5] During the late 1840s, the ties that bound and separated California's social classes during the Mexican Period served to polarize them within the newly imposed Euro-American racial spectrum, a system that designated Mexicans as either Indians or white.[6] Within the new racial hierarchy, Californio elites called themselves "Spanish" as a way to keep their social status. While this helped them temporarily keep their property and social status, it forced lower-class Mexicans into a racialized labor force.[7]

After the U.S.-Mexico War ended in 1848, the ideologies of Manifest Destiny and American white supremacy prompted incoming Americans and elite Californios to negotiate the new politics of land within a racialized system. Both groups viewed land as something that provided benefit and enrichment. For Californios, the benefit was social status, while for Anglos, it fulfilled the vision of the yeoman farmer. Both groups contested their positions in society and sought to use land as a means to integrate themselves into the new sociocultural and political circles.

Between 1860 and 1870, elite Californio families, many of whose daughters had intermarried with Euro-Americans in previous years, worked to redefine their social position within the ideology of Manifest Destiny and Euro-American white supremacy.[8] Aspiring to prove their status, elites attempted to maintain a façade of wealth and a white racial identity within an increasingly racialized capitalist economy.[9] As Californios lost their lands through Euro-Americans' unscrupulous business practices and legal maneuvers, aspiring Euro-American elites claimed these rich lands and carved a place for themselves within California's emerging American economy. It was within this context that Rancho San Pascual changed hands and became American.

Distribution and settlement of Rancho San Pascual's land during the 1870s and 1880s followed Southern California's broader settlement trends based on small-scale suburban agriculture or gentleman farming. This racialized vision of land use emphasized the development of the region through the establishment of small homesteads by white middle-class landowners.[10] In 1873 the Indiana Colony purchased Rancho San Pascual and established its homes, renaming the land Pasadena in 1874. By the 1880s, citrus groves, the American homestead, and the farmer had replaced the rancho, displacing the historical presence of the Californio population that had built the area. The opening of the railroad in the region in 1885 and subsequent land booms brought a steady flow of Euro-American tourists and settlers into Southern California, prompting a new vision of land use. The Pasadena of the 1890s moved away from its agricultural roots toward becoming a commercial tourist destination. This vision of optimal land framed Pasadena's future into the twentieth century and beyond.

Pasadena Before the Roses contends that subjective ideas about race, culture, and land use produced social identities that created, maintained, or dismantled the spatiality of the dominant order. Each dominant group's ideas about race, culture, and land use were tied to specific social identities and hierarchies and determined how the physical land would be used. Rancho San Pascual and later Pasadena's landscape represents the physical manifestation of the racial and cultural ideals of each group that controlled the region over the course of 120 years. This contention is informed by spatial and landscape theories proposed by scholars such as Edward Soja, Denis Cosgrove, Michael Dear, and Jennifer Wolch, who understand space as a location for the production of social meaning, social formation, and territorial power.[11] The processes of Spanish colonialism, mission secularization, and the American Conquest—each imbued with its own ideologies of colonialism, liberalism, and Manifest Destiny—produced a specific organization of space to help establish power.[12] Each of these spaces—the Mission, the Rancho, and the American Homestead—became a site for the production and negotiation of identity. They are part of a sociospatial dialectic in which missionaries and Indians, rancheros and the landless classes, and American farmers and land speculators gave meaning to the spaces that they inhabited in their daily lives during a specific historical moment.[13]

This comprehensive study of the dynamics of identity and land use in the Pasadena region over time and place makes an important contribution to understanding how this region and its peoples were marked by multiple moments of colonization. Employing the decolonial methodology suggested by historian Emma Pérez, this work expands the temporal and spatial parameters of what is considered California's Colonial Period to show the far-reaching effects and physical materialization of colonialism.[14] It examines how the power of colonialism and colonial institutions or colonial projects created specific relationships between those defined as colonizer and colonized through different historical eras. The Spanish colonial project of the mission, the rancho and settler-colonialism of the Californios, and the ideal of the American gentleman farmer and American homestead created power dynamics that determined societal hierarchies based on colonial constructs of difference.

Recognizing the different manifestations of colonialism across these different eras, this work adds to the larger historiography of Chicana/o studies and California history that illustrate both the imposition of dominance and the contestation of power.[15] It contributes to scholarship that examines the regional development of the greater Los Angeles area and the lived experiences of the Mexican and Mexican American populations. Influenced by Albert Camarillo's foundational text *Chicanos in a Changing Society*, it examines community formation and adaptation to changing social, political, and economic structures.[16] It contributes to a historiography of regional scholarship that decentralizes Los Angeles and studies the creation of community and social identity outside the city proper, focusing on more rural and suburban areas and how they are shaped by their specific dynamics of race, class, and gender during different historical moments.[17] Specifically relevant to the present work are Garcia and Romo's studies on the San Gabriel Valley and East Los Angeles, respectively—both areas that are located on former San Gabriel lands, the first consisting of Rancho San Pascual lands. Both studies focus on the twentieth century while *Pasadena Before the Roses* provides an examination of the region's Spanish Colonial and Mexican Periods. This work adds to the knowledge of this specific region and its influence in the development of the regional economy and patterns of settlement.

Similar to Lisbeth Haas's study on the San Juan Capistrano Mission's connection to the city of Santa Ana, this book provides an important understanding of the San Gabriel Mission's role in the development of Pasadena and the larger San Gabriel Valley region. It examines how, over time, changes in land use affected the meaning of place and resulted in the continuous redefining of race and identity in these spaces.[18] Additionally, by utilizing the concepts of rural urbanism and gentleman farming as applied by Laura Barraclough in her study on the development of twentieth century San Fernando, *Pasadena Before the Roses* interrogates the racial discourse connected to the Pasadena region's development during the 1870s. By combining gentleman farming with the Jeffersonian concept of the yeoman farmer, it illustrates how Pasadena's land speculators attracted potential settlers by utilizing a racialized discourse reflective of Manifest Destiny.[19]

Although focused on the emergence of the Pasadena and San Gabriel region, this work is in dialogue with scholarship that examines the emergence of Los

Angeles. Most of this scholarship focuses on Los Angeles's development as an urban area after 1850.[20] David Torres-Rouff's recent work *Before L.A.*, examines the development of Los Angeles from 1781 to 1894.[21] Similar in period and topics, Torres-Rouff's work focuses more on racialization, land use, and cultural change in Los Angeles as an urban center. Most of the change is marked through public policy and municipal development after the 1840s. *Pasadena Before the Roses* complements this work in that it provides a more in-depth examination of the region from which Los Angeles came. It situates the mission as the center of the regional economy and shows how the early Pueblo de Los Angeles survived and thrived through foodstuffs, goods, and labor provided from the San Gabriel Mission. Rather than looking at Pasadena as a suburb of Los Angeles, *Pasadena Before the Roses* shows that the present interconnectedness of the cities of Pasadena and Los Angeles is a consequence of the historical links created throughout the Spanish (mission/colonial), Mexican (rancho), and early American (homestead) periods. It details the development of social, economic, and political relationships that affected community settlement; land speculation; and most importantly, the distribution of power within the region during each era. It examines the multiple ways in which people in the areas that once were part of the San Gabriel Mission lands negotiated relationships with each other and with the land.

Along the same vein as recent studies that use a methodological approach informed by intersectionality, *Pasadena Before the Roses* looks at the history of the region through an analytical lens that examines race, class, gender, and sexuality. Following the methodology of Chicana historians who investigate land ownership, dispossession, and women's rights during different waves of conquest and colonization, I look at how racialized visions of land reflected the dominant group's patriarchal structure through its ideas of land ownership. Expanding on the work of Chicana scholars such as Deena J. González, Antonia Castañeda, Miroslava Chávez-Garcia, Angelina Veyna, and Linda Heidenreich, all of whom discuss land and gender dynamics in different areas of the Southwest from the colonial period to the American conquest, I show how men and women in the San Pascual/Pasadena region continuously negotiated their space through land ownership and visions of land use.[22] Contributing to this scholarship, historian Louise Pubols utilized a gender-based framework to interrogate the role patriarchal power played in the establishment of wealthy Californio families' political and social power.[23] Pubols argued that a stable yet malleable patriarchy helped create the political, social, economic, and cultural order of

Spanish and Mexican California. Building on this work, *Pasadena Before the Roses* conceptualizes gender not only through its effects on the roles of men and women but also by analyzing how visions of land use impacted the shape of masculinity and femininity. Specifically, this work examines the construction of gender roles and the deployment of masculinity and patriarchy through men's land ownership and the establishment of a stable, respectable homestead based on patriarchal control in the ranchos surrounding San Pascual.

Pasadena Before the Roses adds another layer to Pasadena's history by studying the interaction between the land and its people. Although people defined the land, this project demonstrates that, through these different periods of conquest and colonization, it was the land that determined how the people lived. This project provides an additional history for this world-renowned city, not in an attempt to erase the pioneer past, but rather to show the city's multiple layers of history. By focusing on the San Gabriel Mission, San Pascual, and later Pasadena, *Pasadena Before the Roses* traces the region and its peoples, transitions, and negotiations through its multiple (re)creations during different historical moments. Examining the connection between visions of land use and identity, it shows how the area that became Pasadena is unique in its transitions from being a center of social, cultural, and economic production during the Spanish colonial era; to acting as an agricultural hub during the rancho period; and to becoming a suburban satellite of Los Angeles in the American age—through it all defining and redefining the region's economy and culture. In this way, the book details the region's historical importance to the greater Los Angeles area. In a broader sense, it adds to our understanding of American history and regional history by moving past the constructed metanarrative of American progress and recognizing that the history of the American Southwest is representative of several layers of political, governmental, social, and cultural ideologies and a vast diversity of peoples and landscapes.

SOURCES

To examine the effect of optimal visions of land use on the creation of cultural and racial classification throughout these disparate periods, I conducted extensive archival research and reviews of public and private historical records for each era. For an understanding of Franciscans' attitudes about Indian culture, conversion, and labor and the missions' role in the region and land, I examined personal correspondence of mission priests and their superiors. Additionally, for economic information on the missions and their financial role in the region, I reviewed annual reports, mission inventories, and business correspondence between mission priests, military officials, and civilian settlers. Sources for the Mexican/Californio Period include *testimonios* of prominent Californias/os and articles from *El Clamor Público*, the first Spanish-language newspaper in Los Angeles after the U.S.-Mexico War. For the American period, I examined personal correspondence among early Pasadena settlers (the Indiana Colony) and land scout Daniel Berry, as well as widely read nineteenth century regional travel accounts. Other sources include the personal and financial papers of Benjamin Davis Wilson, a prominent Los Angeles politician, businessman, and owner of San Pascual. Lastly, to explore the links among land ownership, race, class, and cultural identity in San Pascual and the surrounding region, I reviewed matrimonial investigations, baptismal records, Mexican land case files, property deeds, and the Spanish and Mexican *padrón* (census), as well as the U.S. Federal Census.

ORGANIZATION

This work is organized into three parts. Each part contains two chapters detailing the manifestation of visions of land use through physical landscape and its effects on social identity and culture. Each part is divided into historical periods and reflects the major land use form that dominated that space: the Mission, the Rancho, and the American Homestead, respectively.

Part I reviews the general social, economic, and cultural role of the missions in Spanish expansion and colonization into the areas north of San Diego, or Alta California. Specifically, it examines the San Gabriel Mission's role in the development of the San Gabriel region from 1771 to 1833. Chapter 1 is largely structured as a synthesis of existing literature on the Mission Period; it provides context and a review for readers unfamiliar with the mission's role in Spanish colonization efforts and its economic, social, and cultural impact on Alta California. Additionally, this chapter analyzes the links between the Spanish colonial project and visions of land use to show that the meaning and purpose of missionaries' imposition of agricultural labor on Indians changed between the years 1771 and 1790. It details how during the early Mission Period labor was part of the missionaries' imposed conversion program, but later became a way to provide for the mission's economic survival. Most importantly, this chapter explores how ideas of land use were integral to establishing the relationships among Spanish missionaries, colonial settlers, and Tongva Indians. Chapter 2 examines the growth of the mission economy from 1771 through 1833. By investigating the development of the San Gabriel Mission's economy within the context of Mexican independence and Mexican liberalism, this chapter illustrates that the growing conflict between missionaries and landed elites was a result of differing visions of land use based on profit.

Part II examines the emergence of the rancho as a physical space and a site of cultural production from 1833 to 1846. It details the patterns of land distribution in the region that became Rancho San Pascual. Chapter 3 demonstrates how mission secularization and Indian emancipation in Alta California facilitated the creation of the rancho system and solidified the Californios' link to the land. It provides a detailed examination of Rancho San Pascual's creation from San Gabriel Mission lands and explores how the processes of economic denouncement and land petition were connected to race and masculinity.

Chapter 4 explores various aspects and markings of Californio culture. Topics include material representations of wealth, as well as the creation of the honorable ranchero and homestead though control of the land, labor, and family. Additionally, this chapter details American immigrants' assimilation into ranchero culture during the 1830s and rancheros' use of pragmatic social cohesiveness to maintain social power and status.

Part III studies American visions of land use framed within the ideologies of Manifest Destiny and white supremacy from 1846 to 1890. I examine wealthy Californios' attempts at negotiating their place within the newly imposed racial structure by using previously established ideas of class unity. Through the example of Rancho San Pascual, these chapters illustrate the implementation of an exclusively racialized land system that legitimized the Californios' dispossession and facilitated the distribution of land for the purpose of creating a region of American homesteads inhabited by gentlemen farmers.

Chapter 5 examines the growth of California's Euro-American population after 1840 and the subsequent U.S.-Mexico War. It studies the continued development of Rancho San Pascual within the context of Manifest Destiny and white supremacy and shows Californios' attempts to navigate the incoming racialized social structure as a means to maintain social status and power. It demonstrates the process of land loss and dispossession through Manuel Garfias's loss of rancho San Pascual to Benjamin Wilson in 1853 and provides a detailed discussion of the distribution of Rancho San Pascual during the American Period.

Chapter 6 analyzes the establishment of the Indiana Colony in Pasadena in the 1870s within the context of a vision of land use rooted in urban ruralism and gentleman farming. It details the broader regional visions of land use in the San Gabriel Valley as well as their influence on the specific ideals held by the Indiana colonists. This chapter also examines the land booms and their role in shifting visions of land use from agriculture to tourism.

PART I

THE MISSION PERIOD

1

THE SPANISH COLONIAL PROJECT

Franciscans, Missions, and Land Use in Alta California

SPAIN'S USE OF CHRISTIAN MISSIONIZING as part of New Spain's colonization dates to 1523, following the conquest of the Aztecs. By 1526, the Spanish Crown issued orders requiring at least two priests to accompany each exploring party.[1] The Franciscan order heeded the call and quickly worked to convert Indigenous groups throughout the Spanish Empire.[2] As missionaries entered into new areas, the Crown issued the Royal Order for New Discoveries in 1573, linking Christian missionary efforts to the Crown's imperial expansion and making missionaries into agents of colonization.[3] Missionaries worked to convert Indians while at the same time helping the military bring new lands under Spanish imperial and cultural control.[4]

In May of 1768, in response to word that Russians had landed on California's coast, New Spain's visitador general, José de Gálvez y Gallardo, who was responsible for administering the affairs of the crown in the Spanish colonies, received authorization to occupy Alta California's Monterey Bay.[5] That same month, Gálvez sent naval and overland expeditions to settle Monterey. Various obstacles impeded the successful launch of the expedition. Gálvez, seeing no other alternative, turned to missionaries to help settle Alta California.[6] Although Gálvez found the missions cost effective because they could "manage Indians at a low cost," he did not fully support their use because he believed that they stunted regional economic growth and delayed Indians' full assimilation into Spanish culture.[7] Despite his reservations, he reluctantly agreed to use both the military and the missionaries to expand Spain's eighteenth century vision of empire into Alta California. Spain's desire to protect its northern border from potential foreign encroachment would lead to the establishment of a twenty-one-mission system spanning seven hundred miles along the California coastline, a system that represented Spain's colonial presence in Alta California.

Franciscan missionaries' entrance into Alta California proved to be the point of origin for the region's civilian settlements. Although the missions were the first Spanish institution in Alta California, eighteenth century colonial policy required the establishment of presidios, or military garrisons, to accompany missions.[8] Presidios were manned by frontier soldiers, known as *soldados de cuera* (leather-jacketed soldiers), who were to protect the northern outskirts of the empire from Indian revolts and foreign encroachments.[9] Due to their geographical isolation, governmental neglect, and haphazard development, the garrison commanders had no real plan on how to provide stability for frontier regions, often becoming reliant on the missions for survival.[10]

Missionaries functioned on the fringes of empire as representatives of the Church and the State. In their religious capacity, they were charged with gaining members for the Church through conversion, assimilation, and eradication of Indigenous culture. As representatives of the Crown, their purpose was to exert Spanish territorial control, expand trade, gain subjects, and incorporate these subjects into Spanish society.[11] In California, missionaries had to negotiate their dual roles to satisfy both their goal of religious conversion and the secular goal of territorial acquisition. As the missions grew in size and production increased, they provided the stability needed for the establishment of secular pueblos at San José in 1777, Los Angeles in 1781, and Branciforte in 1797. As missions became self-sufficient and were recognized as hubs of regional production on which settlers depended for survival, missionaries' dual roles merged.

As mission profits rose due to increased demands for supplies, missionaries concerned themselves with gaining wealth to support the mission and by extension the growing number of colonial settlers and soldiers. This prompted a change in Franciscans' vision of land use from one focused on subsistence agriculture and ranching to one producing surplus agriculture and the sale of tallow and hide. This shift in land use led to increased reliance on and exploitation of Indigenous labor.

Franciscans' vision of land use resonated with the centuries old *Leyes de las Indias* that guaranteed Indians access to land they needed for their subsistence, lands that missionaries held in trust until these converted neophytes were ready to manage them.[12] This vision hinged on the idea that missions were temporary institutions that could be used to quickly convert and assimilate Indians into Spanish Christian society within ten years. Because the missions were seen as temporary, there was no immediate discussion of missionaries' prolonged control of these newly conquered regions.[13] The conflict over land arose as early as the 1780s, when Fray Junípero Serra stated that Franciscans could not assimilate Alta California's Indians in the allotted ten-year period.[14] As colonization progressed and more Indians came into the missions, Franciscans asserted strong claims over mission lands and Indian labor. The expanding population of newly converted Indians, compounded by the mission system's growing self-sufficiency and continued missionary presence on the frontier, brought an array of questions and conflicts over how much land missionaries could hold for their mission neophytes.

Franciscans' use of mission lands for agricultural production and grazing livestock reflected the merging of their spiritual, economic, and political goals. By controlling mission Indians' labor, Franciscans filled regional needs and created an economy based on horticulture, agriculture, ranching, and regional trade.[15] As the demand increased during the late 1790s, the meaning and importance of Indian mission labor changed. While at first missionaries had perceived Indian labor as proof of their assimilation, this labor now represented a way for missionaries to maintain regional economic control. The growth of regional economic self-sufficiency changed the mission project and the Franciscans' vision of land use, making the mission institution a very powerful socioeconomic structure in Alta California.

THE MISSION PROJECT: CONVERSION, LABOR, AND LAND

Franciscan missionaries, the military, and the government entered San Gabriel with the goal of territorial conquest through social control.[16] As Alta California's first settlement, the mission institution was charged with creating the foundation for other Spanish institutions. The extraction of Indigenous labor was at the center of missions' success. To this end, the most important step towards achieving settlement was the *reducción* or segregation of Indians into Christian settlements in the missions. Once semi-sedentary hunters and gatherers were collected from their *rancherías* or villages, the work of appropriating their labor

FIGURE 1 Exterior view of San Gabriel Mission, ca. 1870. Courtesy of the University of Southern California Libraries and California Historical Society. Digitally reproduced by the USC Digital Library; from the California Historical Society Collection at the University of Southern California, http://digitallibrary.usc.edu/cdm/singleitem/collection/p15799coll65/id/6419/rec/2.

for the colonial mission began. Successful implementation of the colonial project required missionaries to change Indigenous peoples' practices and control their labor, measures that proved detrimental to Indian subsistence and culture.

In August of 1771 the Portola expedition, consisting of ten Spanish soldiers and two Franciscan priests, encountered armed Tongva Indians on the banks of the Santa Ana River, near present-day Los Angeles.[17] One month later, Franciscan missionaries founded the San Gabriel Arcángel Mission (see fig. 1). This was the fourth of twenty-one missions built between 1769 and 1823 and the first established amongst the Tongva people. At first contact in 1771, the Tongva people numbered over five thousand. The Tongva were part of the Uto-Aztecan linguistic group, speaking dialects from the Takic dialect family.[18] Their village settlements were in a vast area of Southern California covering the entire Los Angeles basin, the area as far north as Santa Barbara, and south toward San Clemente.[19] Each village had its own distinct name and *tumia'r* (chief) and was politically autonomous.[20]

The characteristics of Tongva settlements and diets were determined by geography. Settlements were often located near water sources and varied from seasonal to permanent village. The Akuranga village, the Tongva settlement closest to the Mission San Gabriel, survived through hunting and gathering. To supply their dietary needs, men hunted small game and women gathered piñones (pine nuts), and acorns.[21] Because the inland groups did not engage in fishing, they participated in a well-established trade network with their coastal brethren who did, giving them access to fish and shellfish. During the winter months, inland groups separated into family units and migrated to the shellfish-gathering areas of San Pedro.[22] Despite the Tongva's widespread settlements, their dialectic variation, and their autonomous structure, villages were bound together by economic, social, and religious ties.[23]

Prior to Spanish arrival, the Tongva had a well-established society, culture, and economy. Religious beliefs, labor practices, economic systems, land use, and gender structures framed a stable society. Upon their arrival, Franciscan missionaries attempted to eradicate what they perceived as ills within Tongva society by establishing Spanish cultural and social practices among the Indigenous population. Through religious indoctrination, labor, restructuring of gender structures, and violence, missionaries aimed to "save" Indians souls by slowly dismantling their Indigenous ways of life.[24]

Tongva religion had evolved over generations and was fused with spiritual beliefs from other Tongva peoples as well as from agricultural peoples from Arizona and New Mexico.[25] Within in a hierarchal structure of deities, Chengiichnegech, the supreme creator, was at the top of a religious cosmology that defined the relationship between the Tongva and the world they inhabited. They believed that "humankind was not the focus of creation but merely a strand in a larger web of life."[26] Therefore, everything they did in this world was connected. This connection influenced societal hierarchy, concepts of morality, labor, and land use.[27]

The Tongva believed that "humankind's primary religious responsibility was to act as wise stewards to earth's living things and sacred places while offering periodic ceremonies of thanksgiving to the creator and earth spirits."[28] Their deep connection to the land imposed on them the responsibility for managing its resources wisely. This connection to the land translated to the larger community in a variety of ways that touched upon the moral code and expected community behavior. For example, as part of the societal values of reciprocity, hunters and anglers were prohibited from eating the animals they hunted or the fish they caught.[29] This rule attempted to prevent food hoarding and encouraged communal sharing. It exemplifies the interreliance and interconnectedness that existed amongst the Tongva and was a rule important to the preservation of life.[30]

Unlike the Spanish, the Tongva were not farmers. They gathered acorns and enjoyed other readily available foods such as yucca root and cactus fruit.[31]

Yet, due to cultural arrogance, the Spanish did not see the stability produced through Indians' relationship to land. Instead they saw them as an uncivilized heathen society in need of improvement. In a letter to Fray Antonio Nogueyra, Fray Francisco Lasuén wrote:

> If we cannot gently withdraw their hearts from their own way of living, how are we to get them to appreciate ours? How shall we teach them Christian obedience, and the ways of a civilized society? The effort entailed in procuring sustenance from the open spaces was incomparably greater than what is now enjoined on them so that they can sustain themselves; but the former is free and according to their liking, and the latter prescribed, and not according to their liking.[32]

Lasuén believed that, if Indians could be taught to use land in a way that provided them regular, steady access to food (i.e. farming, and the domestication of animals), they would have more time to dedicate to learning Christianity.

Land was important to achieving stability in Alta California. Throughout California, missionaries received about 100,000 acres of land as part of Spanish colonization efforts. According to the Leyes de las Indias, missionaries held these lands in trust for their Indian charges during the conversion process. Upon conversion, Franciscans were to distribute the lands to mission Indians, keeping only enough land for the mission parish.[33] Missionaries believed that their goal was to teach neophytes how to work and to maintain land that eventually would be theirs.

Franciscans considered agricultural land use a way to cultivate civilization and Christianity among Indigenous peoples. In an early letter to the guardian of the Colegio de San Fernando de Mexico, the headquarters of the Franciscans in Alta California, Lasuén described the land as "beautiful" and the Indian population as "plentiful and docile."[34] He continued that, if they could "cultivate the thousands of acres of land," they could also "plant our [their] voices" and "with the favor of God cultivate eternal harvests." Here Lausén made the connection between successful cultivation of land and Indigenous labor but also alluded to successful cultivation of Christianity amongst the region's "docile" populace. The desire to convert Indians while achieving successful land cultivation emphasized the Franciscans' connection among neophytes, land, and civilization. Land ownership became a racialized indicator of civilization.

Throughout Alta California, the mission institution served as the site for the missionaries' goals of conversion and civilization. Because Franciscan missionaries believed that Spanish culture and civilization depended on Catholicism, productive agriculture, and disciplined labor, they used a strict regimentation program combining religious conversion and labor. By making Indians perform a variety of work, ranging from constructing buildings to working agricultural crops and tending livestock, they sought to transform them into strong, reliable Catholic workers who spoke Spanish, used Spanish labor forms, and adhered to Spanish cultural tenets of behavior.[35] Missionaries used labor as a means of replicating Spanish society and teaching Indians their subordinate position within the society.[36]

The link between labor and imposed assimilation in Spanish colonialism dates to the earlier colonial period. Prior to 1542 Spain implemented the *encomienda*, a system of grants requiring Indian tribute and labor by which Indigenous peoples were placed under the tutelage of Spanish encomenderos or landowners.[37] In exchange for labor and tribute, encomenderos were expected to show their Indian charges how to become civilized Christian farmers. Vast corruption and exploitation led to the deaths of thousands of Indians and eventually to the system being outlawed in 1542.[38] In mid-eighteenth-century California, the mission represented a form of Spanish tutelage attempting to civilize Indians through labor.[39] By placing Indians into the missions Franciscans believed they could instill in them the fundamental principles of Christian vassalage, sedentary living, and productive labor practices.[40] Mission Friars' paternalism veiled the increasingly exploitative dynamic that justified using Indian labor to develop mission lands, first for subsistence and later for profit. Despite geographic and temporal separations, both the encomienda and mission systems were part of similar colonial processes seeking to profit from Indian exploitation under the guise of a civilizing project. Both were inherently exploitative because they were based on perceiving Indians as "uncivilized heathens" who required the civilizing effects of Spanish society.[41]

Early colonization efforts reflected a variety of attitudes about Indians. As noted by David J. Weber, Spanish missionaries and soldiers settling the fringes of the empire did not simply use the term *indios* when identifying Indigenous groups; they placed them in a variety of taxonomies reflective of their level of exposure to Spaniards or missionaries. Spaniards classified Indians as *indios bozales* (wild and ignorant Indians), *indios infieles/gentile* (heathen Indians), or *indios salvajes/bárbaros* (savage Indians).[42] Each term implied a stage of development but also placed these Indians lower on the social scale than Spaniards, termed gente de razón, and Christianized Indians. Spaniards regarded all

Indians as "never fully escaping their barbarism."[43] In eighteenth century Alta California, military and religious officials brought their visions of "civilization" into these uncivilized regions with the intention of remaking the Indians and placing them outside the parameters of Spanish civilized society.

The first step in religious conversion was baptism. Baptismal instruction was often superficial and did not require neophytes' full understanding of the tenets of Catholicism. Missionaries often disagreed over how much knowledge an Indian convert should have before being baptized. Lasuén wanted Indians to have an understanding of the twelve articles of the Apostles' Creed, while others, such as Fray José Francisco de Paula Señán, felt that knowledge of only the main Catholic prayers and the Ten Commandments was necessary.[44] Although Franciscans desired more assurance of Indians' acceptance of Christianity, most missionaries settled for Indians' renunciation of their lifestyles, beliefs, customs, and behaviors as sufficient evidence that they were prepared for baptism and for Christian life in the missions.[45]

Franciscan missionaries regarded work as vital to human society and essential to creating good Christians. Their conversion and civilizing efforts focused on the eradication of culture through modification of inappropriate and unchristian Indian converts' behaviors.[46]

Franciscans used a strict regimentation program, cued by bells, that controlled every aspect of Indians' lives in the mission.[47] Mission neophytes began each day with prayers, daily mass, and "spiritual instruction led by a missionary or well instructed Indian."[48] After morning prayers Indians ate their morning meal of atole, a cornmeal gruel served hot. After breakfast men left to labor in the fields or were assigned other tasks. Women ground and roasted corn, all the while caring for their children.[49] Indians worked thirty- to forty-hour weeks five to six days a week. Dinner was at noon, followed by a rest period from one until two or three o'clock; work was then resumed until five o'clock. At six o'clock supper was served. After the meal, neophytes had evening prayers and then could do as they pleased until bedtime at eight o'clock.[50] This regiment was meant to control Indigenous peoples' activities and keep them from succumbing to "spiritual decay and temptations" that Franciscans believed resulted from idleness and laziness.[51] Missionaries' dislike of idleness and laziness was not unique to Alta California.

In Spain preachers spoke to rich and poor alike, pointing out the ills brought on by idleness. Social ills were not limited to vice and disorder, but also included lack of economic production that hurt agriculture and trade as well.[52] In Alta

California, Franciscans' perceptions of Indians as "free and lazy"[53] originated from their perceived ideas of Indians' cultural inferiority and their misinterpretation of Indian culture.[54] For example, in a letter to Fray Junípero Serra, Visitador General José de Gálvez referred to Indians as *viciosos y chupadores* (depraved drunkards).[55] These widespread ideas about Indians failed to recognize the specifics of precontact Indigenous labor practices. The Tongva were accustomed to directed labor "of intermittent effort rather than consistent exertion."[56] Their labor went toward completion of necessary tasks such as hunting; gathering; building shelter; and manufacturing clothing, utensils, and weapons. For Native Americans living a seasonal existence, this labor structure worked quite well. The Tongvas' knowledge of their environment and the seasonal availability of fish and acorns allowed them to work tirelessly to accumulate foodstuffs, live off their reserves until they were depleted, and then set out to collect more. These practices clashed with Spanish ideals that defined labor according to industrial standards of the early modern era.[57]

These ideas of Indians' cultural deficiency and backwardness undergirded Franciscans' daily routine steeped in religious instruction, reinforcement of Spanish cultural practices, and labor to convert and mold Indians into model Christian citizens.[58] From this perspective, labor, religion, and food production and distribution were part of a larger colonial project of conversion.

Labor was crucial to the development of social identity at the San Gabriel Mission. In the missions, Franciscans placed Indians into four different laboring categories: skilled artisans, semiskilled laborers, horticulturalists, and general laborers/field hands. Skilled artisans, at the top of the labor hierarchy, were knowledgeable masons, carpenters, blacksmiths, weavers, and tanners.[59] Below them were semiskilled workers such as herdsmen, tallow workers, butchers, vaqueros, and hide cleaners.[60] Horticultural workers comprised the third level of labor; they tended vineyards and gardens and kept pigeons and poultry.[61] General laborers and field hands, who performed work referred to as *labores mecánicos*, comprised the lowest level on the hierarchy. These workers plowed and cleared fields, worked with crops, and made adobe bricks for mission buildings.[62] Despite their specialized training, most Indians knew how to do a variety of jobs when compelled by the Franciscans. This labor structure reflected Spanish society's ideas of cultural progress and corresponded with Spanish ideals of race, culture, gender, and sexuality.

Franciscans divided mission labor along gender lines. Men performed manual labor including plowing land, planting and harvesting crops, and tending to livestock. They also labored in construction projects, building chapels, living quarters, granaries, and work spaces.[63] Women worked in groups inside the mission walls; they attended to their children, ground and roasted corn, wove shirts and woolen blankets, hauled water, prepared food, and performed other duties related to the domestic realm.[64]

Franciscans, concerned with eradicating perceived Indian indolence, closely supervised Indigenous charges to ensure that daily tasks were completed. Missionaries used coercion, violence, and intimidation to compel Indians to work.[65] Failing to complete assigned tasks often resulted in physical punishment at the hands of the missionaries. Fray Lasuén believed that physical punishment was necessary to eradicate the behaviors of "a people without education, without government, religion, or respect for authority . . . such is the character of the men we are to correct and whose crimes we must punish."[66] Flogging, shackling, hobbles, and stocks were common methods of social control in the missions. These devices aimed to mentally and physically intimidate Indians into compliance with Spanish cultural expectations.[67]

The significant changes in precontact and postconquest labor were the meaning behind the work and its compulsory nature.[68] Franciscans used their presumed authority to compel Indians to work on the missionaries' schedule. Labor was no longer used for the maintenance of Indian communities, but rather to provide for the missionaries and by extension the region. Because Indian labor was now compulsory, if Indians did not complete the tasks as directed they were beaten.[69]

The testimonio of Eulalia Pérez, pictured in figure 2—the culturally Spanish mestiza *llavera* (keeper of the keys) at San Gabriel from 1821 through 1833[70]—provides a closer look at the interrelated dynamics of labor, gender, economic production, religious conversion, and cultural assimilation. Born in Loreto, Baja California, Pérez settled at the San Diego Mission in 1802 with her soldier husband, Miguel Antonio Guillén.[71] Over the years she became an integral part of the missionizing process in the Alta California borderland. In 1818, at the request of mission priests, Pérez came to the San Gabriel Mission to serve as main cook. By 1820, she was assigned to oversee a variety of processes at the mission including distributing food rations, wine pressing, sewing, and supervising Indian laborers at mission factories.[72]

Pérez described the variety of goods produced by mission Indians including "sarapes, heavy blankets, saddles, horse brindles, boots, shoes, and other similar items."[73] There was a soap-making workshop and both a large and small

FIGURE 2 Portrait of Eulalia Pérez, keeper of the keys at Mission San Pascual, ca. 1870. At the time of this photo, she was 139 years old. Courtesy of the University of Southern California Libraries and California Historical Society. Digitally reproduced by the USC Digital Library; from the California Historical Society Collection at the University of Southern California, http://digitallibrary.usc.edu/cdm/singleitem/collection/p15799coll65/id/13269/rec/2.

carpentry workshop.[74] Indians also made wine, oil, and adobe bricks.[75] Each department had a neophyte teacher who was an *indio ya de razón e instruído* (Christianized and assimilated). When Pérez, who identified herself racially as *blanca pura* (pure white), referred to skilled Indian workers with the racial and cultural designation of indios ya de razón e instruído, she indicated that they were part of a larger complex hierarchy divided by occupation and that their labor and skill ascribed a certain amount of cultural credibility.[76] Labor's racial implications kept order in mission society. As seen through Pérez's account, Indians who engaged in certain occupations or adopted Spanish dress, speech, or mannerisms could become defined as de razón. Mission Indians' negotiation of Spanish cultural tenets helped them gain recognition as being closer to "civilized" Spaniards. Indians who did not have the social status as de razón were not considered at the same level of those who did.

While labor was used to measure mission Indians' levels of assimilation, it reflected only one aspect of social control. Missionaries' concern with transforming Indigenous gender practices provides an additional way of gauging the effect of their efforts. Interestingly, the gendered division of mission labor did not in and of itself change the gendered structure or undermine Indigenous labor. Precontact Tongva society had a sexual division of labor framed within gender parallelism. This system recognized, respected, and valued both men's and women's contributions as part of "separate but complementary realms within the society."[77] Tongva women were responsible for gathering acorns and pine nuts, weaving baskets, and preparing food, while men hunted and fished. Women's labor roles were pivotal to the survival of the Tongva because they were responsible for the bulk of the native diet. Additionally, women's efforts were significant because the "caloric importance of female food procurement" dwarfed men's hunting and fishing activities.[78] Because women's roles were respected, the efforts of both men and women were seen as important elements of the Tongvas' overall well-being.

The missions changed the concept of gender differences by implementing a Western patriarchal power dynamic that devalued women and their labors. It was a system that distinguished between men's and women's labor as a means of asserting a dynamic based on broader Spanish ideals of gender propriety and gender order.[79] Spanish ideals of gender and sexuality were based on a foundation of patriarchal authority. In a patriarchal system, men assert institutionalized control over women and dominance over women in larger society.[80] Women were considered the property of men, and their value lay in their ability to bear children and maintain men's honor and culture.[81]

Within the context of conquest, the assertion of patriarchy manifested itself through a racialized sexual violence. From the early days of missionary activity in Alta California, presidial soldiers sent to colonize the region repeatedly engaged in acts of sexual brutality against Indigenous women. At San Gabriel soldiers targeted Tongva girls and women; they "swooped into villages, chased, lassoed, raped, beat, and sometimes killed women."[82] These violent acts of colonial domination were rooted in a patriarchal ideology that doubly devalued Indigenous women as an extension of conquered land and subjugated men's property.[83]

In the missions, as part of conversion, Franciscans imposed various types of gender indoctrination that sought to eradicate premarital and extramarital sex, frequent and casual divorces, polygamy, and lax attitudes about sex. They perceived these Indigenous practices as immoral and "immodest exhibitions" of "extravagant Indians."[84]

Among Southern California Native groups such as the Tongva, "females enjoyed a large measure of freedom, respect and independence."[85] The respect and value accorded to women was part of the larger ideology of gender parallelism.[86] Tongva women were allowed to participate in important religious ceremonies and rituals that gave them cultural authority among the Indigenous population.[87]

While divergent labor duties separated men and women during the day, at night Franciscans resorted to more drastic measures to force women to conform to Spanish gender norms and propriety. With the aim of protecting Indigenous girls' and young women's virginity, missionaries physically separated Indian girls from their families. Girls as young as six or seven were forced to live in a *monjerío*, a sex-segregated living quarter where they were isolated from all male contact until they married.[88] Under the watchful eye and guidance of the llavera, Indigenous girls and young women were instructed and socialized in Spanish ideals of gender and sexual comportment.[89]

In her testimonio Eulalia Pérez, llavera of the mission's monjerío, related that girls and young women were segregated in these dormitories under the direction of a matron. They slept in the dormitories at night and were kept under lock and key until morning when they were taken to mass and to breakfast; they then proceeded to their daily work.[90] By separating Indian women from men, Franciscans sought to eradicate Indigenous traditions that recognized women's value, strength, and control over their own bodies.[91]

Missionaries' exertion of control over Indians' bodies through conversion, labor, and gender were attempts at reproducing "the social and physical environment of Spanish society" as well as the "ideological and institutional bases of Hispanic life."[92] Pérez's descriptions of missionaries' efforts, Indians' labor, and the imposition and enforcement of Spanish ideals and practices within the mission reflect a larger colonial process in which race, gender, and differing levels of assimilation intertwined to solidify a rigid system of discipline and labor directly connected to ideas of land use.

The need for a disciplined labor force evolved from missionaries' specific land use patterns and growing regional dependence on the mission for survival. Franciscans' use of mission land supported their agricultural visions of land use. They designated lands closest to the mission for the cultivation of corn, beans, and wheat. Lands farther away from the main mission buildings formed the mission ranchos—thousands of acres dedicated to grazing cattle, sheep, goats, pigs, horses, and mules.[93]

By 1790, the San Gabriel Mission had become the main source for goods and supplies for the region, including the settlement at El Pueblo de Nuestra Señora la Reina de los Ángeles. The steady rise in demand for a variety of mission products throughout the 1780s opened missionaries' eyes to the profit that could be made from neophyte labor. The mission's incorporation into the regional trade resulted in economic growth that blurred the line between the missionaries' financial purpose of self-sufficiency and their spiritual mission of Indian conversion and assimilation.

Although religious conversion and assimilation premised the demand for labor during the early years, the mission's changing economic landscape during the 1780s, 1790s, and early 1800s produced a change in the meaning and significance of Indian mission labor. With the mission's growing self-sufficiency and the region's dependence on mission goods, Indians could more successfully challenge coercive labor practices and leverage their relationships with missionaries.[94]

Since the early Mission Period, Indigenous groups resisted missionaries' attempts to fully control their world. Despite missionaries' use of coercion, intimidation, and violence, they were never able to assert full control over Indigenous populations. Mission Indians were able to maintain their autonomy and resist full colonial subjugation.[95] Despite the rigid labor regiment, mission Indians continued to gather roots, acorns, and grasses and hunt fowl, game, and fish even as they worked in the missions' fields and workshops.[96] However, Indian resistance was not limited to mission neophytes.

During the 1780s local shamans around San Gabriel, distressed over the declining resources, prohibiting of neophytes from non-Christian tribal ceremonies and rituals, and widespread death from disease, moved to organize rebellion.[97] In 1785, Toypurina, a powerful shaman and medicine woman of the Japchavit rancheria, organized an armed rebellion against the San Gabriel Mission.[98] Despite her success in recruiting villages to participate in the rebellion, the plot was discovered, and on the day of the attack, she and her followers were arrested.[99] Although the Tongva rebellion was put down, its causes reflect the broader complexities that existed in the relationship between Indians and missionaries.[100]

As the mission became more reliant on Indian labor for its economic success, Indians were able to affect change in their treatment. The day-to-day activities in the missions were not a display of one-way power relations, but rather ongoing interactions and negotiations. Increasingly Indians used their labor to resist and destabilize colonial power and to maintain a greater level of cultural autonomy. Through acquisition and incorporation of Spanish knowledge, techniques, tools, and schedules,[101] as well as adapting to new economies of labor and survival, Indians actively contested their position in the mission social hierarchy, challenged absolute missionary control, and negotiated their survival on their own terms.

As the San Gabriel Mission entered the nineteenth century, missionaries focused more on obtaining the most from Indian labor and less on the conversion project. At San Gabriel from 1810 to 1814, statistics show that only an average of 11 percent of 1,325 adult Indians received communion annually.[102] This low number of Indians receiving the sacrament coincides with periods of heavy regional reliance on mission supplies, mainly from 1810 to1832.[103] Similarly at Mission of Nuestra Señora de la Soledad, historians Paul Farnsworth and Robert H. Jackson found that "missionaries diverted labor from surplus food production to diversified agricultural production, craft specialization, and the specialized production of livestock."[104] This shift reflects an increased production of goods traded with regional settlers. Additional "archeological records show that between 1800 and 1810 the missions changed their emphasis from attracting, controlling, and changing the culture of California Indians to exploiting their labor for economic production."[105] By the end of the 1820s, the desire for labor rather than for conversion had made the mission into a lucrative business venture.

As demands for mission products increased, Franciscans insisted that Indians give more of their time to working at the mission. When these demands became too invasive of Indians' time outside the mission, they resisted the long hours and labor regimentation by feigning illness or resorting to absenteeism. Both methods proved to be successful in depriving the mission of its productive labor and negotiating a more moderate workload. Franciscans tolerated these behaviors, albeit grudgingly, because they relied on Indians for the mission's productivity and self-sufficiency.[106] Soon the shifts in the regional economy prompted many Indians to seek work outside the mission. Mission Indians took the skills they had acquired in the missions and pursued work in nearby presidios and pueblos.[107]

As Alta California's colonization unfolded through the missions and pueblos, labor became a crucial factor in determining a person's social and cultural standing. Early in the Spanish Colonial period, soldiers did much of the necessary work building the presidios and settlements. They were deeply resentful of this strenuous backbreaking work and felt that it was beneath them. They soon began assigning menial and distasteful work to Indians, as was the practice in other areas of New Spain.[108] Throughout the colonial Mission Period, neophyte Indians and non-Christian Indians alike had sought work in military garrisons and civilian settlements. This labor ranged from coerced, unpaid labor to voluntary, paid labor.[109]

Convict labor was one of the ways in which the presidios obtained Indian labor. If an Indian was accused or found guilty of minor crimes, he was forced to perform unpaid heavy labor as punishment. Franciscans did not agree with convict labor and believed that soldiers often wrongly accused Indians of committing crimes simply to exploit their labor.[110] Despite Franciscans' displeasure with the presidios' use of Indian labor, they directly contracted neophyte workers to the presidios.[111] Contracts ranged from a few days to a month and sent workers to labor on larger institutional projects. In these formal contracts monies paid to workers went directly to the missionaries.

As time went on, individual soldiers and officers began to contract Indian workers for personal everyday tasks, giving rise to an informal labor market. Indians who covertly labored for military personnel gained access to corn, wheat, cloth, and beef—goods that they used to supplement their mission rations.[112] Often the lure was too great and mission Indians shunned their assigned mission tasks in favor of working at the presidios. The availability of jobs outside the mission gave Indians a means to contest Franciscans' increasingly excessive labor regiment at the mission, and while the work at the presidio was backbreaking and the pay meager, they kept what they earned and lessened their dependence on missionaries for survival. The resultant competition among missionaries, military personnel, and settlers for Indian labor provided the Indians with leverage in labor relations and helped them negotiate the changes brought on by shifting economies.[113]

While the presidio competed with Franciscan missionaries for neophyte laborers, the greatest threat came from civilian communities. For San Gabriel, the settlement of El Pueblo de Los Angeles in 1781 provided Indians the opportunities to labor and subsist without the mission. Los Angeles's inhabitants, many of whom disliked farming and land cultivation, focused instead on pastoral pursuits and needed Indian labor to work the land.[114] By 1790 the pueblo had grown, and it infringed on surrounding Native lands and restricted the Tongva's traditional subsistence practices. For non-mission Indians, this spelled the decline of traditional subsistence patterns and made their work for settlers necessary for survival.[115] Indians worked at the pueblo in occupations such as *vaqueros* or cowboys, cooks, domestics, muleteers, and water carriers.[116]

Indian labor played an important role in the pueblos growth. As related in a letter from Lieutenant Francisco Ortega to Military Governor Fages, early *pobladores* (settlers) refused to plant or irrigate their crops. The successful cultivation of wheat and corn is credited to the "aid of the gentiles."[117] Ortega credits Indians with the growth of the pueblo but also chastises its settlers for relying on the native population to do settlers' work.

Despite the exploitative conditions they faced in the pueblo, Indians were afforded a much higher level of autonomy and independence. Settlers did not care to change Indians' cultural and religious behaviors and looked more toward exploiting their labor.[118] Ironically, it was at the pueblo, not the mission, where one clearly sees Indian adoption of Spanish culture. Extensive interaction between Indians and settlers resulted in Indians' use of Spanish, their wearing of settler-style clothing, and in some cases their intermarriage with the Spanish population.[119]

Indian presence in the pueblos caused some worry about the blurring of boundaries between Spanish and Indian populations. After his 1787 visit to Los Angeles, Fages, troubled by the large numbers of Indians in the pueblo, issued a law regulating proper Spanish and Indian behaviors and interactions.[120] This law forbade settlers from allowing Indians inside their houses and required that any work had to be done outside in corridors or patios, even if the workers were women. Additionally, Indians could not sleep in settlers' houses and were required to sleep in the fields near the guardhouse.[121] Although these guidelines represented governmental attempts to firmly delineate the difference between Spanish settlers and Indian laborers, continued interaction created a new cultural identity that was "subject to the continuous [inter]play of history, culture and power."[122] By the mid-1790s, extensive interactions between Spanish pobladores and Tongva laborers were continuing and in some cases resulting in Spanish settlers speaking Indian languages and marrying Indian women.[123]

As the colonial project expanded and mission profits increased, missionaries tethered Indian converts to the land, resulting in immense wealth for the San Gabriel Mission. Franciscans' interest in conversion gave way to the regional economic interests, leading to greater demands on Indian labor. The San Gabriel Mission's wealth and importance to the regional economy is evident in mission ledgers. Mission profit and regional stability were the economic goals of the mission and the Crown alike. As the economy grew on the backs of Indian labor, the ideas of optimal land use changed with it, creating a ruling landed class.

The missions' economic development and the growth of the civilian settlements changed Alta California's colonial structure during the early nineteenth century. As Indians recognized their important role in the changing colonial economy they created a malleable relationship with Spanish missionaries, pobladores, and soldiers as a way of exerting some control over their labor and resisting complete colonial control. It is within this context that the mission system became Alta California's dominant economic institution and facilitated the growth of landed elite who spearheaded calls for secularization.

(RE)CREATING SOCIAL IDENTITIES WITHIN COLONIALISM

The interactions among Franciscans, soldiers, settlers, and Indians in the late eighteenth and early nineteenth century San Gabriel region perpetuated the rise of specific regional identities based on colonial hierarchies. Prior to conquest, Spanish and Tongva people had their own distinct sociocultural systems. Each group's societal organization reflected the values and customs that served as the basis of its society. The conditions created by conquest and colonization created a process of transculturation in which each group's cultural practices and ideas were adapted and altered according to social, and in this case, geographical conditions.[124] The dynamics of colonialism and settlement existed alongside those of acculturation and resulted in regional inhabitants' (re)creation, reconfiguration, and reappropriation of people's social and cultural identities.

Social identity refers to how people define themselves or how others within their own cultural groups define them. Identities are representative of power relations within a specific context and change in accordance with sociocultural fluctuations.[125] During the Spanish Colonial Period society was largely controlled by españoles or Spaniards, followed by criollos (persons of Spanish descent born in Mexico). As racial mixing occurred, and colonial Mexico's racial diversity increased, the *casta* system, a classification system based on race and ethnic identity, was used to determine ones' social status and position and to maintain social order. The *castas* included anyone who did not belong to the español or criollo groups, but rather were part of the mixed-race population. At the top of the castas were mestizos, people of Spanish and Indigenous descent. The categories below mestizos consisted of people of Indigenous, African, and other mixed-race descent. Although the system was intended to keep societal order by creating socio-racial hierarchies, it was not absolute and often the categories and social identities were affected by various other factors.[126] Because social identities are dynamic, changes in government, economics, and land policy directly influenced the factors that constituted each identity. As a site of conquest and colonization, the San Gabriel Mission influenced the social identity of those who functioned within its sphere of influence at specific historical moments.

During the early Mission Period, those regarded as being part of the dominant racial group distinguished themselves from subordinate racial groups using the categories of Spanish and Indian. As the mission institution grew and regional conditions changed, these categories of white Spanish colonizers and Indian colonized failed to capture the San Gabriel mission's sociocultural complexities and diversity.[127] The growth of the regional economy and civilian settlements around San Gabriel prompted a redefinition of the term *Spanish* and decline of the colonial casta system.

In Alta California, separated from the economic and governmental stability and sociocultural distinctions of the metropole in Mexico City, people slowly shaped their new identities based on their lived realities on the fringes of the Spain's colonial empire.[128] In the California borderlands the term *Spaniard* referred to a diverse group of missionaries, presidial soldiers, and pobladores; its racial meaning came to represent a more cultural designation. This new cultural designation also implied a specific place in the social order. For example, terms such as *soldado* (soldier) encompassed a multitude of other interrelated identities and social standings such as occupation, gender, nationality, colonial status, rank, and class, all of which were defined by colonial ideologies.[129] The terms used as markers of social identity—fray, soldado, indio, *neófito* (neophyte), and poblador—were imbued with the rhetoric of colonialism and changed in accordance with the social, economic, and cultural transformations taking place during Alta California's Mission Period.

The colonial system's influence on the casta system solidified the imposed sociocultural inferiority of California's Indian people. Although Indians had been defined as an inferior social group throughout New Spain since the mid-sixteenth century, the dynamics of the borderland racialized Indians according the conditions that existed on the fringes of the empire.[130] The blurring of the boundaries among the castas prompted colonists to use the terms *gente de razón* and *gente sin razón* to distinguish between españoles and indios. Although emerging from theological differences between Christian and heathen, these terms evolved into cultural designations that "implied an insurmountable divide between civilization and savagery."[131] Indians, as perpetual cultural *others*, became laborers tethered to the land and subjected to exclusionary policies and societal marginalization. The reconceptualization of cultural codes and legal classification within a framework of de razón or sin razón displaced the casta system but furthered the construction of an exclusionary regional and ethnic identity.

In Alta California, the accelerated breakdown of the racial hierarchy created a malleability of racial/cultural designations that afforded mestizo and mulatto soldiers and settlers opportunities to define themselves as Spanish, gente de razón, and later *hijos* and *hijas del país* (sons and daughters of the land) and Californios and Californianas.[132] These cultural signifiers provided a means for castas to firmly root themselves in the land and region while simultaneously making Indians into permanent cultural outsiders. The formation of these social identities reflects the interplay among the larger colonial ideas about race, culture, status, and community membership, showing how colonialisms' multiple discourses resulted in the layering of identity.

DE ESPAÑOLES, CASTAS, Y INDIOS

During the early colonial period in New Spain's interior, the Spanish casta system organized society through a racialized hierarchy that placed Spaniards or white Europeans at the top, castas in the middle, and Africans and Indians at the bottom. Despite its aim, the casta system was not as rigid as it seemed and could be influenced by social context and occupation. During the mid-eighteenth century, people could use their occupation to influence their designation into one of the main categories.[133] Soon the system expanded to include more than forty different social classifications.[134] By the late Spanish Colonial Period, the system began to break down throughout New Spain because the racial and economic aspects of the Spanish casta divisions were inconsistent.[135] Increasingly mestizos and mulattos entered into diverse occupations that allowed them to negotiate the racial hierarchy and change their racial classifications.[136] As the colonial project expanded northward into places like Alta California, the social diversity of the borderlands made racial identity something that could no longer be determined primarily through labor.[137]

In the northern areas of the empire "the casta system collapsed into a small handful of designations most commonly mestizo, mulatto, indio, and español."[138] Because many of California's inhabitants came from the racially mixed castas of Mexico's northern provinces, the designation of *español* took on a broader meaning that allowed mixed-race populations to define themselves in relation to Indians.[139] People designated themselves españoles to gain access to a social and economic privilege and a position at the top the colonial hierarchy.[140] However, self-designation alone did not suffice as such designations were linked to social and cultural attributes. A person's culture, a "complex whole which includes knowledge, belief, art, morals, law, custom, and any other capabilities and habits acquired by man as a member of society" had to reflect Spanish norms.[141] Between 1760 and 1790 the social designation of español transitioned from birth or ancestry and was linked more closely to cultural practice.[142] Culture, social behavior, and practice determined a person's racial designation and allowed for social mobility.[143]

Despite the collapse of the casta system and the changes in determining who could be Spanish, creating a social identity on the Alta California borderland proved difficult because regional identities were still informed by the colonial power relations created through the mission.[144] San Gabriel's Matrimonial Investigation records provide a glimpse into how the dynamics of race, culture, and community membership were used to designate one's identity and connection to the land.[145] They show how the structures of colonialism produced a system of social stratification that made Spaniards out of castas and positioned Indians at the bottom of the colonial order.

These investigations, often recorded by a mission priest, are replete with applicants referred to as *vecinos*, *naturales*, or *existentes* of a particular region, presidio, or mission. Although these terms do not explicitly designate a racial/ethnic identity, they are imbued with racial meaning and indicate a person's relationship to the land/region in which he or she lived. The term *vecino*, used throughout the northern Spanish provinces, indicated a non-Indian Spanish-speaking colonist permanently settled in a region.[146] *Naturales* was a Spanish term for Indians, people who were natural or Indigenous to the land.[147] *Existentes* referred to the region in which a person lived but also implied a transient status.[148] Each term reflected the applicant's and his or her family's status in the society and designated a cultural classification. From the 1760s through the 1780s Spanish colonial documents reflected the use of two classifications, "Indios and Vecinos y castas or just Vecinos (Españoles)."[149] As the Spanish Colonial Period continued, these classifications transitioned from an implied racial designation to one reflective of specific cultural characteristics.[150]

Areas throughout the northern borderlands used the term *vecino* to indicate land ownership. Aside from its economic implications, this term reflected cultural ones as well. In areas like New Mexico and the Rio Grande region of Texas, one of the defining characteristics of the vecino identity in the late eighteenth century was the appropriation of Indigenous lands.[151] The acquisition and control of Indian lands created a crucial link between the vecino designation, land ownership, and community membership. By emphasizing their land ownership colonists created a distinction between themselves, non-Indian colonists who held land, and Indigenous peoples who did not. The term asserted that the vecino was a de razón landowner. This link provided the cultural characteristics needs to allow castas to be accepted as españoles.

In the San Gabriel region during the late eighteenth century the term *vecino* was used in a similar fashion.[152] Marriage petitioners used it to establish their status in the community. The November 11, 1798, marriage investigation of Juan José Duarte and María Gertrudis Moreno illustrates how people used this term to assert their identity.

> Juan José Durate, unmarried son of José Duarte y Juana Gertrudis from Real de Los Alamos, stated of his own volition he wishes to enter into the contract of marriage according to the order of our Church with Gertrudis Moreno, daughter of José Moreno and María Guadalupe, vecinos, permanent citizens of Los Angeles.[153]

This early marriage investigation indicates that Duarte had moved into the region after his appointment as a presidial soldier. Because his parents were not from the area, he was considered an outsider with little community status. During the investigation, he evoked his familial lineage, established his legitimacy of birth, and presented a witness who could vouch for his good character as a way to establish himself as a respectable community member.

Comparatively, Moreno's parents are referred to as *vecinos del pueblo*, indicative of their higher status as permanent settlers in the community. At play here are the dynamics of social and cultural identity formation. By using specific language and terms, each person staked a claim to his or her place in society. We can surmise that both Juan José and María Gertrudis were "Spanish" because one was a soldier, and the other was the daughter of vecinos. They were identified as being de razón, were not Indians, and in all likelihood were culturally Spanish and racially mixed mestizos.[154]

While the Duarte family's racial identity is not clearly stated, there is evidence that Moreno was of mixed racial ancestry, yet culturally Spanish. In the investigation, her parents were referred to as vecinos; they were not, however, referred to in this manner in other documents tying them to the community. The 1781 Padrón of El Pueblo de Los Angeles's founding families listed José Moreno as a mulatto from Sinaloa and María Guadalupe Pérez as a mulatta; they were aged twenty-two and nineteen, respectively.[155] The 1790 Los Angeles Census describes Gertrudis Moreno as the mestiza daughter of José Moreno, a mestizo farm worker and his wife María Gertrudis Pérez, a *coyota* (a person of mestizo and Indian descent), both from Rosario, Sinaloa.[156] The shift in the meaning of Spanish identity accounts for the Moreno-Pérez household's ascent in the community from mulattos to vecinos. As racial boundaries blurred, culture became the basis for social identity. In a society where the Indigenous population was the racial and cultural other, mulattos and mestizos became part of the dominant colonial system through their relation to land. Because José Moreno and María Guadalupe Pérez were vecinos, they became less African as the colonial period continued. This designation allowed their daughter to become a mestiza despite their ethnic mixture. The use of the term *vecino* defined them as culturally Spanish and established them as community members.

Commoners such as María Guadalupe Moreno were not the only mixed-race castas who could become españoles. Tracing the origins of one of California's most famous Spanish Californio families, the Picos, shows that as the region grew, ethnic boundaries blurred.[157] On October 31, 1794, priests at the Santa Barbara and San Gabriel Missions began the matrimonial investigation for José Miguel Pico and María Casilda de la Cruz Sinoba:

> José Miguel Pico, single man from Sinaloa, son of Santiago Pico de la Cruz, and María Jacinta Bastidos, and soldier from Santa Barbara presented himself for the purpose of contracting marriage following the order of our Church; he stated that of his free and spontaneous volition he wished to marry María Casilda de la Cruz, single woman, inhabitant of Los Angeles, originally from the Santa Clara Mis-

> sion in New California, daughter of José Francisco Sinoba, y de María Gertrudis Bojoya, permanent, Spanish citizens of said pueblo.[158]

José Miguel, one of the elder Pico brothers, was born in Sonora and lived at the Santa Barbara Presidio. Although the investigation omitted the racial identity of José Miguel and his parents, Santiago and Jacinta, the 1790 United States Census lists them as a mulatto, mestizo, and mulatta, respectively.[159] In this case, these family members' racial classifications had not changed, but were merely absent from the investigation. This omission may indicate that José Miguel Pico had a good reputation and belonged to a family of high *calidad*, a status comprising a combination of characteristics such as "birthplace, wealth, occupation, acculturation, legitimacy, conduct, and personal honor."[160] His legitimacy of birth, occupation, and more importantly his cultural identity as Spanish, kept him in good standing in the community.

The 1794 investigation identified José Miguel's future bride, María Casilda de la Cruz, as the daughter of José Francisco Sinob[v]a and María Gertrudis Bojoya, "vecinos del mensionado pueblo [Pueblo de Los Angeles]."[161] In the 1790 census, José Francisco was listed as an español from Mexico City, while María Gertrudis, from Villa Sinaloa in northern New Spain, was identified as a mestiza. The couple's four children, including nine-year-old María Casilda, were listed as españoles. The structure of the casta system would lead one to deduce that these children were mestizos, the outcome of a racially mixed relationship between a Spaniard and a mestiza; however, the document shows that in el Pueblo de Los Angeles they were designated as Spaniards. The origin of José Francisco's classification as Spanish may be explained by multiple factors. His classification may stem from his skilled occupation as a blacksmith and his origin in Mexico City. Alternatively, one could also argue that upon moving north the great distance from the colonial society in Mexico City may have accelerated his racial designation.

María Gertrudis's birth on the fringes of empire may have contributed to her social distinction as a mestiza. She may have been an Indigenous woman reclassified through her marriage to an español. This relationship sets up many suppositions, yet what is most important here is her daughter María Casilda's racial designation; she was a Spanish woman intent on marrying a man descended from a mestizo father and a mulatta mother. The marriage investigation does not indicate any conflict over the union, suggesting that racial designations were not employed as a means of indicating racial difference but rather signified a distinction in cultural terms.[162] The couple's union was not contested because both the bride and groom were from respected families with similar cultural status.

These examples of settlers' racial designations show that those living in the borderlands participated in creating racial and social identities that correlated ethnicity and superiority. These mixed-race castas negotiated the racial hierarchy and designated themselves as culturally Spanish, gente de razón. Using the term vecino helped them create a higher position in the emerging social order, especially in relationship to Indians.[163]

At the Mission San Gabriel and in its surrounding area, the malleability of racial and cultural designations proved crucial to creating and sustaining a hierarchy that privileged non-Indian vecinos and relegated Indigenous people to the lowest rung of Spanish colonial and mission society. While colonialism's dichotomy of colonizer and colonized allowed mixed-race castas to become Spanish, its designation of Indians as cultural others made them into racialized laborers tethered to the land and subjected to exclusionary policies and societal marginalization.

2

MAKING THE REGION

The Mission Economy, Independence, and Liberalism

DURING THE PERIOD FROM 1769 to 1775, the mission institution and the presidio solidified Spanish settlement in Alta California's Spanish borderlands.[1] The region's isolation from the Mexican interior resulted in missionaries and military personnel experiencing a scarcity of resources, scant economic support, and sporadic delivery of supplies. This instability created a dire situation for regional inhabitants. Due to their control of Indian labor and their vast land holdings, missions' production of food and goods soon supplied regional needs and supported the creation of a largely self-sufficient economy. By the late eighteenth century, the missions had become crucial to the regional inhabitants' survival. By co-opting Indigenous labor and controlling the regional economy, the mission created the foundation for continued civilian settlement and the establishment of cultural hegemony.[2]

The first thirty-five years of the nineteenth century proved very lucrative for the San Gabriel Mission, with much of its development occurring during the push for Mexican independence. Between 1810 and 1832 the mission experienced its golden age, an era that saw wheat and corn production grow and remain steady. Following independence in 1821, when other regional missions focused solely on expanding their livestock production for sale in the tallow and hide trade, the San Gabriel Mission continued producing agricultural goods at a steady rate (except during the 1824 wheat harvest, which declined due to inclement weather).[3] The mission also concurrently expanded its livestock and participated in the tallow and hide trade by maintaining a large number of cattle, sheep, and horses.[4]

After Mexican independence, the San Gabriel Mission's success rested on missionaries' effective management of emerging merchant capitalist markets. San Gabriel Mission priests provided items similar to those imported from San Blas or Mexico City. They also bartered a variety of locally produced supplies, such as wheat, wine, grains, and tallow by-products, to presidios and El Pueblo de Los Angeles. These activities transformed San Gabriel missionaries into successful businessmen and changed their vision of land use to one focused on production of surplus rather than subsistence.[5] Through its control of production and trade, the San Gabriel Mission became the hub of regional trade and the most economically powerful institution in the area.

The post-independence rise of Mexican liberalism and its accompanying vision of land use, focused on private land ownership, placed Franciscans at odds with aspiring landowners. Californio elites regarded the missions as the archetype for a broken colonial system marred by avarice and socioeconomic limitations. The mission's economic success, garnered through monopolizing the regional economy, and dominating trade networks, controlling vast acreages of land and Indian labor, stirred the resentment of aspiring Californio landowners who sought their own prosperity and fortune in the Alta California borderlands.

THE EARLY COLONIAL MISSION ECONOMY, 1765–1810

Between 1765 and 1772 the mission institution functioned under a system created by Visitador General José de Gálvez's administration. Under this plan, each mission site received two missionaries, a governmentally provided 150-peso annual stipend, and a set amount of supplies shipped from the Mexican port at San Blas, Nayarit, on the Pacific Coast.[6] Reliance on supplies shipped by sea created an economic system marked by shortages and inflated prices. In addition to complaining about the inconsistent arrival of supplies and the unscrupulous practices of those charged with distributing them, missionaries contended that the annual stipend was unrealistically low and did not allow them enough money to supply the missions.[7] Despite repeated complaints, the government did not make any efforts to address the situation.

In 1773, Father Presidente Junípero Serra traveled to Mexico City and presented a thirty-two-point report consisting of missionaries' complaints and demands, ranging from economic concerns, labor issues, and social matters, to the central government.[8] Serra's presentation attributed the nascent mission system's problems, economic or otherwise, to weak military presence and command in the north. Serra indicted Military Governor Pedro Fages's lack of control over his troops and pointed to their drinking, gambling, and sexual assault of Indigenous women as an indication of their immoral behavior.[9] Serra believed that these actions decreased missionaries' effectiveness at congregating the Indians into the missions. In an effort to pacify Serra, Viceroy Antonio de María Bucareli y Ursúa addressed the complaints by approving a formal set of regulations, known as the Echeveste Reglamento of 1773, recognizing the priests' authority over mission Indians and removed Fages from command.[10]

Aside from addressing some of Serra's concerns about missionizing efforts, the viceroy sought to solidify the Crown's economic power in Alta California by attempting to incorporate the region into New Spain's larger economy. The reglamento set soldiers' salaries and missionaries' stipends, delineated governmental fiscal support of the presidios and missions, and regulated prices of products and goods imported into and exported from the missions.[11] The newly instituted regulations indirectly affected the missions' increased economic power in the late eighteenth century by doubling mission stipends and rations for the first five years after their establishment. They increased presidial soldiers' buying power by providing them money to purchase mission items. Increased demand for mission goods required missionaries to work their Indian charges harder to produce more supplies.

The situation in the late 1770s and early 1780s illustrates the connection between the mission system's economic growth and Franciscans' visions of land use. Each mission's wealth and the survival of the nearby presidio and pueblo depended on successful mission production. The government came to expect the missions to provide for the presidios, leading to increased mission production.[12] The cultivation of crops and the grazing of livestock correlated with shifting economic markets, labor structures, and sociocultural categories on the Spanish frontier. These economic and social dynamics produced immense conflict between missionaries and secular groups, with the latter demanding increased production from the mission and its neophytes.

For the San Gabriel Mission, the mid-1770s and 1780s proved to be a period of growth and self-sufficiency. Increasingly, presidial soldiers, and after 1781, colonists at el Pueblo de Los Angeles depended on the mission for an array of agricultural products, livestock, and other goods, such as soap, candles, cattle, sheep, and mission-produced wine.[13] As early as 1773, the regional presidios had agreed to purchase all their food, clothing, and leather products from the regional missions.[14] Aside from increased regional demands for everyday goods, a growing international trade brought Franciscans into Russian, French, and English trade networks. Missionaries' participation in international trade increased their sales of tallow and hide and bolstered foreign demands for mission products.[15] This economic growth directly challenged the Crown's control over the regional economy by giving mission priests rather than the Crown the power to set prices and create regional trade contracts benefiting the mission institutions.[16]

Missionaries' ability to provide products at the same price as those imported from San Blas during the 1770s illustrated the missions' growing productivity and economic power.[17] While investigating presidial complaints of unfair pricing, the government discovered missionaries' excessive charges for their goods and products. Recognizing that by 1781 the missions had become the main supplier of food and goods for presidios and settlements, Spanish Governor of California Felipe de Neve issued a reglamento that aimed to keep missionaries from exploiting their monopoly.[18] Issued in January 1,1781, Neve's reglamento reset prices for goods such as beans, corn, and garbanzos, and regulated the price of livestock.[19] These price adjustments were an indirect attack on mission wealth. Missionaries alleged that price regulations and artificially low prices for mission goods reflected a governmental dislike of the mission's growing enterprises and they perpetuated anti-mission prejudice among the presidio and growing settler population.[20]

As the regional population grew and private land holding increased between the mid to late 1780s, mission production and trade posed a growing threat to the stability and profit of the private ranches. Despite the growing resentment by the ranchero class and the government's attempts to curb the mission system's wealth, Franciscans continued to participate in the lucrative tallow and hide trade.[21] Amid accusations of price fixing, most missions, including San Gabriel, negotiated for higher prices, especially in times of food shortages at the local presidios.[22]

The conflict over price regulation illustrates that, although the missionaries, soldiers, and civilian settlers were not completely satisfied with their situation, they created a beneficial and functional relationship through which they negotiated and contested their positions. Missionaries' concerns about attracting and keeping Indians at the mission and maintaining their individual settlements, presidios' interests in supporting their soldiers, and civilians' desires to subsist left missionaries and military authorities no choice but to coexist.[23] Missionaries' leverage in obtaining higher prices illustrates that, despite governmentally imposed regulations, the regional economy was subject to the borderland's volatile forces and conditions.

During the late 1780s, Alta California's missionaries found an additional way to continue building their wealth by participating in the lucrative international sea otter pelt trade. In 1786, Viceroy Bernardo de Gálvez granted missionaries permission to officially enter the fur trade as designated trade agents in charge of collecting the highly valued sea otter pelts. Missionaries utilized Indigenous labor to hunt otter and then trade the pelts for beads.

The trade proved highly profitable. Between 1787 and 1790, Franciscans traded more than 2,000 otter pelts, which garnered them 6,000 pesos of credit.[24] Missionaries were unable to monopolize this trade. Despite laws prohibiting non-missionaries from intercepting or directly trading with mission Indians collecting the pelts, unscrupulous soldiers and settlers, resentful of their exclusion from such a lucrative market, took pelts from Indians and then sold them to the missions themselves.[25] Missionaries, suspecting the illegal methods used to obtain the pelts, had no other choice but to pay the 7 pesos per pelt to soldiers and settlers. Although unhappy with their lack of control over the trade, the increasing conflict with settlers and soldiers, and the number of neophytes who left missions to hunt for sea otters, missionaries continued trading and making tremendous profit.

In 1790 a royal decree officially ended the viceroy's otter trade project. Although legitimate trade ended, missionaries, presidial officials, and foreign traders participated in illegal smuggling well into the period of Mexican independence.[26] Between 1800 and 1810, the total profit from illegal trade between Franciscan padres, at both the Alta and Baja California missions, and American and British traders was estimated at about 25,000 pesos a year.[27] Moreover, in his 1804 journal, American smuggler William Shaler alluded to Franciscans' continued active participation in the illegal trade. He referred to them as "principle monopolizers of the fur trade." He added that "anyone acquainted with the coast can easily obtain provisions," indicating that, despite official orders to refuse foreign ships entrance into California ports, missionaries were very willing to continue their trading practices.

Illegal trade with Shaler and other Americans brought missionaries a variety of goods, ranging from frying pans to rum and tobacco. In addition to goods exchanged for otter pelts, missionaries also received hard specie. Recorded transactions between the American ship the USS *Mercury* and the San Gabriel Mission in 1806 and 1807 show a sum of about 58 pesos exchanged in cash and provisions.[28] Although the individual mission totals are not very high, the combined sum for all missions was approximately 4,936 pesos, of which 3,000 pesos were paid in cash and 2,000 pesos in goods.[29] The profit from clandestine trade, consisting of both merchandise and hard specie, explains the origins of the monetary reserves held at the missions and the wealth of each respective institution.

The increased liberalization of trade restrictions at the turn of the century allowed ships to carry extra cargo into Alta California's ports and facilitated missionaries' continued trade with Russians and Anglo-American traders on the California Coast.[30] Franciscans' continued participation in this underground trade greatly increased the regional missions' production by requiring them to create larger surpluses to meet growing demands by international traders.[31] This trade contributed to the missions' continued growth as powerful economic institutions in the California borderlands.

INDEPENDENCE, TRADE, AND THE RISE OF MEXICAN LIBERALISM, 1810–1833

Mexico's War for Independence, from 1810 to 1821, produced three key developments that created a prime economic situation for the growth of the mission economy and the Californio elite. First, the devastating war disrupted long established yet tenuous trade routes between California and the Mexican interior. Secondly, it destabilized commercial agriculture and export markets in Mexico.[32] Lastly, independence severed ties with Spain, creating an unstable economy marred by the loss of capital as Spaniards fled the country. Individually, each of these conditions is not unique to countries engaged in wars for independence from imperial powers. However, when they are examined collectively in the context of nineteenth century Alta California, it becomes evident that they converged and deeply influenced ideas about optimal land use. In turn, these convergences determined the region's economic growth, power distribution, and institutional development and collapse.

The War for Mexican Independence exacerbated the difficulty of bringing supplies into Alta California. At San Gabriel, plentiful wheat and grain harvests supplied both military personnel and the nearby Pueblo de Los Angeles with much-needed food.[33] At the same time, an abundant cattle supply provided settlers and traders alike with much desired tallow and other mission goods.[34] As the economy collapsed, and military personnel did not receive their salaries, soldiers and settlers, facing hunger and uncertainty, desperately looked to the mission for help.[35] Franciscans, concerned with providing for mission neophytes, hesitantly entered into a business relationship with the presidios and El Pueblo de Los Angeles as a way to help provide for the region's military and civilian population.[36]

Between 1810 and 1830, the San Gabriel Mission provided badly needed supplies worth approximately 56,600 pesos to the Santa Barbara and San Diego presidios.[37] Missionaries faced increasing pressure to provide supplies to the military and the larger region. Despite the high demand for goods, regional inhabitants, military personnel, and settlers often paid for mission goods using notes drafted from Mexico's bankrupt treasury. This practice put missionaries at a disadvantage because they often received no remuneration for their items.[38] Despite the uncertainty of the regional economy, missionaries looked to maritime trade to supplement their coffers.[39] Although Franciscans did not always find prices agreeable, they were happy to be able to keep trading.[40] This continued trade proved to be very beneficial to the growth of the missions because it prompted expansion in production to meet increased foreign demands.

In response to increased regional demands for goods and their participation in foreign trade, Franciscans dedicated more land to agricultural production and ranching. Similar to other California missions, the Franciscans used land nearest the mission building for the cultivation of crops and grazed livestock on the outlying land. Dedicating the majority of mission land to these enterprises reaffirmed missionaries' views of optimal land use based on agricultural production and cattle grazing.

By the end of the War for Independence, the San Gabriel Mission (see fig. 3) had reached its highest point of development, and missionaries were successfully cultivating crops in the surrounding region. In 1821 mission Indians successfully harvested crops, measured in *fanegas*: wheat (5,000 fanegas), maize (3,000 fanegas), beans (150 fanegas), and lentils (30 fanegas)—a total of 8,180 fanegas.[41] These numbers reveal important information regarding San Gabriel Mission's production and land use during this period. For example, despite

FIGURE 3 San Gabriel Mission (east entrance), ca. 1884. Courtesy of the University of Southern California Libraries and California Historical Society. Digitally reproduced by the USC Digital Library; from the California Historical Society Collection at the University of Southern California, http://digitallibrary.usc.edu/cdm/singleitem/collection/p15799coll65/id/6348/rec/1.

there being no standardized measurement until the mid-1840s, scholars such as J. N. Bowman indicated that, in 1830s California, the fanega area for wheat was 1.74 acres and the fanega area for corn was approximately 6.94 acres.[42] If these calculations are applied to San Gabriel's harvest of wheat and corn, 5,000 and 3,000 fanegas, respectively, represent the cultivation of about twenty-nine thousand acres of land, a plausible amount considering San Gabriel's significant land holdings. The fact that San Gabriel's missionaries used this vast acreage to produce corn and wheat, as well as other crops, indicates that agricultural production constituted their vision of optimal land use.

Aside from influencing missionaries' use of land, foreign trade during the war affected the development of the economy outside the mission as well as Franciscans' relationships with secular agents. Although largely autonomous in their participation in clandestine maritime trade, missionaries sought help from people looking to profit from the underground trade network. The region's two strongest missions, Santa Barbara and San Gabriel, expanded and maintained their foreign trade with the help of a purchasing agent who managed monies and nongovernmental trade.[43] Missionaries at Santa Barbara designated José de la Guerra y Noriega, a man familiar with the trade activity off California's coast, as their agent. As comandante of the Santa Barbara Presidio, de la Guerra's official responsibilities included enforcing governmental trade restrictions and combating smuggling. Despite his sworn responsibility to the Crown, de la

Guerra played a key role in regional smuggling and, as a result, became a wealthy landowner.[44] Commander de la Guerra's amicable relationships with a bevy of foreign traders made it easier for him to secure trading relationships for the Franciscan missionaries.

As trading agent, de la Guerra handled transactions between missionaries and foreign business agents and received a portion of the profit as his commission. His responsibilities at Santa Barbara often required him to work with the San Gabriel Mission as well. For example, in 1817 de la Guerra oversaw the shipment of more than 3,000 pesos' worth of goods to San Gabriel. He obtained the merchandise from the foreign traders, brought the supplies to San Gabriel, and sold them at a competitive price, netting 522 pesos for himself. Because he traded the items on consignment, de la Guerra instructed missionaries to buy what they wanted and return the rest to him.[45] Similar to Santa Barbara's missionaries, San Gabriel's mission priests worked with de la Guerra to sell their mission products and purchase foreign staple goods and luxury items.[46] These trade networks were among the many from which Mission San Gabriel profited during this period.

In addition to international smuggling, San Gabriel's missionaries supplemented their profits by establishing contracts with San Diego and Los Angeles residents for the slaughter of cattle. Missionaries sought these contracts as a way to reduce the number of mission-owned cattle grazing on mission lands.[47] The agreements stated that settlers would slaughter the cattle, keep half of the hides for themselves, and give the other half to the mission. Missionaries then traded or sold these hides to foreign traders who entered the region. The San Gabriel Mission quickly became the region's key tallow producer and engaged in extensive trade with foreign companies.

Most of the San Gabriel Mission's trade was with a Chilean company, represented by English-born agent William Hartnell. While other trading companies were restricted to either the Port of Monterey or San Diego, Hartnell's company had obtained a license to conduct business at any California port. Often, he traded out of the Port of San Pedro, located in San Pedro Bay about thirty-five miles south of the San Gabriel Mission. In 1822 San Pedro Bay became a bustling commercial center and served as an outlet for local goods and a source of imported foreign products. Tallow and hide produced at the San Gabriel Mission and regional ranches found their way into foreign markets through the vessels docked at this port.[48] Hartnell's exclusive access to San

FIGURE 4 Branding iron and Father Serra's cup, San Gabriel Mission 1890. The dark-colored brand rests on the cup at center. The cup is ornately decorated with carvings. The objects rest on a wooden platform and an adobe wall can be seen in the background. The objects are from Plaza Mission Museum. The branding iron is TS for St. Temblor. Courtesy of the University of Southern California Libraries and California Historical Society. Digitally reproduced by the USC Digital Library; from the California Historical Society Collection at the University of Southern California, http://digitallibrary.usc.edu/cdm/singleitem/collection/p15799coll65/id/15128/rec/1.

Pedro Bay meant that in all likelihood missionaries did not have much of a choice in deciding whether to trade with him.[49]

Letters between San Gabriel's Fray José María de Zalvidea and Hartnell illustrate the volume and variety of trade during and immediately following Mexican independence. Hartnell's company brought items into the region that were also available from the Mexican interior, but it was their quick availability that made them appealing to California's missionaries. Easy access to these items was tempting, but by no means were missionaries at the trader's mercy. For example, an 1823 letter requesting knives, iron, and sugar indicated that Zalvidea believed the prices were too high; in fact, he stated that he could obtain them at a lower cost.[50] Regardless of how appealing this trade was, Zalvidea asserted that, as the main producers of tallow and hide in the region, San Gabriel's missionaries had an advantage in the trade relationship and would not be disadvantaged by overpaying for these goods.[51]

This trade and the missionaries' relationship with Hartnell reflect the changing relationship between the missionaries' regional power and the interconnectedness of political, social, and cultural spheres during their era. Politically and economically, the decision regarding Hartnell's exclusive trading license came from Provincial Governor Pablo Vicente Solá and head of the mission system Fray Mariano Payéras rather than from authorities in Mexico City. This reflects the assertion of local power over economic affairs, a factor that fueled conflict throughout the Mexican period. However, this decision was directly linked to California's growing elite class.

Socially, Hartnell, an Anglo, had managed to develop a good reputation with the business community in California based on his interaction with the Santa Barbara trade agent, José de La Guerra. Over time, with the support of local elites, Hartnell assimilated into the tight-knit Californio community, even changing his name to Guillermo Eduardo Hartnell.[52] In the 1820s, during one of his visits, Hartnell met fourteen-year-old María Teresa de la Guerra and subsequently, as traditions of the time dictated, submitted a letter to her father asking for permission to wed her.[53] Hartnell converted to Catholicism in 1824 and wed María Teresa in April of 1825.[54] He went on to become a landowner and school teacher in Alta California.

These factors speak to the rising conflict between missionaries and aspiring elites. They also indicate the solidification of economic and social power among Californio politicians and regional elites during the post-independence period. Social networks became increasingly important in gaining and maintaining political and economic power. The inclusion of José de la Guerra, William Hartnell, and others in the free trade that been dominated by missionaries provided secular access to the immense profits missions had reaped during the first part of the nineteenth century.[55]

By 1830 as part of the tallow and hide trade, missionaries and other landowners dedicated more mission lands to ranching. Despite this change they were still criticized for adhering to an archaic colonial system that allowed them to control the region's best lands and profit. At this point it became clear that the issue was not how the mission used the land, but rather that they were the only ones who profited from it.

The escalating conflict between missionaries and those calling for the secularization and privatization of mission lands was a competition over visions of land use and especially visions of the profit they could reap from the land. The generation before secularization regarded missionaries' presence in the area as valuable to the establishment of regional settlements. This view contrasts with that of the second generation of Californios, who saw the mission and missionaries as impediments to their financial opportunities. Although these critics emphasized the evangelical project's ineffectiveness in their complaints against the mission system, it was an increasing attitude of secularism and a desire to control mission lands and neophyte labor that was at the core of these critiques.

The differing attitudes about missionaries is exemplified in Teresa de la Guerra Hartnell's testimonio.[56] Her narrative described the great endearment and sense of debt that her family—some of California's earliest colonists—felt for the missionaries. She took issue with those seeking secularization, stating that their denigration of mission priests was a result of historical ignorance.[57] She asserted that Franciscans represented the interests of their Indian pupils, and credited them with the establishment of civilization and progress:

> I am confident that the people of my race who have valued the conduct of those dignified missionaries of God will recognize that civilization is indebted to them for the progress that our country has made here. That without any exception were the fathers' observed good conduct in Alta California from the 3rd day of 1770 to 1833; I have no impediment in making this assertion that my grandparents and relatives, the true founders of this country, have told me. I, myself, have referred to and value the many dignified acts of the mission fathers whose virtues I admired when I was young and enjoyed the joys of this world, and that I was mother of 20 boys and 5 girls, with one foot in the grave I remember with complete satisfaction.[58]

Teresa de la Guerra Hartnell not only attributed the region's progress to the mission priests but she also tied her families' identity to the land by stating that the original founders recognized the mission system's importance in establishing the region. She regarded the calls for distributing mission lands as something foreign to the region, believing that it was a sentiment emanating from the region's younger aspiring landowners rather than from well-established families such as hers. Her words illustrate broader attitudes about changing regional economic structures and ideas about land.

Doña Teresa's narrative and her family's legacy as one of Alta California's *verdaderos fundadores* (true founders) reflect the interconnectedness that existed between the mission and early regional elites; landed families such as the de la Guerras felt tremendous respect toward mission fathers. Conversely, missionaries respected landed families by allowing some of these patriarchs direct and continued participation in their trade networks. For example, de la Guerra's role as purchasing agent for the Mission Santa Barbara provided both him and William Hartnell the opportunity to participate in this lucrative trade.

The cooperation between mission and regional authorities, with implicit or explicit backing by regional elites, created a mutually beneficial business relationship for the missionaries and traders. The relationship that developed between men like Hartnell and missionaries at the Santa Barbara and San Gabriel Missions during the 1820s illustrates the interwoven nature of business and sociocultural interactions, a link that continued after mission secularization. Prominent Californios, men like Juan Bautista Alvarado and José Castro, who supported mission secularization and were deeply involved in the politics of the time, supported Hartnell's permission to both trade without restriction and maintain an exclusive trade license. Increasing interest in an economy focused on the cattle industry displaced the vision of California as a place for farming.[59] Emphasis on an industry that required a great deal of uncultivated land changed the vision of optimal land use; the age of the rancho had fully emerged. Aspiring oligarchs sought to displace the mission, professing a shift toward liberalism after Mexican independence.

After independence, liberals supported either federalist or republican ideologies. In 1824, under a newly established federalist yet conservative constitution, Mexico took shape as a republic that reflected nineteenth century liberalist thinking.[60] In Latin America and Mexico, liberalism developed in complex and contradictory ways. Often there was a clear distinction between political and economic liberalism.[61] Far from espousing a cohesive ideology based on the universalist Enlightenment ideals of democracy, political equality, free trade, and economic development, liberals differed in their conceptualization of political liberalism and did not always agree on concepts of social and political change.[62] Some supported more liberal ideas such as "public education, popular suffrage, and the abolition of slavery," while others "supported a constitutional liberalism that guaranteed equality and freedoms for the few."[63]

Interestingly, despite their disparate views on societal change and political access, both groups agreed on limiting the wealth and privileges of the military and the Church. The liberals' anticlerical ideology did not manifest itself in the more conservative faction of the party immediately after independence, but rather developed after 1830 when liberal constitutionalism gave way to liberal anticorporatism.[64] Early Federalist attempts to limit individual clerics' power and resulted in the Church using the rhetoric of liberal republicanism to defend its rights to due process under the new liberal system, showing that the Church and secular government were not immediately at odds after independence.[65]

Despite its liberal federalist foundation, the 1824 Constitution declared Catholicism Mexico's official religion and maintained the *fueros*, or special privileges for the military and the clergy. The fueros' connection to the military is of primary concern to the study of California because the special privileges blocked open access to mission lands and made it easier for these groups to obtain land grants. This accounted for the numerous private land grants issued by the Spanish government during the late 1780s and 1790s.[66] Most of California's aspiring landowners were sons of ex-military officers, who had benefited from the fueros to receive the region's best land. The fact that many of these advocates of Mexican liberalism came from such families reflects a major contradiction that existed in Californios' articulation of liberalism.

Californios' liberal ideology was one in which aspiring landowners only rhetorically supported equality, but rather actively implemented ideologies of economic liberalism as a way of maintaining privilege and distinction in their everyday practice. Californios' emphasis on economic liberalism made the Church, specifically the missions, with their vast wealth, property holdings, and social power, the main target of liberalism's anticlerical efforts.[67]

Liberalism often reflected the specific needs and agendas of those who articulated it. Accordingly, Mexican and Californio liberals alike contoured liberalism's political and economic tenets in ways that furthered their respective interests. As Rosaura Sánchez contended in her work on liberal discourse, not all Mexican revolutionaries were concerned with eradicating societal and political inequities, but rather some were more interested in ending colonial domination to promote capitalist development that benefitted the criollo ruling class.[68] To California's aspiring landowners, liberalism did not mean democracy but rather an opportunity for regional autonomy and the removal of obstacles that stood in the way of economic progress.[69] In the Mexican interior, various ideas of how to enact liberal political and economic reforms in the Mexican Republic often resulted in contentious and chaotic struggles for power and wealth between the Catholic Church and the government; this would be the case in Alta California as well.

The broader calls for secularization of Church lands in the Mexican interior manifested themselves on the California borderland through calls for mission secularization. The mission institution represented a repressive system that inhibited liberal visions of social progress and economic development. To many liberals the right to own property represented the right to life itself.[70] Alta California's aspiring landowners shared the ideas of their liberal compatriots in the

Mexican interior who believed that secularization of Church and mission lands would end monopolistic land practices, encourage individual initiative, engender trade, and create a naturally stratified labor system that encouraged general wealth.[71] Aspiring Californios, such as liberal-minded Juan Bandini, believed that missionaries unnecessarily, selfishly, and "insensitively appropriated all the area," and have "sinister[ly] occupied the best lands and water sources . . . desiring exclusive control over the productions of the country."[72] Bandini argued for the decentralization of commerce and the expansion of regional production through private traders. Bandini's critiques of Franciscans' selfish and monopolistic practices reflected early nineteenth century liberal ideas of private land ownership and free trade.

The rise of nineteenth-century Mexican liberalism clashed with missionaries' horticultural and agricultural views about land use, resulting in repeated quarrels over land access and allegations of unfair price setting. The San Gabriel Mission's dominance of the tallow and hide trade in the 1820s and early 1830s motivated local aspiring landowners to assert their liberal visions of land use based on the potential an "inexhaustible" rancho economy.[73] Continued critique of missionaries' control of viable land reflected liberal elites' desires to take, redistribute, and privatize mission lands.[74]

The San Gabriel Mission's position as the region's center of production and missionaries' possession of premier lands bred aspiring landowners' resentment of mission wealth. The economic competition posed by Franciscan missions within the context of economic liberalist thought prompted Californios to replace missionaries' vision of land use and purpose with one that emphasized individual wealth and private land ownership.[75] Ultimately, this power struggle resulted in the Secularization Order of 1833, which dealt the deathblow to the Mission Era in the nascent Mexican Republic.

PART II

RISE OF THE RANCHO

3

SECULARIZATION AND THE RISE OF THE RANCHO

Creating San Pascual, 1833–1843

AMID MEXICO'S LIBERAL-CONSERVATIVE political conflicts of the 1820s and 1830s, Mexican and Californio liberals found common ground in their calls for mission secularization. As early as the 1820s, the rise of Mexican liberalism had given rise to anticlerical sentiment that sought to limit the power and wealth of the Catholic Church in Mexico. After an 1832 coup toppled the conservative pro-clerical government, liberals got an opportunity, albeit short-lived, to implement their secularization plans.[1] After assuming presidential duties from Antonio López de Santa Anna, Vice President Gómez Farías implemented his liberal plan of ending fueros for the military, establishing a secular mentality that emphasized utilitarian rather than religious values, and destroying the power of the Church.[2] On August 17, 1833, Congress issued a secularization order that dismantled the mission system in Baja and Alta California, opening former mission lands for privatization.[3]

Gómez Farías's efforts for secularization fell apart when estranged President Santa Anna returned in 1834. Santa Anna quickly ousted the vice president and did away with a large portion of the secularization plan in the Mexican interior. These developments did not affect the secularization of mission lands, which he allowed to continue.[4] In the years following the 1833 secularization order, Californios supported the implementation of a locally controlled secularization process friendly to the property and economic interests of the aspiring elites.

Independence and secularization helped establish a system of haciendas and ranchos parallel to those dominant in nineteenth century Mexico.[5] Between 1839 and 1851, the land was reorganized and distributed in accordance with a highly racialized and classed system that privileged upper-class blancos and hijos del país, and increasingly left Indigenous people on the margins of Californio society and culture. Economically, the demise of the mission system and the rise of the rancho in California allowed aspiring oligarchs to take control of the land, exploit Indian labor, and replace the mission as the wealthiest institution in Alta California.[6] The emergence of the rancho as the site for the generation of wealth and the physical representation of honor created a society in which people used land ownership to negotiate their place and status within changing social, economic, and cultural systems.

The creation of the private rancho system (see fig. 5) resulted from several pre-1833 secularization act regulations that determined the process and requirements for receiving land grants in California. Under the Mexican Colonization Act of 1824 and the supplemental regulations of 1828, territorial governors were given the power to distribute land grants to settlers at their discretion within the set parameters of the laws.

The colonization act and regulations set the legal basis for the creation of the private land system. They set up the protocol for requesting land, defining ranchos' physical boundaries, and determining who was eligible to receive land grants.[7] Individual grantees could be awarded anywhere from one league (approximately 4,428 acres) to eleven leagues (about 48,708 acres).[8] These laws required grantees to maintain and improve the land to preserve their title. The core requirement of land development was crucial to ensure greater regional growth and the expansion of economic markets. Additionally, it ensured that large land parcels would be held by families who could afford to develop the land. Wealthy Californio families such as the Picos, de la Guerras, and Carrillos claimed 532,000, 326,000, and 320,000 acres of land, respectively.[9]

These families' land holdings not only illustrate the oligarchies that developed in California after secularization, but they also give insight into the link among land ownership, wealth, and honor. Wealthy and powerful oligarchs such as these, as well as smaller scale rancheros interested in keeping their land titles, had to work hard to develop their lands and meet the land grant requirements or run the risk of losing their land titles and by extension their honor.

In the frenzy of activity that developed after secularization, landed Californios throughout the region defended their land grants against claims of

FIGURE 5 Map of old Spanish and Mexican ranchos in Los Angeles County, ca. 1919. This image shows the San Gabriel Mission in the center of the region; Rancho San Pascual is located directly above. Courtesy of the University of Southern California Libraries and California Historical Society. Digitally reproduced by the USC Digital Library; from the California Historical Society Collection at the University of Southern California, http://digitallibrary.usc.edu/cdm/compoundobject/collection/p15799coll65/id/386/rec/1.

abandonment and neglect from aspiring landowners interested in dispossessing them of their premium lands. Charges of neglect were based on a variety of factors, but most were based on accusations of physical neglect of the land or juridical neglect in the petition process. Commonly, petitioners alleging physical neglect cited that a plot of land was in a state of deterioration (i.e., lack of cultivation) because of owner negligence. If upon review authorities verified these accusations, petitioners received title to the land, dispossessing previous land owners.

In cases of judicial negligence, grantees were accused of failing to follow the formal protocol solidifying the land grant.[10] Failure to follow these procedures often resulted from territorial governors' very irregular bureaucratic processes. These arbitrarily defined and implemented processes repeatedly opened grantees up to denunciation by a better prepared party. It is within this context that the Rancho San Pascual took shape on the former lands of the San Gabriel Mission.

While land denunciations were common throughout Alta California between 1833 and 1846, records for San Pascual show that there were two denunciations lodged against the land's owners. In both cases, petitioners claimed abandonment and failure to develop the land.[11] These denouncements were lodged by parties wishing to place San Pascual in the hands of a well-established network of landed oligarchs. The redistribution of mission lands would keep San Pascual in the hands of wealthy landed men and perpetuate a social and cultural system in which social position depended on their relationship to land.

THE RHETORIC AND REALITIES OF SECULARIZATION

As early as the mid-1820s calls for secularization of California's missions prompted protests from Franciscan missionaries seeking to keep control of mission lands and Indian labor. Governor Echeandía's arrival in 1825 marked a move toward preliminary secularization of mission lands and emancipation of mission Indians. Under Echeandía's plan, missions were to be made into pueblos populated by mission Indians, non-Christian Indians, Californios, and colonists.[12] Mission land and livestock would be distributed to the pueblos' Christianized Indian settlers in the form of "two plots of land, one for a house and one for crops"; additionally, "each family of former neophytes would receive a specified number of sheep and goats, one yoke of oxen, two horses and a mare, and instruments for carpentry and cultivation."[13] This plan was supposed to ensure that neophytes gained access to former mission lands prior to non-Indian settlers. Undistributed land was placed under the control of an administrator who answered to town councils and the territorial governor. Secularization required missionaries to relinquish their claims over the land and the vast wealth the mission had garnered during its time as the region's dominant economic institution. Mission priests could retain control only over the church and living quarters.[14]

Part of dismantling the mission system required that a plan for Indian emancipation accompany secularization. Echeandía sought to help Indians separate from the mission and remove themselves from under the Franciscans' authority.[15] Through his Decree of Emancipation in Favor of Neophytes in July 1826, Echeandía declared that mission Indians who had lived in the missions for more than fifteen years or from childhood and could provide for themselves were allowed to leave the mission.[16] Additionally, the decree prohibited Franciscans from using corporal punishment against married or adult Indians and set limits on the whipping of Indian children.[17] Echeandía's limiting of Franciscan control over Indians' bodies influenced mission Indians' perception of missionaries' authority. By the time the California territorial deputation passed full-scale emancipation in 1831, the rhetoric of liberalism and Mexican independence had imbued many Indians with a sense of freedom, individuality, and autonomy. Specifically, mission neophytes defined their freedom as linked to the control of their own labor, entitlement to land, and the ability to move about freely.[18]

As partial emancipation and territorial secularization decrees gave way to a national secularization order in 1833, Indians defined their identities within a liberalist context as Franciscans struggled to exert control over those whom they still regarded as their charges. News of Indian emancipation encouraged mission Indians to challenge priests' efforts to control their actions and labor.[19] Resistance took many forms: some mission Indians refused to work and others petitioned for their freedom, while many openly revolted against missionary control.[20]

In her testimonio, Eulalia Pérez, San Gabriel's llavera, recounted the day Captain Barroso arrived at the mission and roused the Indians to revolt by telling them that they were no longer mission neophytes but free men and women. San Gabriel's Indians reacted to Barrosa's news with violence against head priest Father José Sánchez. According to Pérez, the Indians surrounded the mission and established a mission guard. When Father Sánchez attempted to leave the mission to administer mass in Los Angeles, the Indian guard confronted him and promptly cut the reins on his horses. In response to the attack, Sánchez jumped off the coach, and the Indians violently dragged him to his quarters.[21] She described Sánchez's desperation and sadness during his last days, having recused "himself to his room for eight days, [falling] ill, his ears . . . [exploding] with blood [with] a pain in his head that did not cease until he died in January of 1833."[22] The mission neophytes' violent revolt and their quick embracing of emancipation points to missionaries' tenuous control over their Indigenous charges and the neophytes' overall dissatisfaction with missionaries' authority.

Perez's valuable recounting of mission Indians' response conveys the symbolic ending of the Mission Period. Similar to Sánchez in his languishing last days, the mission had grown increasingly weak, declining in a liberalist climate that defined it as a part of an archaic irrelevant past. Sánchez's passing symbolized the death of the mission's old guard and the end of the Franciscan Order's leadership and control in Alta California.

Secularization and emancipation ushered in a new era of land use and wealth for the region, as well as a new way of understanding peoples' connection to the land. This new system required that Californios take control of the land as well as reorganize and appropriate ex-neophyte labor and loyalty. Throughout the struggle for secularization, Californios endorsed a policy that ensured local control over secularized mission lands while the federal government advocated for distribution of former mission lands to a broader variety of people.

According to federal secularization and emancipation plans, "mission lands were to be divided amongst former neophytes and other Indians; soldiers in the garrisons of California to whom the federal government owed pay; Mexican residents of California who owned less than the minimum acreage allotted under the secularization plan; Mexican and foreign families who emigrated to California; entrepreneurs who brought people into the territory; and convicts who completed their terms of imprisonment in California and wished to stay."[23] As part of the plan the federal government organized and sent the Híjar-Padrés colony to establish a settlement in Alta California in 1834. Under the leadership of liberal leaders José María Híjar and José María Padrés, two hundred colonists consisting of artisans, teachers, merchants, farmers, and other skilled men and women migrated north toward Alta California. The colony was a liberalist experiment to immediately colonize former mission lands by establishing pueblos and opening them up to settlement.[24] This colony illustrates that the liberal federal government intended a wider distribution of former mission lands rather than the creation of a landed class. Although liberal Californios such as Bandini, Vallejo, and Alvarado favored secularization, they resented the centralized government's plan and rejected the colony. They perceived these outsider colonists as a threat to their access to former mission lands and by extension to their economic self-interests.[25]

In a move to ensure that former mission lands would go to local men, Californios in the territorial deputation passed a law enabling "only Indians, rather than the region's soldiers, settlers, or recent immigrants, to receive mission lands and goods."[26] With this law the deputation determined that only Indians would inhabit the former mission pueblos. Land provided to Indians could not be sold and upon the neophyte's death it was to revert to the public domain.[27]

While this law seemed to benefit Indians, Californios were creating a means to ensure their access to land by linking land ownership, Indian emancipation, and territorial sovereignty. They did this by using specific terms and language. Californios argued that, as natives of the land, Indians were entitled to receive mission lands. Although the use of this label implied Californios' recognition of Indians as the rightful inhabitants of the land, and to a certain extent their entitlement to it, their intention was not to give former mission Indians claim to mission lands. Rather, Californios used this label to frame their own claims to mission lands and gain the labor of newly freed Indians. The words *native of the land* or *nativo* later became a standard part of elite Californios' identity and were often used to describe their native connection with and entitlement to the land. Through this rhetorical naming, Californios designated themselves, not Indians, as the rightful heirs of these lands. Rather than using the phrase as a means of claiming space for themselves *and* Indians, Californios increasingly used it to distinguish themselves from Indigenous populations and to maintain a superior sociocultural status. After secularization, despite the deputation's proposed allotment of land to former mission neophytes and Californios' liberalist rhetoric of the importance of Indian emancipation and land ownership, many Californios held fast to condescending ideas about Indigenous populations to deny them land ownership.[28]

As Californio identity took shape within the context of secularization, many Californios increasingly rearticulated Franciscans' paternalistic and negative attitudes about Indians as uncivilized as a means of placing themselves at the top of the social structure.[29] Despite liberal Californios' anti-missionary attitudes, many saw and credited the mission as a site for Christianizing and pacifying uncivilized Indians.[30] Similar to the missionaries before them, Californios imposed a racialized cultural hierarchy that solidified neophytes' sociocultural inferiority through their relationship to the land. Prominent Californios then used this hierarchy to link their familial roots in the region to the mission itself. Californios traced their origins to the San Gabriel Mission walls by defining themselves as nativos of the land, a claim that legitimated their right to access secularized mission lands.

During the period between secularization and the advent of the U.S.-Mexico War, recognized as the height of the Rancho Period, several prominent well-respected Californio families divided millions of acres of former mission lands among themselves. Some of the largest land grants went to men from families such as the Picos, Yorbas, de la Guerras, Lugos, Bandinis, and Sepúlvedas, most of whom had long social, political, economic, and historical roots in the region.[31] By the beginning of the U.S.-Mexico War in 1846, these and other well-known families controlled "some ten million acres of land, or 10 percent of the surface area of present-day California."[32]

Conversely, for most Indians, implementation of secularization and emancipation policies resulted in landlessness, poverty, and coerced labor. Many were forced to negotiate their survival in the rancho system and pueblos as laborers, a role similar to their previous one in the missions.[33] Although some Indians who petitioned for former mission lands did receive plots, most of their requests for land were denied. Of forty-one rancho patents issued to Indians, only twenty-nine were for former mission lands.[34] Most Indian-owned ranches founded on mission lands were located in the areas between San Diego and San Luis Obispo.

In addition to ranches, Christian Indians established thirteen villages in southern California. Only four of these villages, located on secularized lands of the San Juan Capistrano Mission, received patents.[35] Despite liberal claims of Indian emancipation and equality, only small numbers of Native people received the land allotments promised by secularization. Regardless of their newly gained political rights and demands for freedom, "the new political ordering of space continued to bind former neophytes to many of the same conditions of coercive labor that had characterized their previous states."[36] Due to governmental restrictions set forth in the secularization act that forbade Indians from selling or transferring their lands, Indians were very rarely able to obtain titles and clear ownership of their allotments.[37]

Distribution of San Gabriel's former mission lands followed the general pattern of land distribution in California, often granted to prominent Californios rather than Indians. An examination of how Rancho San Pascual changed hands during the Mexican era shows that land ownership was part of a larger oligarchic system founded on sociocultural and economic hierarchies that kept the land in the hands of deserving gente de razón. Land ownership, one of the liberal tenets supporting secularization, was synonymous with freedom; in California's emerging merchant capitalist environment this translated into economic power and freedom for aspiring Californio elites, not Indians. By placing former mission lands under the jurisdiction of Californio administrators, elites quickly mobilized themselves into a political and social force to determine who would hold power and own land in Alta California.[38] Distribution of San Gabriel's lands reflected racialized visions of land use and maintained the racial hierarchy by keeping parties deemed undeserving from benefiting from land privatization.

EL RINCÓN DE SAN PASCUAL IN THE RANCHO SYSTEM

Rancho San Pascual (see fig. 6), comprising approximately 14,000 acres of premier lands and accompanying livestock belonging to the San Gabriel Mission, was one of the largest land allotments resulting from secularization. Local

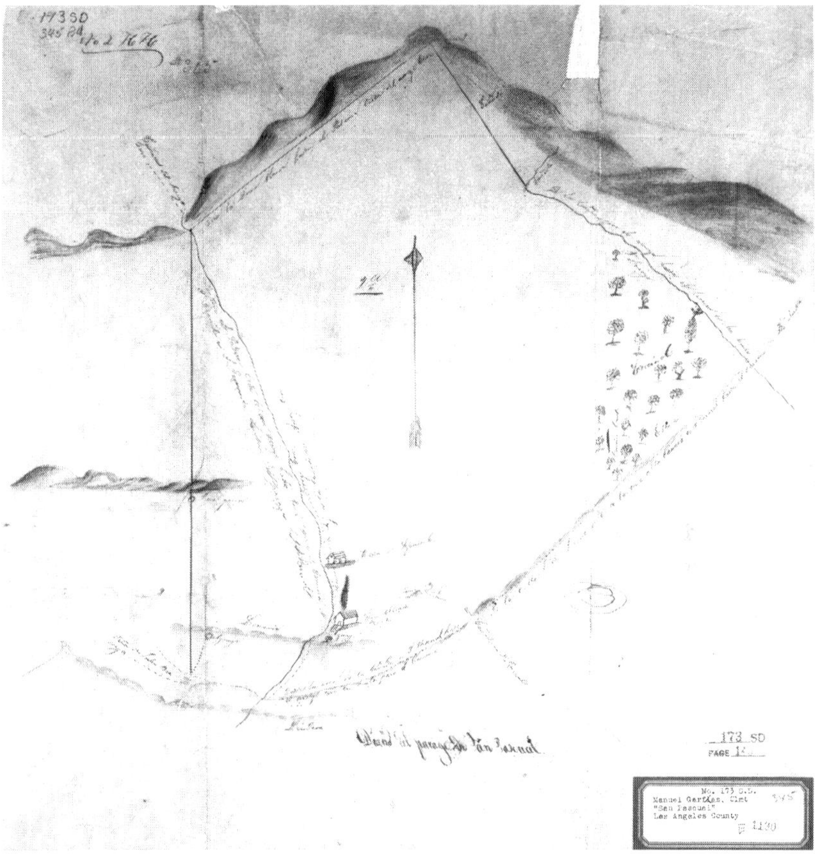

FIGURE 6 San Pascual *diseño* (map) illustrating the rancho's boundaries, landscape, and terrain. Maps of private land grant cases of California, Land Case Map E-1190. Courtesy of the Bancroft Library, University of California, Berkeley, http://content.cdlib.org/ark:/13030/hb0s20029b/?order=1.

folklore posits that Rancho San Pascual took its name from the fact that mission priests made the grant on Easter Sunday in 1833.[39] Historian James Guinn argued that the Rancho's name gained its significance from the baptismal name of Chief Hahamov, the Indian leader of the Hahamog'na band of the Tongva who encountered Spanish Captain Gaspar de Portolá's land expedition in the Arroyo Seco area of present-day Pasadena.[40] Regardless of the name's origin, both stories attribute the naming of the site to religious events—to the rebirth of Christ on Easter or the spiritual rebirth of Hahamov as a Christian. Both naming stories illustrate a clear vision of the land and by extension its people;

both were Christian. The conversion of the Indigenous population to Christianity through the work of the missions and the observance of the Easter holiday at the time of the allotment symbolize the successful establishment of Christianity in the region. This bridges the missionaries' historical presence in the region and the results of their work. Even though the San Gabriel Mission was secularized and missionaries were relieved of their duties and land, their impact and imprint on the land was still recognized: the historical narrative acknowledged the sociocultural importance of the Christian missionizing project to regional settlement.[41]

Interestingly, the land craze engendered through secularization did not occur in San Gabriel in the same way it did in other mission areas. At secularization, mission priests gave San Gabriel's mission lands to Spanish Army Lieutenant Juan Mariné, an allotment whose origins and details are still widely debated.[42] Similar to the way that missionaries' control of the land had kept local settlers from gaining access to it during the Mission Period, Mariné's ownership now posed an obstacle to local settlers' opportunities to develop this rich land. By giving land to this loyal former soldier in gratitude for his service, missionaries attempted to control what happened to their lands after secularization. In San Gabriel, requests for land parcels did not begin in earnest until after Mariné died and his heirs sold San Pascual in 1836. The sale of the land completed what secularization had started. This land allotment speaks to the contestation of power over secularization and provides a glimpse into the societal dynamics during that that historical moment.

The first official deed related to San Pascual was awarded to Juan Mariné by the Mexican governor of California in August of 1835.[43] While this transaction is not in dispute, as there are plenty of governmental documents to support it, the assumption that Mariné was the original intended grantee is a point of disagreement. Popular Pasadena history and local folklore contend that, in 1827, years before the implementation of the federal secularization order, mission priests designated mission llavera Eulalia Pérez as the grantee of El Rincón de Rancho San Pascual as a way of thanking her for many years of devoted service to the mission.[44] Despite the story's popularity, there are no governmental documents, aside from Peréz's testimonio, to substantiate it.

In 1907, historian James Guinn dismissed the narrative of Pérez's grant as a romanticization that many believed without any real proof simply because it was part of local folklore.[45] Guinn argued that "missionaries had no power to deed away mission lands" because "these lands belonged to the government and in theory at least were held in trust for the Indians."[46] Guinn's point is valid because, under the Leyes de las Indias, mission lands were held in trust by missionaries for their Indian converts. The missions were governmental institutions, ultimately belonging to the Spanish Crown and later to the Mexican government, that represented the government's interests in the region.[47] As a result, the missions, missionaries, and Church never held legal or formal title to mission lands.[48] Although Guinn's point is valid, he failed to acknowledge that missionaries' usufructuary occupation of mission lands enabled them to control them at their discretion.[49] Missionaries' perceived ownership may have prompted them to give away the land, albeit unofficially, to Pérez.

As mission secularization loomed, mission priests desired to give land to Eulalia Pérez.[50] Concerned that Pérez would be unable to maintain the land herself and that as a widow she had less ability to administer the land, Father Sánchez encouraged her to marry Lieutenant Juan Mariné, a widower with a family, whom he regarded as being of a man of good character.[51] In her testimonio Pérez noted Father Sánchez's insistence that she marry Mariné. Despite her repeated assertion that "she [did] not want to marry," she stated that she ultimately acquiesced and married Mariné out of her deep-rooted feelings of loyalty, respect, and appreciation for the priest whom she regarded as both "father and mother" and who had supported her and her daughters until they were married.[52] It is clear that Pérez entered into this marriage of her own volition and not out of duress.

Popular retellings of the story contend that the Franciscans required Pérez to marry Mariné in order to give her San Pascual.[53] A closer examination of the politics of land ownership and gender provides a space for reconceptualizing this argument. In her testimonio Pérez stated, "when Father Sánchez gave me two ranchos, rather, land for a ranch and one for an orchard . . . ; when he delivered the land, I was already married to Juan Mariné"[54] Such an allocation to a woman was not uncommon because under Spanish and Mexican law women were allowed to keep their family names and to own land in their own right, leaving their husbands to administer it.[55] Pérez indicated that she was following this practice when she said "later, he [Mariné] only gave me half the land and kept the other half."[56] This implies that Mariné administered Pérez's land, albeit in a way that did not benefit her.

Within this context, Sánchez's encouragement of Pérez's marriage to Mariné may have been a way of protecting the property and not necessarily a condition for acquiring the land. As González found in her study of New Mexico, "women did not surrender their property in marriage; property was defined and protected in the context of a relationship sanctioned by the Church and the state, a relationship, in other words, that served men."[57] If this is the case, Pérez's marriage to Mariné allowed him access to land allocated to her.

Despite women's ability to own land, Pérez seems to have never officially petitioned for San Pascual in her own right, following the custom that legal documents and court proceedings were men's responsibilities.[58] Although Pérez was entitled, both legally and culturally, to all of the land, Mariné gave her only half and kept the rest for himself because it was he who officially petitioned for and was awarded title to it. His public title to the land allowed him complete control of San Pascual, leaving Pérez with no official claim to it. By giving Pérez only half of San Pascual's lands, Mariné essentially dispossessed her of the rest.

In her testimonio, Pérez did not explicitly indict Mariné for his unjust actions, but she regarded him as an avaricious man who never shared his wealth with her, stating that Mariné had "some money, but never gave me possession of the [cash] box."[59] Her testimonio reflects the gendered dynamics of land ownership and marriage by showing that, although women did hold certain rights within the society, they could exercise those rights only at the discretion of their husbands. Using patriarchal control to restrict Pérez's command of the land and limiting her economic means allowed Mariné to build his social status as an honorable landed man.

In 1833, Juan Mariné solicited the regional government for official title to San Pascual. The solicitation named him as the sole interested party and contained no reference to Pérez or her allotment by the mission priests. By claiming San Pascual for himself, Mariné exerted patriarchal control over the land and rendered Pérez invisible, removing any legal claim she may have had to the land. Comparing Pérez's testimonio and Mariné's solicitation shows that, because legal documents and proceedings were men's domain, Mariné could officially separate Pérez from her land in the governmental records.

Following are passages from Pérez's testimonio and Mariné's solicitation from the expediente for San Pascual. Pérez asserted that

> To grant them [land for a ranch and an orchard] to me, Father Zalvidea gathered all the mission Indians and, addressing them in their language, he asked them if they wanted to give me the land for an orchard and a rancho because I had always cared for and attended them; he directed those who did to raise their hands. All of the neophytes raised their hands at once, indicating that they did.[60]

Mariné's solicitation stated that

> Juan Mariner, retired lieutenant of the Mexican artillery in Alta California, and resident of the San Gabriel Mission, and having had the misfortune of losing my orchard in Los Angeles during the flood of 1831, I went to the San Gabriel Mission and spoke with Reverend Father Sánchez, so he could do me a favor and give me a piece of land to cultivate, construct a house, and graze livestock. Upon this request he organized a group of [Indian] alcaldes . . . the alcaldes stated that it would be done and they would give it [land] to me. Father Sánchez told them that it was not for one or two years but forever; they all responded that it was good; later they took to measuring the lands and gave me the site measuring three leagues, called el Rincon San Pascual on which to graze livestock.[61]

In his solicitation, Mariné set himself up as a deserving member of the community, qualified for the land as a citizen of the territory, a distinguished soldier, and a person of good character. Together these attributes embodied Californio masculinity and qualified him for land. After citing the loss of his land in El Pueblo de Los Angeles because of a flood, Mariné explained that he had asked Father Sánchez for land. Both statements indicate that Sanchez gathered the Indians to ask permission to distribute the land, confirming that this event did happen. The question is whether it happened to Pérez or to Mariné. Historians often privilege official documents to determine accuracy and credibility. The fact that Mariné's claim is part of official record—and not personal memoir like Perez's claim—validates his story. It is possible that Mariné co-opted the story from Pérez and used it to legitimize his claim for the land. The fact that Mariné's version is present in the *expedientes* (land records) helps to erase Pérez from the historical record pertaining to ownership of San Pascual. Pérez's name did not appear in the public records relating to San Pascual until Mariné's death in 1836 made her a widow for a second time and she lost claim to *his* land.

The gender dynamics described above explain only part of how Mariné successfully received the land allotment. In keeping with the established racialized vision of land use, it is clear through the expedientes that ethnic, cultural and social identities were also major factors in qualifying Mariné for the land. In the original land solicitation, dated July 15, 1833, Mariné defined himself as a "retired artillery lieutenant of the Department of Mexico in Alta California and resident of the San Gabriel Mission."[62] By defining himself as a retired military officer and vecino, he situated himself within Alta California's sociocultural hierarchy.

Although Mariné did not explicitly identify his race, his status as a *teniente*, or lieutenant, implied that he was an español. On January 8, 1834, at the direction of the *jefe político* (or local prefect), Mariné produced two witnesses, Máximo Alamos and José Manuel Silva. Both were Mexican citizens and vecinos del Pueblo de Los Angeles who had met Mariné during their military service. Alamos and Silva affirmed that Mariné was an español from Catalunya [Catalonia] who had been married to a hija del país with whom he had a large family.[63]

Mariné's testimony contains several important points that helped him obtain San Pascual; it also provides a view of politics and culture in Alta California's land grant process and society. The witnesses first identified Mariné as an español by birth; they immediately followed this with a statement connecting him to a hija del país. Although this seems to be routine information one would provide to attest to a person's character, the language used to describe Mariné holds tremendous significance. As an español by birth, Mariné held a high social status during the Spanish Colonial Period. In post-independence Alta California, when aspiring oligarchs claimed land as part of their birthright as naturales and hijos de país, their Spanish nationality did not hold the same significance as it once had. By immediately connecting Mariné to a hija del país and mentioning his having a family with her, witness testimony solidified his deep roots in Alta California. It must be noted that, although it was Mariné's marriage to Pérez that gave him claim to San Pascual, the testimony emphasized his first marriage to Maria Antonia Sepúlveda. Mariné's marriage to the daughter of distinguished Californio Francisco Xavier Sepúlveda linked him to the regional elite and gave him much needed cultural legitimacy.

In their testimony, Alamos and Silva discussed Mariné's loyal military service. Emphasis on military service in land solicitation was common. Secularization policy stipulated that ex-military men were to be awarded land allotments, and as a result many of these men received land grants throughout Alta California. While common practice in many expedientes, discussion of Mariné's military career served the purpose of presenting him as a loyal Mexican committed to the larger republic and to Alta California specifically. With these words, witnesses helped to remove the stigma connected to Mariné's nationality and better qualified him to obtain land.

On May 6, 1834, the regional governor granted Mariné title to Rancho San Pascual. This land grant detailed several provisions specifying his rights and responsibilities pertaining to the land. The provisions called for the productive development of the 2,214 acres of land. Within one year, Mariné was to have established a homestead, maintained a mill, and planted fruit trees and other useful plants. These provisions recognized Mariné as the sole owner of the land and stated that he could enjoy and develop it without any impediment. The government used these provisions to ensure that San Pascual's owner developed the land in a timely manner. Stipulations in the San Pascual land grant, like other such grants, stated that if the land owner failed to meet these requirements another more suitable petitioner could denounce the land grant.[64]

This provisional grant, not unlike others for former mission lands, reflects larger societal ideals and values for land use. Although the development of viable crops and the establishment of a private homestead demarcated by fences and boundaries were part of broader federal land requirements, the manifestation of these requirements in Alta California reflects post-secularization Californios' racialized visions of land use. A private homestead, set up by a vecino—a term reflective of a racial, ethnic, and class status—was to many the foundation of a civilized society. This was not unlike the visions held by missionaries and early pobladores during the early Mission Period.

Early in the Spanish Colonial Period, because many did not want to settle in such a distant region, missionaries attempted to establish a civilized Spanish society by impressing Spanish cultural identity onto mission neophytes through religion, discipline, and labor. In the post-secularization period, Californios attempted to establish their view of a civilized society on the outskirts of the Mexican Republic through racialized, classed, and regionally defined land requirements. The difference lay in the political, social, and economic factors of each of the periods. By the 1830s, pobladores had become Californios, determined to implement their vision of society. As exemplified in land allotments after 1836, vecinos applied for land grants around the San Gabriel region, including San Pascual, citing land as crucial for the "support of themselves and their families."[65] This phrase emphasizes the cultural importance of establishing permanent homesteads in San Gabriel—homesteads belonging to vecinos and hijos del país who had the wealth to develop the land.

Land grant requirements mandating that original grantees or denouncing parties show their economic potential to develop awarded plots into productive acreage tied economic wealth and stability to land distribution. Land case denouncements and petitioners' use of phrases emphasizing a landowner's lack of means to cultivate land or the petitioner's sufficient means to cultivate the land when contesting or responding to a land claim indicated, indirectly at least, the importance wealth played in land ownership. The strategy of basing land challenges on neglect prompted many rancheros to funnel money into their properties lest they be accused of abandonment, or worse, of poverty. To maintain the appearance of wealth and luxury, landowners built elaborate ranch houses and estates. These estates and the items in them came to represent a Californio material culture inextricably linked with land ownership and labor. Using the rancho as a representation of one's wealth placed it at the core of Californios' visions of optimal land use.

Rancheros' visions of a thriving productive economy with the rancho at the center had broader social and cultural implications. In attempts to keep their land grants, landowners created and emphasized a sociocultural identity based on the links among land ownership, labor, whiteness, and gender. The convergence of these factors combined to create San Pascual's social boundaries. Through social ritual, symbolism, and the display of material wealth, Californios subordinated the lower classes in an attempt to exert and maintain an outward appearance of power and control. Visions of optimal land use premised on creating and developing productive land could be used to dispossess original grantees of their land and place it into the hands of others who could develop it. Grantees who failed to maintain the land, or at least to outwardly reflect their good fortune and ability to maintain it, found themselves forced to give up their titles; San Pascual's story follows this common trajectory.

Two years after Mariné received the grant for San Pascual, the land stood vacant and abandoned, boasting nothing but a rundown shack and some livestock. Mariné's failure to develop the land violated his provisional land grant and left him open to denouncement, but he died before that could happen. Upon Mariné's death in 1836, his heirs—the five children from his marriage to María Sepúlveda (Fruto, Filomeno, Rafaela, Candelaria, y María Antonia)—held legal title to San Pascual.[66] In April 1836, Fruto, Mariné's eldest son, sold half of San Pascual— consisting of "pastures, watering places, lumber, streams, four brindle horse, two double rein horses, and ten heads of cattle"—to Eulalia Pérez's nephew, José Peréz.[67] Fruto Mariné maintained that as an active duty soldier he did not have the time to work the land. Having no desire to keep any portion of San Pascual, his siblings acquiesced to the sale. On April 3, 1836 Fruto Mariné relinquished his families' "ownership, right, possession, domain, and title over the land," leaving José Pérez owner and *apoderado* (official representative) of San Pascual.[68] Mariné's sale of this portion of San Pascual allowed the family to maintain its social status by avoiding a denouncement of the title and opened the rest of the acreage to settlement. Between 1834 and 1846, José

Pérez, Enrique Sepúlveda, and Manuel Garfias vied for ownership and control of Rancho San Pascual's rich lands.

MASCULINITY AND LAND OWNERSHIP: SAN PASCUAL CHANGES HANDS

As Alta California's hierarchal land-based economy grew, the San Gabriel region experienced the growth of a rancho society in which men sought to gain control of vast tracts of land and the honor that came with being a large landholder. San Pascual's change of ownership during the last years of the Mexican period reveals two things about Californio rancho society. First, land documents pertaining to San Pascual reflect that Californios' status and eligibility for land stemmed from their wealth or their perceived wealth. Landowners constructed, maintained, or lost their social distinction through their livestock, vineyards, and the land itself. Secondly, documents show that racialized masculinity affected men's attempts to gain access to San Pascual. For Californio men, ideals of dominant ranchero masculinity required them to provide for their families, control their women, and be *hombres de bien*, or honorable men of means. Both racialized gender norms and ideals of ranchero class masculinity show that, in Alta California's land-based economy, ethnicity, masculinity, class, and land ownership were linked to societal honor, distinction, and status.

A Californio's masculinity and honor depended on his ability to successfully claim and keep his land, fending off potential interlopers. Juan Mariné's death and the subsequent sale of Rancho San Pascual brought José Pérez, Enrique Sepúlveda, and Manuel Garfias into a competition in which each man attempted to distinguish himself through this one parcel of land. Each man, socially and politically respected in his own right, experienced land politics in similar ways; each gained title to San Pascual thorough denunciation and each lost the land because of denunciation/mismanagement. Although economic denouncements were common in Alta California during the 1840s, the story told through these documents indicates how a person's status could quickly change and how easily one's honor was questioned.

Owners of highly desired lands such as San Pascual needed to be wary of people who established themselves near their ranchos' boundaries only to then attempt to claim a portion of the land for themselves. José Peréz, who purchased a portion of San Pascual from Fruto Mariné in 1836, found that keeping the land was more difficult than obtaining it. In 1838, Peréz faced a small-scale challenge from vecino Francisco Villa's petition for 1,000 varas at the northwestern point of Peréz's San Pascual.[69] Villa, a retired soldier who had served at Santa Barbara and San Gabriel, premised his land request to the governor on his years of service and sacrifice to the missions. In his petition Villa contended that Peréz had given him permission to develop the land as his own and establish a *ranchito*, or smaller scale rancho. Villa contended that he had since cultivated the land and established a "provincial house made of adobe."[70] To further support his claim, Villa pointed out that, because he had put all his efforts into developing said land, he had abandoned his home and crops in Los Angeles and wanted title to the portion of San Pascual that he had made fruitful.[71] Villa stated that Peréz did not object to his working the land until he saw that it was fruitful and that, out of envy and greed, Peréz decided to deny him any official claim to the land.[72] Villa ended his petition by asking for help with the situation and stated that he was not acting out of malice toward Peréz. Interestingly, Peréz did not formally respond to this petition but rather let the process go through official channels.

The governmental response to Villa's claim came in July of 1838. First, Juan Bandini, administrator of the San Gabriel Mission, responded that the land, located on the boundary between San Pascual and San Gabriel, could not be conceded to Villa because the mission still used it to pasture domesticated horses.[73] Although Bandini's recommendation did not support giving Villa title, it did state that he should be allowed to continue working and developing the land. Governor Alvarado, heeding Bandini's recommendation, responded that, because "it is the government's objective to partition all vacant lands for cultivation," Villa would be granted permission to use the land under the condition that he could never own it as long as it belonged to the San Gabriel Mission.[74]

From this response, it is evident that, although the land sat on the boundary between former mission lands and San Pascual, José Pérez deferred to the mission's right to contest the ownership. The reason for this may stem from the fact that secularization policy had attempted to control the distribution of mission lands in the interests of reserving it for ex-neophytes; therefore, in this case, mission administrators had a greater claim over the land than a private landholder. Bandini's response to Villa's claim all but ensured that the land would be kept out of private hands because it represented the mission's interest. Although Bandini responded on behalf of the mission, it must still be considered that he was one of the largest landowners in the Los Angeles and San Diego areas. Like Pérez, Bandini was part of the political and land-owning class; therefore, class interests may have informed his recommendation. The resolution of Villa's claim allowed him to stay on and develop the land, something beneficial to whoever claimed it later, while reserving it for settlement by better qualified parties. In this instance, the complex alliances among the Californio oligarchy, as well as their regional interpretation and implementation of secularization and land distribution, kept San Pascual from falling into the hands of an outsider. The next claim, based on a denouncement by a member of the prominent Sepúlveda clan, would end very differently.

In 1839 Enrique Sepúlveda, a native and vecino de Los Angeles, submitted an economic denouncement against the owner of San Pascual. In his claim, he asserted that the land's owner lacked the means to develop the land and that he, having the wealth to make it productive, should be awarded the land.[75] Additionally, Sepúlveda stated that he needed the land to make a better living for himself and his family and to support horses and livestock.[76] Sepúlveda's charge of neglect was standard in economic denouncements, as was his emphasis on his role as a patriarch who needed to provide for his family. While on the surface this seems to be a standard denouncement, certain dynamics of the case illustrate just how tenuous honor and status were in Alta California rancho society.

In his denouncement Sepúlveda identified Juan Mariné and his heirs as San Pascual's owners, completely ignoring José Pérez's ownership. The Commission of Vacant Lands was not so remiss; it quickly responded by stating that San Pascual was occupied by Peréz's livestock and horses.[77] Determined, Sepúlveda took another avenue to contest Peréz's ownership. Sepúlveda claimed that he, not Pérez, was the rightful apoderado of Juan Mariné and by extension of San Pascual.[78]

Sepúlveda's move to usurp Pérez's position as apoderado required him to publicly challenge José Pérez's honor and position among California's landed elites. His claim of being San Pascual's rightful apoderado originated in the complex web of social relations created through intermarriage. Wealthy Californios used intermarriage to solidify their social network and reputations, maintain alliances, and increase their land holdings.[79] The challenge in this case dates back to original grantee Juan Mariné, who had been married to María Antonia Sepúlveda, member of the of the Sepúlveda family. This relationship gave Enrique Sepúlveda a basis on which to contest José Peréz's ownership of San Pascual. Sepúlveda claimed that Peréz's purchase from Mariné's heirs had not given him title to the entire rancho, but only to the portion sold to him by Fruto and his siblings. He argued that Peréz had taken over only a portion of the land and was wrongfully acting as representative as a means of obtaining all of San Pascual.[80] In his attempt to remove Pérez, Sepúlveda focused on besmirching his character and by extension questioning his honor.

In his letter to Governor Juan Alvarado, Sepúlveda stated that Peréz had no real interest in developing San Pascual but simply wanted to control it so that he could distribute it to his brothers-in-law, Antonio María Silvas and Desidero Velverde. Sepúlveda claimed that Silvas lived on the rancho and was the caretaker of two "güilos dementes, un hombre y otra mujer" (mentally incapacitated people, one man and one woman).[81] From the documents, it seems that the mentally incapacitated woman was Silvas's sister-in-law. Sepúlveda alleged that Silvas had taken sexual advantage of his sister-in-law's mental incapacitation and violated the sacred family bond, acts that resulted in the birth of a child.[82] Sepúlveda cited this alleged sexual abuse to indicate the type of dishonorable persons that Peréz and his family were. He stated that, because these men acted in their own interest and could devalue the sanctity of family to such an extreme, they should not be entitled to hold San Pascual or even have a say in what happened to the land.

Honor is important in this case because Peréz also had connections to the landed elite. Nephew of Eulalia Peréz, he was married to María Merced Lugo, daughter of Californio Antonio María Lugo. This familial connection made any claim against Peréz's honor a very serious matter as it tainted the reputation of the entire clan. Although the existence of the child that resulted from the illicit union between Silvas and his sister-in-law is not mentioned in the documents, the fact that Sepúlveda made this claim was enough to call into question the family's honor and integrity. The behavior Sepúlveda described was not that of a respectable patriarch; an honorable man charged with controlling and maintaining his family would not have permitted this type of behavior to occur. Relying on this claim, Sepúlveda's petition steered away from the economic conditions necessary to denounce Peréz's claim and instead focused on his masculinity and failure as a patriarch.

Sepúlveda's claiming of San Pascual allows a closer look into the societal and cultural dynamics of Los Angeles' oligarchs. Sepúlveda's accusations against Peréz did not elicit a response defending his honor or his land. Interestingly, in a petition dated April 10, 1840, Peréz and Sepúlveda filed a joint economic denouncement against Juan Mariné's heirs for the rest of San Pascual. In response to the denouncement, local land officials ordered an investigation into Mariné's heirs and their ability to develop the land. One by one, three witnesses testified that Mariné's children, including Fruto, the person who had sold a portion of land to José Peréz years earlier, were unemployed and therefore could not develop the land. This testimony helped legitimate the economic denouncement and moved Peréz and Sepúlveda closer to owning all of San Pascual. Further land surveys and economic investigations found that the land was vacant and that the two petitioners had the economic means to develop it. land. In October of 1840, during the investigation, Eulalia Pérez appeared and made what would be her last attempt to hold onto Rancho San Pascual.

In her petition, Eulalia Peréz, as Mariné's widow, requested a share of the vineyard and house left behind by her late husband. Sepúlveda's response to her claim revealed that the land was in a "state of deterioration, due to the lack of care by the owner."[83] Because societal gender norms considered the maintenance of a rancho to be men's work, it was common for widows who owned land in Alta California to face denouncement due to neglect. When a woman's husband died, responsibility for the land fell to her sons or brothers because it was not proper for women to perform agricultural labor.[84] For the elderly and financially unstable Eulalia Pérez, maintenance of San Pascual was not possible, making José Peréz and Enrique Sepúlveda's economic denouncement a viable one. José Peréz's denouncement of his aunt's ownership of San Pascual did not differ from other economic denouncements; what is unique is that the widow withdrew her claim once José presented his. Peréz's withdrawal of her claim illustrates her negotiation of Alta California's gender dynamics. In her studies on New Mexico, Deena González found that women removed themselves from court cases and allowed their male relatives to set up the initial proceedings; they returned once the parameters of the case had been established.[85] Peréz may have retreated from the claim once she saw that a family member, not an unrelated third party, had claimed her interest in the rancho. Her withdrawal allowed José Peréz and Sepúlveda to receive the land concession, ending her hold on San Pascual.[86]

By late 1840, Sepúlveda had successfully obtained the land he desired. This claim is rather interesting because in the end both José Peréz and Sepúlveda were given title to the land. The way this came about addresses several issues that arose within California's close-knit oligarchy class. It exemplifies how the desire for land and wealth strained familial ties and called into question a landowner's honor. When Sepúlveda's attempt to initiate an economic denouncement failed, he utilized gender concepts and ideas of propriety to pressure José Peréz into an agreement that required him to share his land, thereby questioning

Peréz's masculinity and patriarchal control. Basing his denouncement on Peréz's character, Sepúlveda sought to uplift his own reputation and become a better qualified candidate for land. In the attempt to save his familial honor, Peréz acquiesced to Sepúlveda.

Aside from descriptions of the claimants as vecinos and *ciudadanos* (citizens of the pueblo), the issue of race/ethnicity did not arise in the official proceedings, indicating that these men were social equals, but also showing that the landed elite held many secrets that could be used to gain the upper hand. The illicit union Sepúlveda pointed to, albeit unsubstantiated, shows how these secrets could potentially devastate one man's social standing and aggrandize another's. In a society in which perception was everything, men competed to show that they had the economic means, social standing, and honor necessary to be part of the landed class. As Sepúlveda would quickly discover, the bases of honor and status in this society were tenuous and required constant reaffirmation. In a matter of a few short years, Sepúlveda's honor would be questioned and he would lose control of San Pascual to a "better" man.

DON MANUEL GARFIAS: THE LAST MEXICAN OWNER OF SAN PASCUAL

Upon receiving title to San Pascual in 1840, Pérez and Sepúlveda built two houses at the southwest portions of the land near the Arroyo Seco and brought their livestock to the rancho. One year after receiving title, José Pérez died; the Lugo family, relatives of his wife, María Merced, took his livestock and moved them a few miles south of San Pascual to Rancho San Antonio. José Pérez's death left a great portion of the rancho abandoned and, more importantly, it left Enrique Sepúlveda susceptible to economic denouncement. Sepúlveda, who had established himself as an honorable man, quickly found himself in a position to lose everything to another man with better economic means and a higher social standing.

In June of 1843 Lieutenant Manuel Garfias, pictured in Fig. 7, lodged an economic denouncement against Enrique Sepúlveda for San Pascual's lands. Following accepted protocol, Garfias denounced the Pérez/Sepúlveda land title and claimed the rancho for "his benefit and that of his family."[87] In his claim, not unlike other economic denouncements, Garfias cited the lack of development and the land's poor condition. However, in Garfias's denouncement,

FIGURE 7 Portrait of Don Manuel Garfias of San Pascual, the last Mexican owner of Rancho San Pascual. Courtesy of the University of Southern California, Libraries and California Historical Society. Digitally reproduced by the USC Digital Library; from the California Historical Society Collection at the University of Southern California http://digitallibrary.usc.edu/cdm/singleitem/collection/p15799coll65/id/13157/rec/1.

unlike that of Sepúlveda, Pérez, and other men who filed papers related to San Pascual, Garfias did not claim the status of vecino of Los Angeles. As seen in previous claims, the term *vecino* reflected an ethno-social status and placed claimants within the racialized societal structure. Using this term when petitioning for land reflected a level of respectability that helped legitimize claims and connect petitioners to the region. Garfias, a high-ranking military officer in Micheltorena's fixed military battalion, Batallón Fijo de Alta California, arrived in Los Angeles in 1842, making him an outsider in comparison to other landed men, including Enrique Sepúlveda. Because of political connections and social maneuvering through the years after Juan Mariné's death, San Pascual had remained in the hands of local elite who were connected to the Lugo and Sepúlveda families. In keeping with the complex web of social relations and the preservation of land for the aggrandizement of the Los Angeles elite, Garfias's economic denunciation of San Pascual should not have been successful. His claim should have met the same end as that of Francisco Villa, the vecino and retired soldier denied land by the Los Angeles Land Commission. Although both Villa and Garfias were military men, albeit one a soldier and the other an officer, Villa was local and a vecino, a status that eluded Garfias.

In order to level a successful economic denouncement against Sepúlveda's title, Garfias needed to rely on his status as a military officer and build his local reputation by becoming part of the local elite. Garfias had the wealth necessary to support his claim, but his status as an outsider was an impediment. Aside from wealth, Californio men desiring land needed to represent a dominant masculinity. Marriage, as an institution, was crucial to the support of masculinity; it helped create the basis of a strong patriarch who in turn represented the stability of the social hierarchy.[88] Aside from supporting a patriarchal system, marriage was a successful method to gain social and political power. Ranging from the marriage of mestizo soldiers to Indigenous women on the California frontier to the intermarriages among elite families and foreign men's marriages to elite daughters, the institution of marriage served a myriad of purposes.[89] In the Mexican Period, Euro-American men assimilated into Mexican society through marriage. Not unlike the outsiders before him, Garfias married into the community to obtain legitimacy and power to complement his wealth.

In mid-November of 1842, Garfias appeared at the San Gabriel Mission requesting permission to marry Doña Maria Luisa Avila, daughter of Francisco Avila and Encarnación Sepúlveda, both from prominent Californio families.[90] In the matrimonial investigation, Encarnación Sepúlveda and Fray Tómas Estenaga referred to Garfias as a ciudadano and "natural de Oaxaca, Méjico."[91] Reference to his legitimate birth into a well-respected Mexican family supported his claim for honor and respectability. Additional references to Garfias began with the honorifics señor or don, indicating Garfias' standing in the eyes of those called to testify on his behalf. Although the witnesses did not directly address his racial and ethnic identity, they referred to him in a respectful manner, as a citizen and a military officer. The respect afforded to him by Sepúlveda and Estenaga indicated that they considered him gente de razón and not an Indian. After priests completed the investigation into Garfias's and his fiancée's character, marriage status, and birth, the couple married in November of 1842.[92] The marriage gave Garfias legitimacy and entrance into the world of the local elite.

In June of 1843, when Garfias filed his economic denouncement, he did so without the status of vecino but with the backing of his bride's family name; Garfias was now part of the Sepúlveda and Avila clans. Within two days, Governor Micheltorena ordered the prefecture's office to investigate Rancho San

Pascual's condition.[93] The prefecture's investigation into San Pascual's condition found land that was undeveloped and abandoned. The investigator, Antonio José Coronel, reported "two adobe houses, one belonging to the deceased José Peréz and the other to Enrique Sepúlveda."[94] Additionally, he said that "there were no head of cattle or flock of any sort on the land," and "that there was no evidence of the families of said men having labored on the land."[95] While on the land, Coronel encountered Sepúlveda, who quickly offered apologies for the condition of the ranch and assured the investigator that there were "thirty heads of cattle in the area."[96] Despite Sepúlveda's assurances that he was using the land, Prefect Manuel Domínguez stated that the "purpose of giving land titles was to make the land grow and that in the course of three years this premier land has sat abandoned."[97] With this vision of optimal land use in mind, Domínguez recommended that Garfias, "an honorable citizen, and a man with the necessary means to make the land thrive," be awarded the land.[98]

After this damning report, Sepúlveda responded with a letter detailing why his land had fallen into disarray. He explained the lack of livestock by stating that it had "either been killed or run off by thieves in the direction of the Avila Rancho."[99] He stated that interlopers had taken over portions of his land and despite his several complaints local authorities had done nothing to ameliorate the situation. Finding himself in desperate circumstances, he decided not to try to develop the land any further.

In his response Sepúlveda failed to take responsibility for the land's condition, opting instead to blame others for its deterioration, an action that does not reflect the control and power of a patriarch.[100] This only further supported Garfias's claim for San Pascual because upon investigating Sepúlveda's allegations authorities determined them to be false. Although the specifics of the fabrication are not contained in the records, Prefect Manuel Dominguez's report to the governor declared that he had the honor of uncovering the lies that Sepúlveda had told pertaining to his land. Domínguez stated that, because Sepúlveda's lies had disgraced the prefecture office and governor, he should be punished according to the law.[101] It is clear from this statement that Sepúlveda's allegations had not been proven and were simply fabricated to save face.

The accusation of lying and its accompanying dishonor put Sepúlveda at a disadvantage, and although he was not punished, this undoubtedly tainted his honor. While the prefecture found Sepúlveda's allegations to be false, there is evidence that some of what he said may have been accurate. After José Peréz's death, his widow, María Merced Lugo, left the land, and her family moved his cattle to Rancho San Antonio. In her official statement approving the sale of her casita on San Pascual to Garfias, she stated that the responsibility of the land had fallen to her male family members and that, although she had the means to cultivate the land, she chose not to do so.[102] Even though Lugo's statement lends some credence to part of Sepúlveda's statement, the fact remains that he lost control of his portion of the land. In the end, Sepúlveda was forced to give up his land to Garfias and was compensated seventy pesos for his adobe house on San Pascual.

Garfias's honor or his ability to develop San Pascual was never questioned. In April 1843, he easily received title to the land, pictured in Fig. 8. Throughout the denouncement process, Garfias used his wealth to reiterate his ability to develop the land. He backed his words with action by offering to compensate Lugo and Sepúlveda for what he termed *casuchas*, or shacks, implying that they were not worth anything.[103] Regardless, Garfias paid two separate skilled evaluators to assess the value of the houses and subsequently remitted payment in full to both parties.[104] These actions showed that he was an honorable man of means.

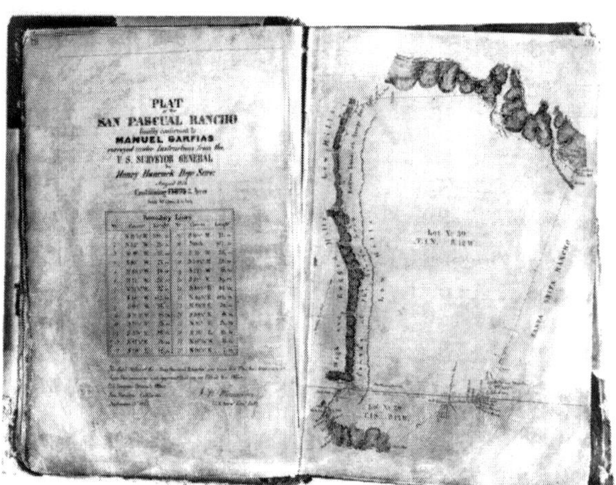

FIGURE 8 Map plate of Rancho San Pascual, Pasadena ca. 1858. Prepared by Henry Hancock for the United States Surveyor General's Office, Pasadena, September 1858. Left page provides identifying information; right page shows surveyor's map. Courtesy of the University of Southern California, Libraries and California Historical Society. Digitally reproduced by the USC Digital Library; from the California Historical Society Collection at the University of Southern California, http://digitallibrary.usc.edu/cdm/singleitem/collection/p15799coll65/id/12761/rec/1.

Garfias's success resulted from a combination of knowing how to maneuver within the political and social systems and having the right connections. As a loyal military officer, he had close professional and personal relationship with Governor Micheltorena, the man charged with distributing land. Upon his arrival in Los Angeles, he married into the prominent Avila family. The Avilas owned Rancho La Ciénega and a large adobe home in the center of the pueblo. Marriage into this family gave Garfias standing in the community and access to Maria Luisa's land, but it also connected him to the wealthy Sepúlvedas. The Avilas and Sepúlvedas were related through marriage, making Enrique Sepúlveda and María Luisa Avila cousins.

The familial connection engendered through Garfias' marriage to Avila may have facilitated his access to San Pascual. He may have had specific knowledge of the rancho's condition, such as the fact that the Lugos, friends and distant relatives of the Sepúlvedas, had removed the cattle. The access he gained to the regional elite's complex relationships allowed Garfias to obtain access to San Pascual by emphasizing his wealth and his honor; this tactic was not unlike the way Enrique Sepúlveda had pressured Peréz into sharing his land. Although Garfias was defined as a regional outsider, his successful acquisition of San Pascual in 1843 indicates that the local oligarchy's power was not absolute, and despite its efforts to maintain control, an outsider could infiltrate it. While Garfias's racial/ethnic identity did not explicitly play a role in his acquisition of land, it was implicitly present in the land distribution process. Local elites used their authority to award the land to those who fit within a racialized class structure.

Allotment of San Pascual to José Peréz, Enrique Sepúlveda, and Manuel Garfias speaks to the different power dynamics involved in access to land in 1840s California. While secularization and liberalism emphasized equal access to land regardless of race and ethnicity, the way San Pascual's lands were meted out points to the existence of racial/ethnic privilege that was inextricably linked to class identity and wealth.

EX-NEOPHYTES AND FORMER MISSION LANDS

As seen during the Mission Period, Indians at San Gabriel occupied the lowest level of Spanish society. Their place within the mission was determined through their relationship to the land. Since neophytes worked mission lands as part of Franciscans' conversion process, they were placed into a social stratum that denied them control of their labor and their bodies. Although some Indians did gain political authority and rose through an Indigenous social hierarchy within the missions, ultimately they were not allowed to attain the same level as the mixed-race "Spaniards" who slowly came to form the regional elite. The implementation of secularization policy in the San Gabriel region did not dramatically change the status of former mission Indians.

After secularization and emancipation, mission Indians were left to make their lives outside the mission. Many Indians who found themselves landless and destitute migrated into El Pueblo de Los Angeles and nearby ranchos in search of work. Other Indians petitioned for allotments of the mission lands that they had helped develop. Indian petitions and their subsequent *diligencias judiciales* (judicial proceedings) reflect the interplay between sociocultural perspectives and Indigenous identity by illustrating how Native petitioners negotiated their status in a racialized society. Additionally, these investigations show how non-Indian governmental officials perceived Indian petitioners. These investigations show that, after secularization, societal perceptions of a person's racial/ethnic designation still determined his or her relationship to the land. Ex-neophytes had to prove that they were racially and thus culturally fit to own land. In other words, while in the mission Indians had to prove that they were culturally Spanish, but after secularization, they had to prove that they were hijos del país, deserving of the benefits of liberalism and freedom.

California State Archive Land Expedientes and Los Angeles County Prefecture Records for San Pascual and its surrounding areas contain several cases dealing with Indian petitions for land. The cases of Indian petitioners Valencia, Manuel Antonio, Próspero, Emilio Joaquín, and Serafíno de Jesús give insight into the negotiation of regional identity in 1840s San Gabriel because they show how Indians presented their identities in land allotment applications. Often ex-neophytes emphasized their connection to the mission and to a certain extent their successful assimilation into regional society and culture. Methods for establishing this connection included applicants' detailed identifications of themselves; adherence to proper protocol in the paperwork; referencing the mission directly; citing the name of an important Californio to whom they were connected; and showing the proper deference to the governor, prefecturía, and other governmental officials.[105]

Suppliants began their petitions with the standard "excelentísimo señor," addressing the governor or prefecture with an honorific that recognized his supreme authority. The greeting was then followed by "con la mayor sumisión y respeto ante usted" (with the highest level of submission and respect), a statement through which the petitioner submitted to the official's authority and showed him the utmost respect of his power. This deference helped the petitioner enter into the political realm and engage the power dynamics involved in requesting land. Although this protocol was part of the larger accepted discursive practice that allowed governmental institutions to maintain power over the population, it took on a different meaning when used by a person from a subjugated racialized group.[106]

Ex-neophytes' use of this discursive practice presented the potential for the destabilization of institutional power because it challenged accepted ideas about Indians as the racial and sociocultural other. Despite liberalism's ideals of equality, society still viewed Indians as ignorant and racially/culturally inferior. Therefore, using this language in their petitions was not enough to support their claims of successful assimilation and ascent into Californio society and culture; they still bore the burden of proving it. For example, whereas non-Indians had to establish their status as vecinos and honorable and hard-working men of means, ex-neophytes were challenged to show that the mission had successfully made them into productive, honorable, and culturally civilized men. At play were the dynamics of race and masculinity manifested through land politics. As historian Steve Stern argued in his discussion on masculinity and power, "men constructed their sense of masculinity on a field of power relations . . . manhood signified rights to power and citizenship."[107] For Californio men, their power and citizenship rested in their identities as gente de razón. To legitimize their status, they simply had to show their commitment to developing the land and that they had the power to control it.

For ex-neophytes in 1840s California, masculinity rested on the labor they had provided to the mission before secularization; their proper behavior; and their ability to show their successful assimilation, through labor, after emancipation. To be described as an hombre de bien was significant because it allowed men to ascend the sociocultural hierarchy. For ex-neophytes, masculinity could potentially serve the dual purpose of establishing them as citizens *and* men, entitled to the same rights as Californios blancos, a socio-identity that proved to very elusive.

Expedientes for San Gabriel show that many ex-neophytes asserted their masculinity in their land claims with varying degrees of success. In his 1845 petition to Governor Pío Pico for a formal grant of a *sitio* (site) on which to establish a rancho, Manuel Antonio, the former mayordomo from the mission, described himself: "a son of the mission, born and raised in her, and during the best of my years, I have provided good services, in the work that has been given to me."[108] Manuel Antonio's statement shows his lifelong commitment and faithful service to the mission. Additionally, he cited the permission given to him by mission administrator Colonel Nicolás Gutiérrez and the Indian community to cultivate the land.[109] Through this statement, he presented himself as a legitimate member of local society. Gutiérrez, a witness in the petition, established Manuel Antonio's relationship to the mission and addressed his development of the land. Gutiérrez proudly stated that, although the number of Manuel Antonio's livestock and cattle was small at first, in time with his hard work they had increased in number. Additionally, Gutiérrez attested to Manuel's successful cultivation of the crops and vineyard that he had planted.[110]

By emphasizing his cultivation of a vineyard and the development of a productive plot, elements directly linked with the emergence of the Californio culture, Manuel Antonio reflected Californios' racialized ideas of land use. Without making an explicit statement, he emphasized the improvement of the land while under his supervision, without the guidance of mission fathers. By attributing the successful development of the land solely to his hard work, he legitimated his claim to the land as an honorable man. San Gabriel missionary Fray Tomás Estenaga substantiated Manuel Antonio's claim to honor in an 1841 letter to the prefecture. Estenaga described him as "a son of the San Gabriel mission [whose] conduct to this critical date of his emancipation, has continued with the same honor."[111] Estenaga's regard for Manuel Antonio gained him cultural legitimacy and provided support to his claim to former mission land.

As an honorable man, Manuel Antonio lodged his appeal to Governor Pico out of concern that, although he had developed the land over the course of eleven years, it was being sold off to others who were not rightfully qualified to develop it.[112] In his concluding statement, Manuel Antonio emphasized his entitlement and natural right to the land based on his sweat and labor in developing it.[113] His statement substantiated that "for Indians freedom meant liberation from the mission and entitlement to own land."[114] The ex-mayordomo believed that he had more right to the land than others who were interested in buying it. He based his idea on his natural right to the land, a reference that suggests his simultaneous support of and resistance to Californio liberal discourse. By indirectly basing his petition on natural inheritance of land, as did the hijos del país in their calls for secularization, Manuel inserted himself into

Californio political ideology and claimed his rights to citizenship, equality, and the land rights of the Californios.

In the interest of preserving the land for themselves and indirectly maintaining their political and social power in the process, Californios challenged claims such as Manuel Antonio's by questioning their integrity. In August 1841, in the process of investigating Manuel Antonio's petition, Prefect Santiago Argüello reported his suspicions regarding the ex-neophyte's land claim. Argüello, a member of a prominent family, reported to the governor that Manuel Antonio and Fray Estenaga had lied about the ex-neophyte's service to the mission.[115] According to Argüello, Manuel Antonio was "not connected to [the] mission after puberty" and since his departure he "disassociated himself from it . . . having not spent the best of his age in service to the old mission."[116] Argüello questioned the one thing that tied Manuel Antonio to the land. By emphasizing Manuel Antonio's disassociation from the mission, he attempted to make the claimant appear less qualified for land ownership by implying that he had not fully assimilated. Argüello's attempts to delegitimize Manuel Antonio's claim reflected the anti-Indian attitudes that permeated Californio society.

Many local inhabitants still regarded Indians as an inferior people who lacked the intelligence, work ethic, and values necessary to successfully develop former mission lands. Some Californio landowners' anti-Indian sentiment brought them to the prefecture to request that Indians be dispossessed of land and that it be given to them instead. In 1842 Rafael Guirado, an influential citizen of Los Angeles and father of future California first lady María Guirado Downey, petitioned the prefecture to "remove the Indian settlement to another location and grant [him] the land now occupied by said Indians . . . in order to plant thereon vineyards and other fruit trees for the maintenance of my needy and large family."[117] Guirado's proposed displacement of an entire Indian settlement to address the needs of his family reflects the larger societal devaluation of Indian people.

In the same vein, in 1842 Antonio María Lugo, politician, landowner, and member of the prominent Lugo family, appealed to the prefecture requesting the removal of Indians from land distributed by Los Angeles authorities.[118] Lugo stated that he wished to "plant an orchard and a vineyard . . . beneficial to society and [his] family." He asked for the removal of Indians from the land in the interest of the "the peace and order of the Pueblo" and stated that "it is not advisable for them to remain where they now live."[119]

Aside from showing the continued discrimination against and contemptuous disregard for San Gabriel's Indigenous population, Guirado's and Lugo's petitions point to Californios' goal of keeping the best lands out of the hands of Indians. Guirado and Lugo applied for land parcels located on former mission lands that had proven to be productive since before secularization. The potential for economic aggrandizement through these lands motivated many to create obstacles to prevent Indians from obtaining or keeping these lands. The larger the land, the more tightly Californios held on to it. This reflected a larger institutionalized anti-Indian sentiment.

Prefect Santiago Argüello, the man charged with investigating claims and distributing land allotments in the San Gabriel region, functioned within the system detailed above. In his challenge to Manuel Antonio's claim for the large portion of the lands of the San Gabriel Mission, Argüello, after describing the land as one of the "best sites known in this vicinity," recommended that they reserve the land for a better *criador* or breeder, who could sufficiently develop it through large-scale use.[120] His recommendation, made after questioning the ex-neophyte's integrity, could be seen as a way of reserving the land for a more deserving and qualified candidate. Although not clearly expressing a bias, and seemingly justifying his challenge to Manuel Antonio on an economic basis, Argüello, in his reference to leaving the parcel for someone who could use a large-scale labor force to develop it, indirectly reflected the racial/ethnic qualification for access to land. Part of what defined Californio identity was their relationship to land and labor; Californios were the rancheros who controlled labor, and Indians were the workers who provided it. This social hierarchy, similar to that which existed in the mission, hinged on a person's relationship to land and labor; it reflected a larger system of social relations employed by countless others throughout California during the Californio period.

Despite Argüello's claims and recommendation against Manuel Antonio, Governor Pico awarded him the land in 1845.[121] Pico's decision to override the prefect's recommendation provides a different view of Californio society by showing that there were times when the local and departmental government supported Indians' rights to land or at least kept vecinos from easily dispossessing them. For instance, in response to Lugo's and Guirado's claims, local authorities decided that "the petitions for lands of the Indian settlements [could] not be granted because they have not been vacated."[122] Support such as this was not consistent, and although Manuel Antonio received the plot he requested, other neophytes were not as fortunate, receiving only small allotments on which to build a small house and cultivate a small huerta.

In San Gabriel, ex-neophytes Serafino de Jesús, Valencia, Próspero, and Emilio Joaquín obtained grants ranging between 200 and 400 varas. The lands distributed to these neophytes were part of the former San Gabriel Mission and adjacent to the Rancho San Pascual. The lands were often *terrenos baldíos*, or vacant lands that no one claimed. This is important because in this case, unlike the case of San Pascual, ex-neophyte grants did not result from economically based denouncements. This fact speaks to vecinos' attitudes about Indians' place in the social hierarchy.

Following the accepted procedure, these ex-neophytes asked for lands connected to the mission that had served as their former home. Similar to Manuel Antonio, each one linked his identity to the mission in the hope of receiving the land he had cultivated under the mission priests. In April of 1843, Serafino de Jesús, "indígena de la Misión de San Gabriel (Indian from the San Gabriel Mission)," petitioned the prefecture asking for land "for the maintenance of himself and his family to cultivate a fruit orchard."[123] Having the necessary witnesses and support, including the testimony of Fray Estenaga, Serafino received his land allotment measuring 200 varas. Two years later, in April 1845, Serafino petitioned for an extension of his land holdings by 200 varas, citing that his previous allotment was too small. In his request for an additional allotment, Serafino identified himself as a "natural y vecino de San Gabriel," a term imbued with racial meaning.[124] These documents, dated two years apart, indicate that Serafino experienced a rise in socio-ethnic status. By calling himself a vecino rather than an Indian convert or ex-neophyte, Serafino placed himself on an equal footing with gente de razón, Californios blancos. Because Serafino followed his petition for land with the necessary documents and inspections, including a letter from the parish priest, Governor Pico awarded him title to the land in December of 1845.[125]

Other petitions for land by ex-neophytes netted results similar to Serafino's. For instance, three claims dated 1843 resulted in distribution of land to the petitioners. The parcels were small but provided for a modest living. The claims of Próspero, Emilio Joaquín, and Valencia share similarities with those of Manuel Antonio and Serafino de Jesús.[126] Each petition identified the claimant as an Indian convert from San Gabriel. Each stressed the labor and service he had provided while in the mission and noted his accomplishments after emancipation from the mission. Each of these men had maintained a portion of land, without title, on the outskirts of the mission lands. As a testament to his successful assimilation and conversion, each emphasized that he had established and maintained a small home, orchard, or livestock on said land; these claims, when verified in the subsequent investigations and surveys, lent credence to their successful integration into Californio society.

In the case of Emilio Joaquín, an Indian who had provided years of service to the mission, the investigator regarded the ex-neophyte as a role model of sorts by stating that issuing title to this Indian served to stimulate his coworkers to take up agricultural pursuits and dedicate themselves to work.[127] The attitude represented in this recommendation supports the contention that land ownership and use reflected racialized ideas about the owner. During the mission period, ex-neophytes' adherence to a religiously based discipline and regimentation indicated successful assimilation. In the post-secularization period, ex-neophytes' ability to adapt to sociocultural expectations, such as maintaining homesteads similar to those of vecinos, indicated their assimilation. For some ex-neophytes, such as those discussed above, the ability to obtain land opened the door into a society that based its identity on a racialized land ownership. Entry into this society required ex-neophyte petitioners to negotiate and identify with the values of Californio vecinos in an attempt to become members of a society that kept them marginalized.

Indian applicants' various attempts to find a common ground, if not a common identity, with Californios are evident from the reasoning they gave when they petitioned for land allotments. Indians based their land requests on their desire to develop the land as a means of supporting themselves and their families. This speaks to the ideals of individualized land ownership and economic development reflected through nineteenth century Californio liberalism. In the hope of obtaining land, ex-neophytes had to show that they too were Californios, invested in developing the land. In the process of moving away from their identities as ex-neophytes and toward those of vecinos or gente de razón, titles that would prove ever elusive to most Indians, they became wedged between the colonial moment and the nationalist project. Ex-neophytes found themselves in an interstitial space in which they were a people without a nation, Indigenous or Mexican.[128]

The period between secularization and the American Conquest served as a transitional moment in which discourses of Spanish coloniality, Mexican nationalism, and California regionalism defined Indians as a marginalized people lacking political and social equality. Indians negotiated their survival in a society that did not desire their fusion or integration into the community. Indians' use of discourse imbued with racialized sociocultural values served as a form of discursive doubling in which they mimicked Californios' agenda for land distribution, seeming to agree, yet in actuality creating a space for themselves within a Spanish and a Californio discourse that sought to silence them.[129] Indian suppliants' use of the term *natural* in their petitions served as a form of resistance in which they challenged the socio-ethnic ideas about Indians as outsiders; *natural*, when used by an Indian, made white Californios into the other, and Indigenous persons became part of the nation, at least temporarily.

Denial of land to Indigenous people allowed Californios to construct and maintain a system that confined Indians to the lowest levels of the socioeconomic hierarchy. Despite the rhetoric of racial/ethnic equality and the granting of full and equal citizenship irrespective of race after Mexican Independence, distribution of secularized mission lands reflected racialized ideas of Californio culture. Men who claimed Spanish elite lineage became landowners, while the majority of Indians became workers in a society that increasingly divided itself along socioeconomic lines.

Mexican independence, secularization, and land distribution shaped Californio society and politics during the 1830s and 1840s. Despite the liberal rhetoric of equality and land for all, land ownership increasingly linked racial/ethnic identity with class. Land ownership gave way to the creation of a regional oligarchy that kept land out of the hands of less qualified men. In the San Gabriel region, local Los Angeles elites used their familial ties and wealth to obtain the highly desired lands of Rancho San Pascual. Hinging their claims on wealth, honor, and masculinity, they vied against each other for San Pascual's vast acreage, blocking ex-neophytes from the land that they had earned through their labor in the mission.

As Californio society divided itself by ethno-class lines and a person's identity was determined through his or her relationship to the land, it became increasingly important for landowning elites to demonstrate their affluence through elaborate displays of material possessions and cultural ritual. Through land ownership, elaborate estates, livestock, and the control of Indian labor, Californios racialized the lands of Rancho San Pascual and the optimal vision of land use was redefined.

4

THE MARKINGS OF CALIFORNIO CULTURE AND STATUS

Constructing Class

IN THE YEARS BETWEEN secularization and the U.S.-Mexico War, Californio landed elites successfully took control of thousands of acres of former mission lands. Members of California's wealthy landed class competed within a very profitable tallow and hide economy, making enough profit to build their ranchos and establish themselves as the leaders of Californio society.[1]

During the 1830s, Californio culture flourished; however, changes in regional demographics and developing political turmoil of the coming decade would compromise the society they had created. During the 1830s, partly due to the growing opportunities for land ownership, the region saw an increased American presence. As a numerical minority, Americans entered into Californios' elite circles through alliances established through intermarriage, acquisition of citizenship, and cultural assimilation.[2] During the 1840s as war between the United States and Mexico became inevitable, these alliances gave way to an imposed American white supremacist ideology that established Americans as the dominant land owners.[3] This ideology left Californios maneuvering to keep the land, wealth, and prestige they deeply valued.[4]

The creation of Californio identity and culture in San Pascual paralleled that in other places throughout Alta California. After secularization, a few prominent Californio families took control of most of the former mission lands. For these families, access to land was a crucial factor in maintaining their status in California's racial, class, and cultural hierarchies. Californios' successful exclusion of Indians from accessing land helped solidify societal relationships based on land ownership and imbued these relationships with racial and cultural meaning. The ability to own land helped many elites shed the confines of their mixed-race roots.

Prior to secularization, emerging elites used their control of Indian labor to construct their status as blancos or españoles. In the post-secularization era, the availability of lands allowed these elites, the descendants of Mexico's castas, the opportunity to uplift their social position in relation to other gente de razón and Indians.[5] By considering themselves Hidalgos or (upper-class people), California's dons and doñas moved to establish a high-class culture that reflected their status and, more importantly, distinguished them from the poor. Solidification of the social hierarchy in this manner linked status to property, class, and ethnicity.[6] By linking these three factors, Californios created a society and culture that embodied the racialized visions of land use that had fueled secularization and land distribution. The existence of a racialized elite class necessitated a system in which their visions of optimal land use were readily discernible. Californio culture reflected this vision.

RACIALIZED LABOR: MEXICAN WORKERS

The rise of an economy based on land tenure during the 1830s gave rise to social distinctions that took on racial and ethnic components.[7] As in the Spanish Colonial Period, a person's connection to the land either as an owner or laborer influenced his or her social position and racial designation. Aside from indicating economic position, the distinction of being a large landowner came to reflect a higher racial status and whiteness.[8]

Under the Spanish colonial system, the term gente de razón indicated that one was a Spanish Christian. Although the term contained an implicit racialized meaning, during the Mexican Period, as racial boundaries blurred and castas gained access to political, social, and economic power, the term reflected the societal changes produced within a changing cultural context.[9]

Prior to the rapid growth and expansion of the rancho economy in the mid-1830s and 1840s, the ranchero elite and the non-ranchero class, comprising small landowners, artisans, foremen, and laborers, found common ground in their identity as gente de razón by emphasizing that they were not Indians.[10] In the late 1830s and 1840s as the rancho economy grew more profitable, elite rancheros sought to "whiten themselves as they moved up the social ladder."[11] They distinguished themselves from other landless gente de razón and Indians by claiming a Spanish ancestry and white skin, identifying themselves as españoles blancos.[12] The growth of a society based on land ownership allowed the ranchero elite to create and solidify societal boundaries based on constructed ethnic and cultural difference.

As California's oligarchy grew more exclusive, elites affirmed their status and distinguished themselves from the landless class through familial stability, social ritual, symbols, strategic use of community fiestas, the compadrazgo system, and material wealth.[13] Motivated by their desire for the affirmation of their social status more than simply the accumulation of money and material possessions, elites used their elaborate estates, herds of livestock, and vast vineyards and orchards to emphasize their position at the top of the social hierarchy.[14] Wealthy Californios' assertion of their social and economic status was premised on their ownership of land and control of labor.

Not surprisingly, racial and ethnic ideas manifested themselves through the complex relationship between landowners and laborers in Californio society and culture. Similar to the Spanish soldiers who delegated their responsibilities to Indigenous laborers in the missions because they considered manual labor degrading, wealthy landed men came to rely on Indigenous and mestizo laborers to maintain their lands, construct their elaborate houses, and ensure agricultural production.[15] In some instances landowners would go as far as "rounding up Indians from a nearby ranchería and force them to work."[16] Californios quickly realized that, without sufficient reliable labor from the working classes, they would be unable to sustain their lifestyles or their honor and status.[17] The work of ranch hands, agricultural workers, and domestic workers was crucial to the rancho's operation.

Largely excluded from land ownership, Indians and mestizos comprised the labor force in places such as El Pueblo de Los Angeles and the former San Gabriel Mission lands, including Rancho San Pascual. The division of labor on the ranchos was based on prior work experience, skills, and gender.[18] Ex-neophyte men skilled in mission tasks performed similar work on the ranchos including rounding up cattle, heading the *matanza* (slaughter of cattle), candle production, smithing, and leatherwork, as well as primary plowing and harvesting.[19] Similarly, mestizo men skilled in ranching worked as vaqueros and ranch hands tending to horses and flocks of sheep.[20] Unskilled Indians and mestizos laborers performed heavy manual labor and assisted in sowing and reaping the harvest, cutting timber, and clearing land.[21] Under the supervision of the woman of the house, Indigenous and mestiza women often worked as domestic servants. They assisted wealthy Californians by laundering and ironing clothing, preparing household meals, sweeping, sewing, making bread, grinding corn, cutting wood used for cooking, milking cows, and performing a variety of other domestic chores.[22] Additionally, former neophyte women made soap and candles, wove baskets, and did hide work using skills they had gained at the missions.[23] Regardless of whether laborers performed domestic, ranching, or agricultural work, they provided the support system necessary for the rancho to function and helped create a stable rancho and home for the ranchero class.

The 1836 and 1844 padrones for Los Angeles and its surrounding areas including San Pascual listed men and women in occupations such as laborers, servants, vaqueros, and field hands.[24] Ranchos Santa Gertrudis, Las Bolsas, and San Rafael, comprising allotments from former San Gabriel Mission lands and proximate to San Pascual, had workers in a variety of occupations ranging from *sirvientes* (servants) and *labradores* (farm laborers) to skilled artisans such as *cigarreros* (cigar makers) and *bordaderos* (embroiderers).[25] For instance, in 1836, Antonio María Nieto's 21,298-acre Rancho Santa Gertrudis had five labradores, nine sirvientes, and one cigarrero.[26] Similarly, the Verdugo family's 36,403 acre Rancho San Rafael had twelve labradores and one bordadero, who embroidered and ornamented the lace shawls, bedsheets, and men's chalecos or vests, women's gowns, and other luxury garments that Californios used as designations of status.[27]

Aside from the consistent labor provided by workers living on the ranchos, landowners had steady access to laborers residing in the San Gabriel Mission region.[28] The 1836 padrón enumerated nine labradores, one vaquero, and two mayordomos (principal servants), workers that ranchers could call upon whenever needed. In addition to this rancho-related labor, the region had several skilled artisans and merchants, including a *jabonero* (soap maker), a *verdulero* (fruit and vegetable dealer), and a *platero* (silversmith), all of whom served the regional inhabitants' needs and supplied rancheros with luxury items essential to their public image.[29] The availability and control of labor helped landowners fulfill provisional land grants requiring land maintenance and improvement. In stark contrast to the ranchos discussed above, Juan Mariné's Rancho San Pascual did not reflect the characteristics of a successful productive ranch.

In 1836, San Pascual was in the hands of the original grantees, Juan Mariné and Eulalia Pérez.[30] Interestingly, the 1836 Padrón did not specify San Pascual as a rancho but rather included it as part of the San Gabriel Mission. Additionally, unlike landowners of similar sized ranches, Mariné was identified as a laborer-proprietor, a farmer who owned his own land, not a rancher.[31] There were no laborers listed in connection with San Pascual. The only others included in the enumeration of the Mariné household were his children, Filomeno, Fruto, Rafaela, Josefa, and María Antonia. Filomeno, the elder of Mariné's two sons, was listed as a laborer, while his younger son, eighteen-year-old Fruto, had no listed occupation.[32] The fact that Mariné's ranch had no farm laborers aside from himself and his sons, as well as the fact that he was not classified as a rancher, speaks to the status of the ranch itself. The information provided in the padrón gave an indication of the ranch's condition and foreshadowed the economic denouncement that soon followed; it also spoke to Mariné's failure to develop San Pascual into a rancho.

By 1844, as the result of an economic denouncement, Rancho San Pascual had changed hands and had been granted to José Pérez and Enrique Sepúlveda. Despite their acquisition of San Pascual, they were unable to make the land profitable or develop it in any significant way. Similar to the 1836 census, the 1844 census did not identify San Pascual as a rancho and in fact excluded it altogether. There are several possible reasons for this exclusion.

One explanation may be that both Pérez and Sepúlveda had died by the time of the padrón's completion. After their deaths, in 1841 and 1844, respectively, their wives took over their lands. Land records for San Pascual show that Pérez's and Sepúlveda's widows, María Merced Lugo and María Bernarda Alanís, gained their husbands' land and livestock and that their husbands' properties were largely absorbed by their respective families. A second explanation is that the rancho did not have a male head of household or elaborate household. Inclusion in the land records of surrounding ranchos, such as Rancho Santa Gertrudis and Rancho San Rafael, indicate that the enumerator visited the area, but either neglected Rancho San Pascual or included it as part of these larger ranchos.

Regardless of the reason behind its 1844 exclusion, San Pascual's status did not change over the course of the eight-year period between the padrónes. Although the land allotment was quite large and had proved viable during the Mission Period, grantees' repeated failures to develop it point to larger societal ideals of optimal land use. Because the 1836 Padrón did not enumerate any laborers aside from Mariné and his son, and the 1844 Padrón did not include the rancho, according to popular definition, the land itself was not popularly considered or recognized as a rancho.[33]

A comparison of San Pascual and surrounding ranchos shows the importance of labor in creating the popular perception of the land and its rancheros. Mestizo and Indian workers sold their labor to landed men who created a society based on the work of others. The growth of ranchos perpetuated elites' visions of land use based on land ownership and control of labor. The exploitation of a racialized labor force helped propel the image of a Mexican California characterized by adjoining ranchos and Spanish dons. The definition of what a rancho was and who was an honorable ranchero emerged from an interaction between the elite and lower working classes. The ranchero created the image and compelled workers to support that image. Laborers were crucial to the realization of elites' visions of the rancho. Without labor to build the homestead and to work the land, the ranch and the rancher did not exist in the public perception. The ranching elite's emphasis on socioeconomic class distinction through expressions of material wealth came after they had successfully managed to fulfill visions of optimal land use and become wealthy rancheros.

CALIFORNIOS RANCHEROS: THE LAND-OWNING ELITE

Class-based ranchero culture during the 1840s reflected racialized and gendered ideas about land ownership and labor. In this social order, Indigenous and mestizo laborers were charged with maintaining the land and livestock and faced long workdays and endless economic exploitation, while blanco elites distinguished themselves through rituals, symbols, and material wealth. Often scholars credit the production of ranchero culture to the efforts of the wealthy class.[34] Contrary to this classic narrative, the creation of culture did not occur in isolation nor did it stem from one specific source.

Cultural production resulted from simultaneous interactions in a specific historical context, in this case labor. As argued by historian Lisbeth Haas, "identities are grounded in the particular relationship formed through histories of race, gender, class, and place; the politics of space is closely connected to the formation of collective identities grounded in particular interpretations of the past."[35] Social and cultural identity emerged from the interactions between laborers and elites.[36] The multifaceted relationships produced through attempts to establish the rancho as a site of economic production directly connected the laboring classes to the production of ranchero culture as social spectacle.

Workers became another crucial element in the production and maintenance of elites' material culture and social status.

Prior to 1834, California's nonindigenous people shared many commonalities based on their relationship to the land and the mission. Following secularization and through the 1840s, a racialized socioeconomic hierarchy tied to land ownership marked the main distinction in Alta California. In the emergent rancho society, land ownership served as its own social distinction. Status and societal perceptions of wealth originated in how much land an individual owned; even modest land holdings set a person apart from the larger landless masses.[37]

As the number of landed families increased through the middle of the nineteenth century, outward reflections of wealth and status grew in importance. Competition to obtain a higher socioeconomic status depended "on the affirmation of social standing, not the mere accumulation of goods and capital."[38] Wealthy men measured their success through societal recognition of their status. Between 1834 and 1846, the golden age of the Mexican rancho, gaining societal recognition became increasingly important because wealthy elites needed to justify their wealth and social power to each other as well as to lower groups. Elaborate estates and homes furnished with fixtures of the finest quality, clothing made of fine expensive cloth, and public ritual and symbols distinguished elites from the lower classes, but more importantly defined them in relation to other wealthy landowners.

LAND, ESTATES, AND HOMESTEADS

In the attempt to distinguish themselves from other more modest landowners, elites attempted to establish a respectable homestead as a way of affirming their societal status. The wealthy invested their money and efforts into building adobe homes instead of the *jacales* or rudimentary wattle and daub huts of the lower classes.[39] Landowners' use of adobe as construction material indicated their economic wealth and augmented their social status. Many wealthy families throughout the el Pueblo de Los Angeles and its surrounding areas built elaborate homes using the durable material (see Fig. 9).

One of the most popular adobe homes of the time belonged to the Avila family. As one of the first men to receive a grant under the Spanish system, Francisco Avila owned the first adobe home built in Los Angeles. The wealthy rancher and grantee of Rancho Las Ciénagas, Avila built the adobe in the

FIGURE 9 An old adobe built by Jose Pérez. Pictured ca. 1900, this adobe was situated south of the Hotel Raymond and was obtained by Manuel Garfias as part of Rancho San Pascual, but it was not Garfias's residence. This building is often referred to as the Flores Adobe. Courtesy of the University of Southern California, Libraries and California Historical Society. Digitally reproduced by the USC Digital Library; from the California Historical Society Collection at the University of Southern California. http://digitallibrary.usc.edu/cdm/singleitem/collection/p15799coll65/id/6737/rec/1.

center of El Pueblo de Los Angeles in 1818.[40] As one of the wealthiest men in Los Angeles, he decorated his home with the finest furnishings imported from the Mexican interior as well as from New England and Europe.[41] After independence and secularization, as the government distributed land grants in greater numbers and aspiring rancheros amassed their wealth, the home became a way to distinguish oneself among other elites. Not to be outdone, other landed families built their own elaborate adobe homes.

In 1828, Corporal José María Verdugo, a soldier who had served at the San Diego and San Gabriel Missions, retired and built his family home at Rancho San Rafael. Naming it the Catalina Adobe after his favorite daughter, Verdugo, he improved the ranch home, using the profits from his lucrative ranching and agricultural ventures, with the help of his many sons. After his death in 1831, his son Julio took over full operation of the rancho and shared the land with his sister. Under Julio Verdugo's ownership, Rancho San Rafael grew in wealth through the cultivation of grape vineyards and cattle grazing. Like the Avilas, Verdugo furnished his home with items imported from New England and Europe.[42] In addition to the main house occupied by his immediate family, he built several smaller adobe homes on the land for his older sons. Having inherited half of the land, his sister Catalina also maintained a small two-bedroom home at the northernmost point of the rancho.[43] The 1836 padrón indicates that approximately thirty-three people, including family members and laborers, lived on the Verdugo land. Julio Verdugo's successful building and furnishing of these homes, as well as his maintenance of a significant labor force, reaffirmed his status as a successful ranchero.[44]

The image of the economically successful ranchero was tied to societal perceptions of gender and masculinity. Attainment of land was the first step in defining a man's space in California's social and cultural society. In their petitions for land, many men referred to their role as head of the family and to their need for land to better the condition of their families. Once a man received land, it became his responsibility to use it to define his identity as a man, a ciudadano, and a ranchero. In nineteenth century California, the stable rancho homestead became the site for affirmation of these identities because the term *homestead* did not simply refer to the physical home but also to the familial relationships and gender roles within it. As patriarchs, men had to control their women and their land and maintain their honor.[45] As argued by historian Louise Pubols in her work on California patriarch José de la Guerra y Noriega, "patriarchy was part of the natural order of things," and the patriarch was "expected to command and dominate others . . . who fell within the bounds of his authority."[46] Patriarchy and dominance of those regarded as lower on the social hierarchy were essential to maintenance of ranchero masculinity. The rancho household represented a private space in which men extended their public dominance and patriarchal power to the confines of their home and family.[47] With the intention of protecting women's virtue and by extension men's honor, patriarchs built large houses that served the dual purpose of reflecting their wealth and controlling their women.[48] The design of rancho adobes supports the idea that the home housed men's honor. The homes, often built in a U or L shape, facilitated men's vigilance over the women who lived there.[49] Vigilance over women's virtue reflected their status as men's possessions; men watched their women as they watched their ranches, their laborers, and their wealth.[50]

Men's protection of women's virtue reflected only one aspect of their assertion of male dominance. Women's activities in the home also directly affected society's perception of wealthy patriarchs. As manual labor determined a man's status, connection to manual labor defined women's status. Elite women were responsible for running the household and controlling the labor of household servants.[51] Women's roles in the home were directly linked to men's honor and public reputation because elite men's wealth determined how many servants worked in the home. The more servants a husband provided, the less direct contact his wife and daughters had with manual labor. Access to manufactured goods and a consistent domestic workforce did not completely remove them from their duties as housewives; it simply redefined their gender roles within a different economic reality. Both elite and working-class women labored inside and outside the home, performing domestic duties such as baking, cooking, cleaning, ironing, sewing, and laundering clothing; elite women supervised servants in these tasks.[52]

Aside from sharing similar labor duties, women from both classes bore the responsibility of bearing children. Within a patriarchal society, motherhood was an important element of women's identity regardless of their economic status. Although all women were responsible for bearing children, elite women were expected to have a multitude of children in order to physically demonstrate their husband's virility and masculinity. Most working-class women bore about four children, while elite women often birthed upward of fifteen to twenty children.[53] The number of children a man had directly correlated with his socioeconomic status because it showed that he was had the means to maintain them.[54]

Women's position within the household and the physical dwelling itself were crucial to reflecting men's honor. Landed men's spheres of influence originated in the household and were informed by societal prescriptions of masculinity. Social ideals about women's behavior and a patriarch's responsibilities to his family created the foundation for a stable household. Landowning patriarchs needed to indicate their ability to control and dominate their household affairs and to provide for those living and working on their land. The honor that came from men's control over their dependents materialized and was legitimated by public recognition of their control.[55] The examples of the Avila and Verdugo homesteads speak to the variety of social and cultural dynamics that combined to create the physical representation of prestige and honor needed to be a successful ranchero in control of a productive rancho.

CREATING THE ELITE: MARRIAGE, THE FAMILY, AND SOCIAL NETWORKS

Although the nexus of a man's identity was rooted in the individual patriarchal unit of his homestead, the creation of the family and familial honor existed within a larger social system. Similar to mixed-race soldiers and pobladores, wealthy Californio men sought to maintain social status and respectability by building networks with other prestigious families.[56] These families often used intermarriage between their children to create important alliances. The creation of these familial networks complemented elites' political connections and helped facilitate the creation of a landed oligarchy. As a result of the successful establishment of these familial networks, most of California's lands were controlled by a small number of elite families.

In Los Angeles and the surrounding areas, sons and daughters from elite families such as the Avilas and Sepúlvedas married each other to solidify their families' socioeconomic status and expand their familial land holdings. Rancho San Pascual fell under the auspices of these families. The connection between Rancho San Pascual and the Sepúlveda/Avila clans dated back to the period immediately following secularization. Juan Mariné, grantee of San Pascual, was married to Francisca Antonia María Sepúlveda, daughter of patriarch Francisco Xavier Sepúlveda. After Francisca's death, Mariné married Eulalia Pérez; after his death, his children with Sepúlveda inherited his stake in the land.[57] José Pérez, Eulalia Pérez's nephew, denounced the land and was given a provisional grant. Pérez was married to María Merced Lugo, daughter of the prominent patriarch Antonio María Lugo.[58] Upon seeing that Pérez was not fulfilling the provisions of the grant, Enrique Sepúlveda, son of Juan José Sepúlveda and nephew of Francisca Antonia María Sepúlveda, denounced Pérez's claim and became co-grantee of San Pascual. Later, Manuel Garfías, a military officer married to María Luisa Avila, the daughter of María Encarnación Sepúlveda and Francisco Avila and cousin of Enrique Sepúlveda, denounced Sepúlveda's claim to San Pascual.[59] The intermarriages and the familial connections between the Sepúlveda and Avila families illustrate how prominent landowning families were able to access San Pascual's premier lands from the Spanish Colonial Period through the Mexican Period. The Sepúlveda and Avila families remained connected to San Pascual until Garfías lost the land after the U.S.-Mexico War.

The fact that the Avila and Sepúlveda families successfully maintained access to San Pascual, as well as to the thousands of acres gained elsewhere in the Los Angeles area through intermarriage, reflects the importance of the family unit in Alta California.[60] The marriages contracted by these families functioned as a symbolic system that helped shape and support social hierarchies and behaviors.[61]

By establishing a stable family unit and strong familial networks, ranching elites transformed the family into a symbolic system that distinguished them from the lower classes. The fact that elites married only within their own ethnoclass circles defined the parameters for broader social and class behavior and interactions. Within Californio society, familial connections were part of larger social rituals and symbols that engendered class-specific relations that allowed the wealthy to maintain a multifaceted grasp on their power.

SOCIAL DISTINCTION, RITUAL, SYMBOL, AND MATERIAL CULTURE

In Mexican California, societal distinction manifested itself through a variety of interactions between the wealthy and lower classes. Wealthy Californios sought simultaneously to emphasize their social status above that of the poorer classes and to distinguish themselves from other elites through a project of cultural production that centered on material possessions, as well as ritual and symbolic interactions. This project served the dual purpose of separating social classes while fostering a pragmatic social unity with the working class. Wealthy rancheros and laborers framed their relationship through a system of complementary obligations. In this system described as *seigneurialism* or paternalism, workers exchanged their labor for supplies and food rations provided by the rancheros.[62] While this exchange financially benefitted rancheros it also served an important social purpose. Wealthy Californios simultaneously reiterated their power and status through material culture and created interclass unity through symbolic events and relationships such as fiestas and the system of godparent relationships or compadrazgo. Californios created a society concurrently based on social deference and reciprocity, a culture in which, regardless of status, every person was interconnected yet classified.

HOME AND RANCH ACCESSORIES

Upkeep of the rancho was crucial to Californios' inclusion among elite circles. Although the physical appearance of the homestead was very important in avoiding economic land denouncements, elites accentuated their homes' aesthetics through an array of imported furnishings. Many Californio elites, because of their proximity to seaports, participated in trade with Americans and Europeans, which allowed them to purchase material items that augmented their economic status. Some wealthy families purchased items that enhanced household aesthetics such as planked floors, carpeting, glass windows, and wooden doors, while the very wealthy purchased luxury items such as mirrors, clocks, glass decanters, silver table services, pool tables, pianos, and organs.[63]

In addition to these items that many could dismiss as frivolous and mere expressions of wealth, some wealthier families' possessions reflected the fundamental inequities in Mexican California. For example, in his 1877 testimonio, Don José del Carmen Lugo described the different types of beds and bedding available in California. Families of means had beds [mattresses] made of poplar covered with leather hide.[64] Less affluent persons used beds "made of small logs placed in a leather hide" while those "who had nothing else slept [literally threw themselves] on a hide."[65] In addition to quality beds, elites also enjoyed lace-edged embroidered pillowcases and bed sheets made of the finest cloth. In his 1877 testimonio, wealthy Los Angeles rancher Don Antonio Coronel recalled the attention paid to decorating household beds and accessories: "Women took particular care in the adorning of their beds; the bed sheets and pillowcases had to be embroidered."[66] The fact that elites took such care in their bedrooms, spaces that in all likelihood were very private and closed off from public eyes, spoke volumes to their commitment to creating and maintaining their image even when behind closed doors.

In addition to the bedroom, Californio elites used material items to emphasize their wealth in their homes' more public spaces. Living rooms and parlors—places frequented by neighbors, friends, business contacts, and relatives—reflected a family's affluence through the display of imported clocks and mirrors. Well-to-do families frequently hosted dinner parties and fiestas that accentuated their wealth through silver table services and glass decanters, items that most of the population could not afford.[67] For example, in describing dinner and silverware, consisting of plates, forks, and spoons, Lugo stated that "generally speaking of the poorer classes, which were the majority of the population, few had plates, spoons, or forks."[68] Lacking these items, the poor used *cajetas* (clay bowls) instead of plates and ate their food using tortillas instead of utensils.[69] These items indicated the affluence of the elites. The wealthy adorned their homes with the finest goods and successfully created a social image that left no question about their status.

The social status reflected through the home and its furnishings was only part of a larger endeavor to distinguish oneself in a materialistic culture; items outside the home also became crucial in creating a well-rounded image of the ranchero and his status. Throughout the region, most rancheros and their laborers had the standard vaquero gear consisting of a saddle, lariat, knife, sword, and serape.[70] The quality of the gear signified its owner's wealth and status. In a culture in which both wealthy men and laborers rode horses, status and distinction were important because wealthy men could potentially be mistaken as being from the same class as laborers.

In a rancho and horse culture, the item that best reflected a man's status was the *montura*, or the saddle and its accessories.[71] According to Coronel, the saddle was a fundamental part of a vaquero's gear. Functionally, saddles were similar in construction and type, made of sturdy materials to resist the harsh conditions of working with livestock. Strong leather reatas, or ropes made of thread crafted from horsehair, attached the saddle to the horse; this harness was laid upon a *vaqueta*, a cowhide that covered the horse on both sides.[72] While saddles were similar in practicality, their adornment often varied. The vaquetas included "bordadas de seda de colores ó hilo de oro ó plata" (silk embroidery of gold or silver) depending on "los recursos del cabalgador" (the [economic] means of the rider).[73] Saddles' intricate decorations often carried over into elaborate vaquetas covering the horse's *anca* (haunches); often these vaquetas matched the color, patterns, and border of the cowhide on which the saddle rested.[74] The saddle reflected the status of the rider and accentuated a social and economic distinction among men on a field that presumed them equal.

CLOTHING

In Californio society, clothing served as the most important way of distinguishing oneself because it was what most people saw. As in other places throughout the Mexican frontier, encounters in the public arena required that one be dressed according to his or her social class.[75] Wealthy Californios dressed in the most up-to-date fashions made of the finest materials as a way of making their status and economic position known to the public. Here, as in the creation of the respectable homestead and family, public perception played a crucial role in creating a person's status among other wealthy people as well as the lower classes. A person's clothing and the public's recognition of that clothing affirmed the thewealthy Californios' social status.

California's agricultural lifestyle and culture determined the type of clothing used in the region.[76] Clothing and accessories were made of light cotton and linen, as well as leather and woolen materials that provided durability and versatility. Influenced by these factors, California's distinct social classes wore clothes that were very similar in style but differed in quality and decoration. The wealthy took great pride in their clothing and used it to emphasize the differences between themselves and the poorer classes.

In his 1877 testimonio, Coronel's detailed description of men's clothing emphasized the disparate quality of clothing among the classes. In describing men's *chalecos* or vests, he detailed the elaborate decoration and ornamental buttons used on the *paño* (silk cloth). Coronel meticulously described buttonholes outlined with colorful silk and detailed the vest's elegant silk hand embroidery.[77] With similar detail, he described the elegant riding sleeves, jacket, pants, and expensive garters decorated with silken flowers, fruits, and animals.[78] After asserting that his careful description reflected the clothing of "men of means that enjoyed more comforts," Coronel continued his description of clothing worn by lower class men.[79] In contrast to his detailed description of wealthy men's vests, Coronel very briefly and simply stated that, depending on their means, laborers wore chalecos made of wool, cotton, or silk and that they "were decorated capriciously."[80] With a similar lack of detail, he described laborers' jackets and pants, stating that they were made of the same material and decorated in the same fashion.[81] By providing a more detailed description of wealthy men's clothing, Coronel very clearly asserted the line between the men who owned the land and those who labored on it.

While men's clothing was often designed with functionality in mind, women's fashions served the dual purpose of asserting both gender roles and class and social status.[82] In 1834 and 1835, women, regardless of economic class, wore dresses. Similar to men's fashions, women's dresses signified class differences by means of the material from which they were made, as well as their detail and decoration. In his description of wealthy women's clothing, Coronel stated that women wore tight-fitting narrow tunics made of cotton or suede.[83] The top of the dress, described as a *corpino* or bodice, was high-necked and sleeveless.[84] Women decorated their dresses with their choice of a *listón* or ribbon or with flowers, whatever they fancied.[85] Frequently they accentuated their clothing with necklaces and earrings they obtained from trading hides with American merchants.[86] Coronel stated that fancy lace rebozos or shawls, reminiscent of those worn by Spanish women, completed their outfits.[87]

While wealthy women wore the most up-to-date fashions, women of lesser means often wore more traditional style skirts and off-the-shoulder blouses, lacking the intricate decorations and detail of higher quality clothing.[88] Poorer women's less elegant and more loose-fitting attire reflected class-specific ideas about gender because it afforded them the mobility necessary to more easily perform their day-to-day activities. Poor women's less modest clothing also indicated their place in the social strata. Elite women's very conservative clothing spoke to the value of wealthy women's sexuality and gender behavior. Upper-class women were consistently supervised in their homes, the place that accorded them their honor and virtue.[89] They were expected to remain sexually pure until marriage and faithful to their husbands afterward. These gender expectations indicate that wealthy women were responsible for maintaining landed men's honor as well as sustaining their own propriety. Wealthy women's tunics were very tight-fitting and restrictive. While wearing a dress, or *medio paso* as it was known, wealthy women could take only half steps.[90] The dress's effect on a woman's mobility affirmed gender and economic status by controlling what she could do. In terms of labor, wealthy women could not freely complete many household tasks, increasing their reliance on their domestic servants and indirectly reaffirming their status as rich women, as well as their husbands' and fathers' status as strong patriarchs.

Lugo's and Coronel's testimonios reveal several things about elites' socioeconomic status as reflected through material items. Both men spoke to the different conditions existing in Californio society and described material items enjoyed by those at different socioeconomic levels. Despite their attempts to supply an all-inclusive depiction of everyday items used in Alta California, their narratives betrayed the privilege accorded to them through their wealth. Their recollections reflect the social distinction they sought during the Californio Period. For example, Lugo used the phrase "according to one's resources" to indicate that not everyone had access to the same standard of living. Lugo first described the goods of the upper class, followed by those of the middle class, and lastly by the those of the lower classes. The order in which he told his story reflected his experiences as a man of means, distinguishing himself from those who could not afford his lifestyle.

Although Lugo's use of the phrase "according to one's resources" and the order of his recollections showed his awareness of the economic inequities of Californio society, they also served a larger historiographical purpose. According to Hayden White, historical work is a verbal structure in narrative form that classifies and explains past structures and processes in ways related to a specific vision and purpose for telling the story.[91] Following this definition, the historian writes history by arranging events in a certain order, deciding which events to include and exclude, and by stressing some events and subordinating others. As part of a project conducted by Hubert Howe Bancroft and his research assistants, Lugo's testimonio made him into a historian whose recollections became part of a history that he was simultaneously telling and making. His role as historian thus allowed him the latitude to create the story however he wished. His formalist argument identified material objects by ordering, classifying, and reclassifying them according to economic accessibility.[92] In other words, Lugo related the history as he saw fit, and his story socially distinguished Californios, including himself, from the lower classes in the past as well as in the future.

Californios' use of material possessions and their establishment of stable homesteads and respectable families allowed them as landed elites to create a public image they used to remain at the top of the social hierarchy. Aside from reflecting Californios' participation in the reaffirmation of social difference through material items, Lugo's and Coronel's testimonios indicated wealthy Californios' relationship with people in lower economic classes.

SYMBOLIC SOCIETAL UNITY

In Mexican California, rancheros utilized a form of paternalism long employed by their fathers to ensure patronage and maintain an amicable relationship with the lower classes, all the while solidifying their honor as wealthy landed men. Based on patriarchal authority and notions of elite masculinity, first and second generation rancheros took responsibility for their workers and their communities. Seeing this responsibility as an extension of their honor, rancheros provided an array of support for their communities. For example, wealthy ranchero José de la Guerra provided money for building churches and gave food to community members as a means of performing his paternal responsibility to those lower on the socioeconomic scale.[93] By seeing themselves as fathers of a large interrelated family, elite Californio men, structured their society "on clear lines of authority and submission, but linked as well by chains of obligation and reciprocity."[94] In other words, landed elites' responsibility for the lower classes resulted from a constructed relationship built on their roles as provider and dependent. Elites' paternalism sought to maintain authority and respect through the giving of gifts, symbolic/fictive kinship networks such as compadrazgo, and community acts of altruism such as fiestas.

Throughout Mexican California, the community fiesta and compadrazgo system served the dual purpose of fulfilling paternal responsibilities and simultaneously publicly reaffirming elites' social status and power.[95] Elites were fully aware that their maintenance of wealth and success often relied on the lower classes' labor and respect. Despite Californios' emphasis on social distinction, differences between the elite and the poor did not fully isolate the two social classes. Elites, seeking to distinguish themselves from the lower classes while maintaining their respect, utilized the fiesta and compadrazgo system in a self-serving attempt to create a symbolic and pragmatic unity beneficial to their social status.

FIESTAS

Californio society marked special occasions such as weddings and religious holidays with lively parties where guests enjoyed abundant food and drinks while they engaged in endless revelry.[96] In the early rancho era, these high-profile celebrations often brought together people from different social classes and provided elites the opportunity to display their wealth. The wealthy hosted these community parties, using their homes to highlight their affluence. The rancho home symbolized the landowner's ability to appropriate and control the land and its resources to establish an elegant homestead. In a society and culture based on public perception, the home became the physical representation of the optimal vision of land use; it illustrated how a man's control of the land's resources could bring affluence, honor, and respectability. As guests enjoyed their time at the fiesta, physical markers of wealth constantly reminded them of the host's status.

In addition to his home, the host used food and drink to display affluence. It was the responsibility of the *encargado* or party host to provide food and drink for the fiesta, which in some cases could last as long as a week. As social custom required, on the first day of the fiesta, the host served a "large meal for important and notable party attendees."[97] For these meals, hosts ordered calves to be killed for food and provided guests with an unlimited amount of imported brandy to imbibe.[98] While providing for guests seemed part of a successful celebration, in Mexican California this too took on an important social meaning. The large elaborate meal was an opportunity for the elite to prove their status by having their social peers mingle in the spacious living rooms furnished with imported furniture and elegant decorations while waiting to dine in the elegant dining room. Although the public could not partake in the meal, they could participate in the rest of the evening's revelry.

After supper, the host organized a dance open to anyone wishing to attend. The *enramada*, a large canopy made of tree branches, served as the site for the evening's baile or fandango.[99] In the 1830s, these dances were inclusive, and all classes of the city's population attended despite social differences. In his 1878 testimonio, José de Arnaz, a wealthy Spanish-born trader turned rancher, described the atmosphere of the Californio bailes of the period as a mix of "rich and poor, honorable women and prostitutes, alike . . . [participating] equally in social diversions. Even women who lived openly as prostitutes and those with reputations as concubines, were easily admitted to public events."[100] Arnaz's recollection indicates that although social distinctions existed in 1830s Californio society these boundaries were not very rigid. His statement reflects a level of disbelief in the intermingling of social classes. He seemed shocked at what he regarded as a very permissive society. His statement indicates the possibility that, as social norms changed, not all elites were happy with the interaction between the classes. Arnaz's use of the term *honorable* in his reference to women showed that he believed in a strong social and cultural hierarchy in which some people deserved to be shunned because of their status. Regardless, these dances created the opportunity for the host to display and share his wealth with the larger community—in many cases with his employees.

To sustain his image as a respectable honorable man, the ranchero had a responsibility to share his wealth with those who helped him make it.[101] The rancho's laborers made the rancher wealthy, and to ensure his continued wealth, he needed to maintain workers' loyalty through the distribution of its rewards. This interaction clearly shows simultaneous maintenance and deconstruction of social distinction. By providing food and drink to the community and his workers, the ranchero provided temporary access to the elite's excess while increasing his social stature in the eyes of the community. Although the ranchero temporarily blurred social distinctions by providing momentary access to food, drink, and the surroundings of affluence, social interactions and behavior reflected through dancing quickly restored the hierarchy and his place as a strong patriarch.

Dancing was an important part of the fiesta and, not surprisingly, it reflected one of the more organized and supervised parts of the social gathering. Even though admission into the bailes was unrestricted, party participants' adherence to class norms was still expected.[102] Despite the proximity between classes and the increased possibility of intimate and/or interclass interactions, party attendees were expected to adhere to specific class norms.[103] These expectations changed the baile's dynamics because they reinstituted the class boundaries between party guests. While adherence to class protocols was an attempt to maintain social class distinction, these protocols were imbued with ideals of gender as well. Men and women's performances in culturally symbolic dances spoke to the gendered and classed aspects of these interclass gatherings in which elites and the *populacho* or the lowest class of the population commingled.[104]

Men and women engaged in a variety of dances with names such as la bamba, la jota, el fandango, and el burro, each with its specific moves.[105] In some dances men performed while women observed, and in others women performed while men observed. Both used the dances as courting opportunities, and because the dances were in public spaces, men and women had to follow a gendered protocol. The design of the enramada provided a place for women to sit under the canopy and a place outside for men to congregate while mounted on their horses; the men's space was alongside the enramada and allowed them to see and be seen by the women inside.[106] Men and women could not form mixed groups and were always separate, except when they danced.[107] Women sat under the canopy while men remained outside on their horses until the master of ceremonies, or *tecolero*, announced a couple's dance.[108] Men dismounted and entered the tent, chose the woman with whom they wished to dance, and proceeded to the dance floor.[109] After the dance was over, men excused themselves from their companions and went back to their horses.

The protocol described above does not seem to reflect the delineation of classes at these social gatherings; however, a deeper analysis shows how class played a major role in the exchange. Men with the resources to own and mount a horse distinguished themselves from lower-class men, who did not own horses. It made them *caballeros*, a term indicating a level of respectability not available to men without the means to own a horse. When on horseback, a man was significantly higher off the ground than an unmounted man. The visibly elevated status provided by riding a horse translated into a symbolic elevation of social status.[110] Within this context, the horse became an accessory, like clothing, boots, or saddle—a way of elevating and indicating a man's social position and means. The baile reinforced a ritualized classed masculinity that reaffirmed wealthier men's status among men of differing social classes. Only men who had the means with which to compete in this show of masculinity could claim access to the higher class and its women. Those who did not were by definition part of the poorer classes.

As mixed-class spaces, fiestas and bailes temporarily blurred lines of social distinctions but did not obliterate them. Although attendees shared a common language, general culture, and geographic space, their relationship to the land continued to determine their interconnectedness with each other. The ranchero who owned the land allowed those who labored on it to enjoy it at these fiestas. His actions were part of a larger system of mutual respect and obligation; the more he provided, the more respect he earned. In his 1878 testimonio, José Arnaz referred to this system with specific reference to the elite's obligation to the poorer classes. Arnaz maintained that, although there were economic differences among inhabitants of Los Angeles, the poor did not lack meat to eat. He stated that, when a man of means ordered the killing of a calf, he directed that men who lacked the means to feed their families would receive enough meat for one or two days.[111] Additionally, Arnaz stated that, "if an individual who needed meat for his family stole and killed another person's cow, the matter could be resolved by giving the owner the cow's hide; in this manner hunger and necessity were addressed in this region."[112] Elites' distribution of food to the lower classes helped them create positive reputations and loyalty among the community.

The system of obligation, in conjunction with the fiesta, reflected the ties that existed between classes during the early rancho period. This bond did not override elites' desire to distinguish between the classes but rather helped improve their social status through self-serving measures that seemed altruistic and paternalistic.

COMPADRAZGO

The desire to create a connection between and among different social classes transcended secular interactions and entered into the ecclesiastical realm through the compadrazgo system. In the compadrazgo system, families created bonds with each other by taking responsibility for the spiritual and material well-being of each other's children. Although this responsibility was articulated through social relationships, religion and spirituality served as the basis of the godparent-godchild bond. Church law delineated the terms of the compadrazgo relationship, creating a sacred bond among the parents, child, and godparents. Despite the religious origins and meaning of compadrazgo, in nineteenth century Alta California it was largely a system meant to fulfill economic needs and create social cohesion between the wealthy and the poor classes.

In the compadrazgo relationship, *padrinos* or godparents needed to provide for their *ahijados* or godchildren, in case they lacked the resources with which to live after the loss of their parents.[113] The fact that godparents might need to provide for their godchildren prompted parents to choose padrinos who had the means to help their children. As a result, workers and poorer relatives often asked their bosses and wealthier familial relations to sponsor their children as padrinos and *madrinas* or godmothers. Elites entered into the agreement as a way of obtaining the lower classes' respect and loyalty.[114] Although elites benefited from their godparent relationship with the poor, the advantage was far from one-sided. Workers also benefited from having the ranchero as a compadre because it reflected a solid long-term bond with the employer, ensuring an increased level of job security.[115] For this reason, the compadrazgo system often served to create a reflexive bond between the upper and lower classes, a relationship through which both the wealthy and poor obtained an affirmation of their status as a ranchero and as a worker, respectively. This is only one way in which the system functioned. Among the elites, the compadrazgo relationship helped solidify political and economic bonds between the wealthy and ensure elite's social status.[116] The dynamics of the system changed depending on the groups that were involved.

The situation differed when elite children needed godparents. The wealthier class chose close family and allies from the same socioeconomic class as godparents.[117] In this respect, the compadrazgo system functioned similar to intermarriage between elites. Uncles, aunts, cousins, and close family friends and associates often took on the compadrazgo relationship, forming a multitude of relationships that linked most Californios by blood or at the very least by custom.[118]

In the case of the landed families directly connected to San Pascual between 1834 and 1845, the ties are readily visible through marriage and baptism. In April of 1791, Juan Mariné, original grantee of San Pascual, served as godfather at the baptism of Juan José Sepúlveda's son, Enrique Sepúlveda, a later owner of San Pascual. Mariné, a military officer, was Juan José Sepúlveda's superior at the San Diego Presidio. He was also married to Francisca Antonio María Sepúlveda, Juan's sister. Interestingly, the baptismal record listed Mariné as a third godparent in addition to fellow soldier José Carmen Araña and his wife, Manuela Astorga.[119] The link between the owners of San Pascual, illustrates how the exclusive circles created through marriages, baptisms, and other affinities helped keep land and wealth in the hands of a select few.

The compadrazgo practice described above paralleled relationships throughout California's elite. As argued by anthropologist Robert Kemper in his comparative study of compadrazgo in urban and rural Mexico, the system served as a means of strengthening already existing ties of kinship and friendship; the expansion of the system outside family or blood relations depended on specific functional and historical circumstances.[120] Mariné and the Sepúlvedas were relatives through marriage, not blood, yet he was still chosen as a padrino, illustrating the expansion of kinship networks among the early soldiers and pobladores. When the Spanish Colonial Period ended and these families slowly came to constitute the landed elite, the system of compadrazgo changed to accommodate the shifting political, economic, and social climate created by independence and secularization. In 1830s and 1840s California, compadrazgo amongst the wealthy became a system that created what Pubols has referred to as kin clusters, interrelated groups of godparents that sponsored children born of kin or fictive kin.[121] The connection compadrazgo provided the wealthy went beyond that of spiritual kinship; it transformed into a political kinship that determined Californios' place in the social hierarchy.

Californios utilized the compadrazgo system in two different ways as a means of determining social status. The system allowed the poor the opportunity to assure themselves of their connection to the ranchero and reflected their pragmatic decision to display loyalty and respect, irrespective of how genuine, for elites' patriarchal authority. For the wealthy, the godparent system supplemented other links among the elite; it assured them of political, economic, and social power and status. Overall, the compadrazgo system reflected the attempt to create an image of cohesiveness on one level while reaffirming and social class distinctions on another.

As spectacle and public ritual, the interactions created through the fiesta and compadrazgo system provided the semblance of cohesiveness while redeploying and reaffirming concrete examples of social hierarchies and social distinction. In this context, the fiesta and godparent relationship were part of elites' self-serving attempts to maintain social appearances of wealth and status by sharing their riches and creating links with people they considered inferior, yet whose loyalty and support they needed to maintain their status.

INCREASED AMERICAN PRESENCE AND PRAGMATIC SOCIAL COHESIVENESS

As regional diversity increased, and the Euro-American immigrant and landless Mexican populations began to increase, the pragmatic cohesiveness created through the fiestas, bailes, and compadrazgo systems during the early Rancho Period began to decline. Over time, wealthy families sought to distinguish and separate themselves from the lower classes with whom they had once commingled. In the Los Angeles area, the influx of Euro-Americans and their acculturation into Californio society began to change the organization of social functions and the community's social structure. Increasingly, wealthy families held their own exclusive parties separate from *la gente común* (commoners). Californio elites mingled with prominent Anglo merchants and land owners at exclusive parties and other social functions.

These social relationships resulted from business interactions and intermarriages between daughters of the Californio elite and acculturated Anglos. Contrary to earlier social custom, wealthy Californios now attended social functions that excluded persons from the lower classes. In his testimonio, José Arnaz, after discussing the mixed nature and lax admission practices of bailes and fiestas, described Los Angeles's preparation for the celebration of Mexican independence in September of 1840:

> Around that time, attempts were made to establish a circle of decent and honorable people. To this effect, on September 16,1840 there were two public dances held—one in the central plaza under a ramada, which the majority of the populacho [rabble] and gente común [common people] attended. The other [dance], hosted at the house of Abel Stearns, was attended by invited outstanding families of the town. In order to obtain this result [invited guests only] he posted a guard at the door as a precaution.[122]

Arnaz's statement spoke to the erosion of societal cohesiveness in 1840s California, but also to Euro-Americans' growing presence and influence among Los Angeles elites. As the immigrant population grew and immigrants entered elite Californio circles, the contours of the elite class changed. Looking at this example within the context of change brings to light the way in which the Californio elite began to change their relationship with the poor during the last years of Mexican rule.

Between 1800 and 1834, foreign traders and merchants migrated into California in the attempt to establish trading relationships with the missions. Many traders found that assimilating into the emerging elite class served to solidify their business interests, and they quickly converted to Catholicism, obtained Mexican citizenship, married into the area's respected families, and in many instances even Hispanicized their names. This pattern, repeated throughout California and other areas of the Southwest, helped immigrants become

Californios.[123] The case of Abel Stearns, the host of the party described by Arnaz, serves as an example of the immigrants who came into Los Angeles in the period before secularization in the 1820s and early 1830s looking to establish themselves as profitable merchants. Stearns, an American merchant who had migrated to Los Angeles in the 1820s and became a prominent member of Californio society, was one of many immigrants who had come to the city in search of social and economic opportunity during the last years of Spanish rule.[124]

In 1836 the Los Angeles padrón enumerated 48 foreigners among a non-Indian population of 1,678.[125] Although the padrón indicates only a person's nativity and not his or her emigration date, it does offer an accurate count of foreigners in the city at the time of the census. Numbering twenty-two, American men constituted the largest of the immigrant groups.[126] The padrón does not list women amongst these immigrants, supporting the contention that immigrant men married into the local population as a means of gaining social legitimacy.[127] Americans held a variety of occupations in Los Angeles society; three were merchants, eleven were skilled laborers or craftsmen, three performed general labor, one was a servant, four were transients, and one was a medical doctor.

In the census, Stearns was listed as a merchant from the United States, alongside another notable member of Los Angeles' elite, Juan (Jonathan) Temple. In 1828, after leaving San Diego, Temple migrated to Los Angeles and established a profitable general store. Both Stearns and Temple quickly became well-respected and wealthy members of Californio society. The stories of Stearns and Temple are not unique in the sense that many immigrants came to Spanish/Mexican California seeking wealth and riches; their uniqueness lies in their success. Stearns and Temple entered into Los Angeles's elite circle through marriage. Stearns' marriage to Arcadia Bandini, daughter of established merchant Juan Bandini, allowed him entrance into the society's upper echelon and gave him access to large tracts of land.[128] Similarly, Juan Temple married Rafaela Cota, daughter of Guillermo Cota and Manuela Nieto, gaining him access to lands owned by his new in-laws. Both men eventually numbered amongst Los Angeles's wealthiest landowners.

By the 1840s, many of the businessmen, like Stearns and Temple, who had migrated during the early nineteenth century, found themselves at the top of California's hierarchy, within its elite circles. The 1844 Padrón, taken two years before the outbreak of the U.S.-Mexico War, lists Stearns and Temple as merchants. Figures provided in the 1850 Los Angeles City Census indicate that they expanded their wealth and improved their social status after 1848. For example,

Stearns was classified as a gentleman with an estimated worth of $80,000, while Temple was listed as merchant worth $50,000.[129] The status that these men held in Californio circles paralleled that of the older established families in Los Angeles.

As the circle of elites grew larger and interactions with American markets increased, Mexican Californios began emphasizing the differences rather than the similarities that existed among the population. Arnaz's example of the 1840 Independence Day Party indicated that Los Angeles Californio elites had entered into exclusive circles with the region's Euro-Americans. Americans, who had been a minority in the region since the 1820s, had finally begun to influence the community's social structure. In his autobiographical *Life in California*, Alfred Robinson, an American businessman who married into the prestigious de la Guerra family, described the growing separation between the classes: As "the country . . . became more settled, a necessary distinction prevail[ed] amongst the various classes; and [the] society was more selective, as in places of greater civilization."[130] Within the context of the 1830s and 1840s, this statement reflects Americans' racial and class attitudes regarding Mexican society. Growing animosity between the United States and Mexico, exacerbated by racially fueled notions of expansion, influenced Americans' and Californios' ideas regarding social organization and propriety. Wealthy Californios sought to place themselves within a new racialized class structure that not only distinguished them from the lower classes, but also emphasized their class similarities with Euro-Americans.

The exclusion described above is not unlike the variety of measures Californio elites used to distinguish themselves from the community's common folk. As shown through this chapter, the wealthy had long used clothing, homes, material goods, and dinners to emphasize the wealth gained from land ownership and control of labor. Despite their desire to distinguish their economic status, they did not seek to eliminate societal cohesiveness. Arnaz stated that "decent and honorable" people wanted a place for themselves away from the rabble; this statement, unlike those of Lugo and Coronel, does not indicate distinction but rather separation. The example above presents a look into elites' changing perceptions of class distinction during a transitional period in the region's social and political history. Changing economic, political, and social forces contributed to a decline in the desire for societal cohesiveness and gave way to ideas based on distinction and separation within an increasingly Anglo-based model.

PART III

THE AMERICAN PERIOD

5

THE AGE OF TRANSFORMATION

San Pascual Becomes American, 1843–1872

AFTER THE U.S.-MEXICO WAR, Californios' attempts to maintain their power and influence in the American system faltered because the racial rhetoric of Anglo-Saxon white supremacy eradicated notions of class-based solidarity. Unlike the Mexican Period, in which Mexican liberalism and independence helped frame visions of land use and ownership within a racialized class status, under the American system the ability to own land rested solely on racial identity.

Within the new American racial structure, Californios' acceptance as social equals depended on owning land. In attempts to assimilate into the American system, Californios claimed whiteness or Europeanness as a way to reframe cultural and class superiority as racial superiority. Californios believed that, through marriages, improvements of land, and links with prewar American immigrants, they would be able to maintain their power and influence. Unfortunately, within the postwar race-based American system, their attempts only temporarily staved off their political and economic loss. Once Californios lost their lands they lost their claims to racial and cultural superiority.

The visions of optimal land use that had fueled the war of expansion and conquest continued into the postwar era, supporting a practice of land dispossession. For Rancho San Pascual, the process resulted in the sale and eventual parceling out of its lands. Garfias, who had tried very hard to assimilate into Mexican and later American society, exemplified the consequences of the transition from a class-based to a race-based system. Garfias's loss of San Pascual to Benjamin Wilson marked the rancho's transition from Mexican to American ownership. American visions of land use had triumphed over Californio ideals of pastoral land use.

THE U.S.-MEXICO WAR COMES TO CALIFORNIA

The tension between Mexico and the United States over land had festered since American annexation of Texas in March of 1845. The war between the two countries began with the American declaration of war on May 13, 1846, and ended with the signing of the Treaty of Guadalupe Hidalgo on June 30, 1848.[1] In California, tension between Mexicans and Americans arose with the steady influx of American immigrants into northern California during the 1840s. Unlike the Americans who had migrated into the region during the late 1830s, these immigrants had no intention of acculturating into Californio society. Many of these post-1840 arrivals did not come prepared to work in agriculture or in skilled professions, but rather were interested in acquiring land. By 1845 the increased American presence gave rise to conflict between Californios and immigrants who sought to assert racial ideologies of white supremacy and Manifest Destiny.[2] These American immigrants considered themselves the great civilizers of the continent and regarded Californios as racially and ethnically inferior to themselves.[3]

The arrival of John Frémont in January 1846 set in motion a series of events that clearly illustrated American desires to overtake the region and expel the Californio government. The American declaration of war in May 1846 emboldened a belligerent group of American squatters and trappers who referred to themselves as Bears to mobilize against Governor Mariano Vallejo and other Californio leaders. On June 6, 1846, launching what would be referred to as the Bear Flag Revolt, the insurgent Americans arrived at the home of Governor Vallejo and placed him under arrest. They declared California independent and named it the Bear Flag Republic.[4]

As the war raged on and Californios organized a resistance movement, American forces slowly took over California's northern presidios and pueblos.[5] On August 11, 1846, the war came to Los Angeles. American troops arrived in the city to find it deserted. Californio troops had fled into the hills and, with both Pío Pico and General Castro gone, American Commodore Robert F.

Stockton's troops took possession and occupied the city on August 14, 1846.[6] Determined to retake the city, the region's vaqueros and rancheros, many of whom were retired military officers and soldiers, mobilized a militia led by Captain José María Flores, Andrés Pico, and José Carrillo. Under the leadership of Flores, Garfias and fellow Californios participated in Los Angeles' defense.[7] In September, Flores's forces retook the city, forcing the Americans to retreat and wait for reinforcements. Moving south from Los Angeles to San Pedro, Stockton waited for General Stephen Kearney's troops, making their way through Arizona, to provide support to his tattered forces.

In December, Kearney's troops reached San Diego and began their march northward to Los Angeles. On December 6, while moving north, Kearney's forces engaged Flores's lancers at the Battle of San Pascual at Rancho Guejito, site of present-day Escondido.[8] After several days of fighting, Stockton's troops arrived, providing much needed support. After taking Rancho Guejito, Kearney and Stockton's combined troops continued north, entering Los Angeles in early January 1847. On January 8, Flores's three hundred lancers engaged nearly six hundred American troops at the Battle of the San Gabriel River, near present-day Montebello.[9] After several failed attacks, Flores, who was outnumbered and outgunned, retreated, conceding the battle to the Americans. Moving westward toward Los Angeles, Flores and his men engaged the Americans the next day at the Battle of La Mesa.[10] After an intense but unsuccessful resistance, Flores concluded that his men could no longer ward off the onslaught of American forces and ordered his men to withdraw. Flores's retreat at La Mesa marked a turning point in the war. It left Mexican leaders in Los Angeles demoralized and defenseless against Colonel John C. Frémont's incoming troops. With no means for a viable defense, American forces overtook Los Angeles on January 10, 1847.[11]

After the fall of Los Angeles, Flores and his remaining contingent of men, including Lieutenant Garfias, met at the Rancho San Pascual adobe, just outside of the city, to decide their next move. Here Flores, José Antonio Carrillo, and Captain Agustín Olvera discussed the Californios' terms of surrender. Fearing that American forces would execute him upon surrender, Flores transferred control of the militia to Andrés Pico and fled south to Sonora with Garfias.[12] On January 13, 1847, Carrillo, Pico, and Olvera met with Frémont at Campo de Cahuenga to sign the treaty ending the war in California. Under the articles of capitulation, Californios were to turn over all their artillery and promise not to pick up arms against the United States for the remainder of the war. The treaty also provided Californios the same rights and privileges awarded to American citizens, including the protection of their rights and property.[13]

After having served as Flores's final headquarters, Rancho San Pascual remained in the same condition as it had prior to the war. Although not of critical importance during the war, it proved to be an important site for regional historical analysis. The rancho's importance lay in the land itself because it had witnessed and contributed to the region's various social, economic, and political changes. Located on the lands of the former San Gabriel Mission, where seventy-five years earlier Spanish friars and Tongva Indians had collided, it provided for the growth of a regional economy that propelled the continued settlement of Alta California. The land itself bore the marks of the political, social, cultural, and economic struggles produced from the previous cycles of conquest and the clash of ideas of optimal land use. Seventy-five years later, scourged by the march of Manifest Destiny, it served as the site at which Los Angeles's last Mexican defenders, ex-military men turned rancheros, small farmers, vaqueros, and vecinos, contemplated their surrender to the American forces that had overtaken their homeland.

Despite the Californios' surrender at Cahuenga and the Mexicans' subsequent loss to the United States, elites continued to negotiate their space within the incoming social, economic, and cultural structure. Californio elites picked up the pieces and worked to keep their land by adhering to Anglo-American norms and redefining their identity in accordance with Anglo-American models of land ownership. As the American Period progressed, elites such as Garfias attempted to use their lands to incorporate themselves into the new social and economic structure only to find themselves in the margins.

SAN PASCUAL BECOMES AMERICAN

Throughout the Rancho Period, rancheros' visions of optimal land use required a man to utilize the land he owned to successfully produce wealth and accumulate goods representative of that wealth. For many well-known rancheros of the era, building a productive ranching operation and participating in the tallow and hide trade brought tremendous wealth and prestige to their families. In the areas around San Pascual, including the outlying areas of El Pueblo de Los Angeles, men from landed Californio families such as the Verdugos, Avilas, Sepúlvedas, and Nietos, along with a handful of immigrants such as

Juan Bandini, Abel Stearns, and Hugo Reid, made their wealth and reputations on these lands. Similarly, Manuel Garfias slowly used the land to the build his reputation among the region's elites.

In 1843, despite receiving the grant for San Pascual, Garfias and his wife, Luisa Avila, moved into his Los Angeles home located on First and Main Streets. Upon inspecting San Pascual, he found the small adobe beneath his standards and decided to live in town, leaving the small adobe ranch house for laborers involved with the day-to-day ranch maintenance. Largely disinterested in ranching and having gained social status from his mere ownership of the land, Garfias committed his efforts to creating social relationships with some of the most powerful men in Los Angeles. Despite Garfias's disinterest, Rancho San Pascual slowly took shape under the supervision and guidance of Doña María Encarnación Avila, Luisa's mother. Not interested in making Rancho San Pascual a huge prosperous rancho like the Avilas' Rancho Las Ciénegas, the widow Avila concentrated on simply developing the land enough to ward off economic denouncements. Despite the rancho's successful maintenance, Garfias largely ignored the land, relying on it only to increase his public image. Garfias would not focus his energies on the rancho until after the U.S.-Mexico War ended in 1848 and the gold rush impacted the cattle economy.

The discovery of gold in northern California in 1848 and the subsequent gold rush in 1849 dramatically affected California's social and economic development in the immediate postwar period. It caused, among other things, a shift in economic markets, visions of land use, and the Californios' position in the new American system. In the north, Californios witnessed an increased migration into the region and quickly found themselves outnumbered.[14] Many found their land rights attacked and became embroiled in litigation and land swindles; they were also affected by legislation that dispossessed them of their ranchos by the mid-1850s.[15] In southern California, the gold rush ushered in a profitable age for the land-owning ranchero class, allowing most to stave off the loss of their lands, albeit temporarily. In places like Los Angeles and Santa Barbara, as well as areas that included San Pascual and the former San Gabriel Mission lands, the massive population explosion in the north resulted in increased demand for beef cattle for food. Demand for cattle was not unique; rancheros had long prospered from a lucrative tallow and hide trade, exporting an estimated "six million hides and seven thousand tons of tallow between 1826 and 1848."[16] During the early 1840s, a ranchero could make about $10,000 a year on about eight thousand head of cattle.[17] Economic dependence on this trade required that the land be used for cattle grazing and ensured that fourteen million acres of California's premier lands were owned by about two hundred California families.[18] After 1849 the cattle boom that lasted into 1856 shifted the composition of the southern California's cattle market from the trade of tallow and hide to the trade of cattle for food consumption in the northern mining districts. This shift positioned rancheros to net nearly $20,000 on the sale of one thousand cattle, quickly dwarfing the profit from the tallow and hide trade and creating an even more lucrative market for southern Californios.[19]

The wealth brought on by the cattle boom further solidified the class divisions between wealthy Californio rancheros and the lower landless classes. Emphasis on material culture as an indication of social class status, while critiqued by American onlookers as improvidence and ostentation, was part of an established sociocultural practice used to define the place of the Californios in the ranchero economy and regional elite.[20] When the war came to California in 1846, Garfias had only briefly been part of the local elite. Following the war's end, he found himself within a transitional period during which many of the city's elite still maintained their control and power for the time being. Within this context, Garfias jockeyed for a position among the Californio and emerging American elites.

The 1850 city census lists Garfias as an agriculturalist owning property worth an estimated $7,000.[21] Of the four ranchers in the city of Los Angeles in 1850, Garfias ranked third in estimated worth. Amongst thirty-nine farmers listed with property values ranging from $200 to $50,000, Garfias ranked fourth. These figures indicate that by 1850 Garfias had successfully become a wealthy member of the elite, and although he was a respected member of the community, he did not have enough wealth to place him among the highest ranking men on the social ladder. The figures recorded in the census data reflect the value of real estate owned by an individual; in this respect, land translated into social status.

In 1850, in the hope of further integrating himself into Los Angeles' political and social circles, Garfias took an active interest in developing Rancho San Pascual. Lacking the capital necessary to build the home, he sold a parcel of San Pascual's less inhabitable northern section to raise money for his project.[22] He sold "a tract [of] one square mile, commencing where the arroyo turns upward on the tillable land," to Americans Carlos Hanewald and John Pine for $2,000 at an interest rate of 4 percent.[23] The terms of the sale required $600 up front with the remainder paid over nine months beginning on March 9, 1850. If the total purchase price was not paid in nine months, the land would revert to Garfias.[24] In 1851, Garfias invested this money into San Pascual and undertook construction of a large estate on the land. The resultant Garfias Adobe rivaled the grand Californio estates of the time in size and elegance. Unlike the Avila and Verdugo adobes that serve as physical representations of the past, the Garfias adobe exists only in the stories of guests who visited the home and authors who wrote about the structure (see fig. 10).[25]

Completed in 1852, the Garfias adobe stood on the banks of the Arroyo Seco in San Pascual. In his memoir, Judge Benjamin S. Eaton described it as a one and a half story adobe building with walls two feet thick, all nicely plastered inside and out, with an ample corridor extending all around. It had board floors and boasted green blinds, a rare thing in those days.[26] This description is one of the most detailed available. Other works comment on the adobe's physical display of wealth. For example, Perry Green noted that "a veranda extending around the building and with a finish costly and somewhat pretentious for the time it was built hinted at the character of the former occupants."[27] Both Eaton

FIGURE 10 Ruins of Manuel Garfias's elegant and elaborate adobe ca. 1886 are still visible on the banks of the Arroyo Seco. Courtesy of the University of Southern California, Libraries and California Historical Society. Digitally reproduced by the USC Digital Library; from the California Historical Society Collection at the University of Southern California, http://digitallibrary.usc.edu/cdm/ref/collection/p15799coll65/id/6155.

and Green spoke of the adobe's grandiose design and expensive appearance and both alluded to the fact that the adobe was unlike those in the surrounding areas.

Garfias spared no expense in building and decorating his home. Although Eaton and Green both provided a view of the level of affluence reflected throughout the home, there is a striking difference in the two descriptions. Eaton, who eventually would live at the adobe after Garfias lost the land, spoke in praise of the adobe; however, Green alluded to the "pretentious character of the owner."[28] Green's comment about Garfias reflected early nineteenth century Euro-American attitudes about Californios' ostentatious ways. In *Two Years Before the Mast*, Richard Henry Dana indicted wealthy Californios as a "thriftless, proud, and extravagant" group, emphasizing his perception that they misused their wealth.[29] Other American contemporaries, such as Alfred Robinson, referred to Californio men as "generally indolent, and addicted to many vices, caring little for their children, who like themselves, grow up unworthy members of society."[30] These remarks reflect American perceptions of Californios as people who used the land to obtain wealth only to squander it on materials and items that they were not industrious enough to make for themselves. In this light, Green's description of the adobe seems to represent larger racialized attitudes about Californios' misuse of their wealth. Describing the Garfias home as costly and pretentious for the time served as a way of dismissing the former occupant's achievements and downplaying his wealth in a larger sense.

In addition to improving the land, Garfias needed to safeguard his ownership of the property within the new American land laws. Despite guarantees of citizenship and land through the Treaty of Guadalupe Hidalgo, elites' land rights eroded under the incoming American system. The Federal Land Act enacted in March of 1851 required Mexican landowning elites to prove ownership of their land grants. As a legal process, the confirmation of land titles was quite tedious. According to the regulations established on January 21, 1852, a claimant was required to file a written petition indicating the date of the original grant and a detailed list of previous landowners ending with the claimant.[31] In addition to this petition, claimants needed to provide a land survey as well as information pertaining to any interfering land claims. The petitioner needed to furnish the original grant and any documentary evidence, including sworn testimony, to substantiate the claim.[32]

In September 1852, Manuel Garfias filed his petition to keep Rancho San Pascual, but inadvertently began the path to its loss. Like many Californios, he committed his money to the time-consuming and costly process of upholding his land title. When Public Land Commission members Alpheus Felch,

Thompson Campbell, and R. Augustus Thompson arrived in Los Angeles in August 1852, Garfias held a large lavish party in their honor at his Los Angeles home on First and Main Street.[33] Aside from the commissioners, many of the city's elite, including Abel Stearns, Pío Pico, and José del Carmen Lugo also attended.[34] The list of attendees exemplifies Garfias's adherence to social protocol in his attempts to keep his land. Utilizing a process similar to that of the Mexican system, Garfias emphasized his connection to the land and to the local elite by publicly displaying his wealth.

While the Southern District land court reviewed his petition, Garfias continued to funnel money into the land and the costly legal proceedings. Like other Californios caught up in the costly confirmation process, Garfias sought the necessary capital to improve his rancho. He approached American businessman Benjamin Wilson for a loan and used Rancho San Pascual as collateral.

Shown in fig. 11, Wilson, known to Californios as Don Benito, had arrived in California in 1841 as part of the Workman-Rowland Party. Upon his arrival in Los Angeles, he sought transport to China to engage in the fur trade, but failing to gain access to any ships he decided to stay in the city.[35] In 1844, he married Maria Ramona Yorba, daughter of prosperous ranchero Bernardo Yorba.[36] Wilson quickly became a prominent community member, landowner, and local politician, serving on the Los Angeles Common Council in 1850 and for one term as mayor of Los Angeles from 1851 to 1852.[37] By 1850, Wilson was one of the region's wealthiest men with real estate valued at $50,000.[38] After the U.S.-Mexico War, he found many opportunities to obtain land through a variety of means, including making loans.

In 1852, Garfias borrowed $8,000 from Benjamin Wilson and his business partner John S. Griffin to improve San Pascual. A few years later, on March 6, 1856, the Southern District Federal Court confirmed the petition, upholding Garfias's claim.[39] Having overcome the confirmation process, the only step left was to receive the most important title to the land, a U.S. land patent signed by the president. While awaiting the patent, Garfias had become heavily indebted to Wilson. By 1859, due to an exorbitant compound interest rate, the $8,000 loan had ballooned to $24,000. With no means of paying off the loan, Garfias was compelled to turn over Rancho San Pascual to Don Benito. On January 1, 1859, Manuel Garfias and his wife, Luisa Avila, signed all right, title and possession to Benito Wilson for a consideration of $8,100.[40]

Garfias's loss of San Pascual illustrates a very common way in which Californios were dispossessed of their lands after the U.S.-Mexico War. In keeping

FIGURE 11 Portrait of Benjamin D. Wilson, landowner, lawyer, and former mayor of Los Angeles, often referred to as the Father of Pasadena. Courtesy of the University of Southern California, Libraries and California Historical Society. Digitally reproduced by the USC Digital Library; From the California Historical Society Collection at the University of Southern California, http://digitallibrary.usc.edu/cdm/singleitem/collection/p15799coll65/id/17813/rec.1

with the requirement of the federal land act, wealthy Californios found themselves in litigation lasting as long as seventeen years, spending an exorbitant amount on legal fees in attempts to prove the validity of their claims in court.[41] The process proved to be a large financial burden for many wealthy Californios and resulted in the transfer of land as payment for personal indebtedness, bankruptcy, delinquent taxes, and other related expenditures.[42]

Attempting to navigate within this new social, economic, and cultural structure, Californios utilized the traditional method of emphasizing affluence. In their attempts to develop their ranchos and maintain their elevated social status, many Californios obtained high-interest loans to develop their ranchos. Looking at the Garfias-Wilson transaction, it is interesting that the amount Wilson paid for San Pascual was a little more than what Garfias had borrowed, yet a fraction of what he owed with interest. This indicates the possibility that the loan was from the onset an attempt to gain San Pascual. As reported in the 1850 census, Rancho San Pascual had never been worth more than $7,000, yet Wilson provided a loan with an $8,000 principal. Between 1860 and 1890, these unscrupulous business transactions increased throughout the American Southwest, successfully dispossessing wealthy Mexican landowners of property rights that had been guaranteed thorough the Treaty of Guadalupe Hidalgo.[43]

MANIFEST DESTINY, AMERICAN WHITE SUPREMACY, AND OPTIMAL LAND USE

Within fifty years of the American Conquest, many of California's wealthiest Mexican rancheros had lost their lands to Anglos. While fraternization with Euro-Americans had not posed a threat during the early nineteenth century because they constituted a minority of the population, by the mid-nineteenth century, Mexican Californios had become the vanquished people in a war of territorial aggression. As the Euro-American population grew so did their access to social, economic, and political power. As Mexican Californios lost control of their lands and by extension their socioeconomic and political control, their visions of land use were displaced.

During the second half of the nineteenth century, the ideology of Manifest Destiny, a term coined by journalist John O'Sullivan in 1845, described the United States' "destiny to overspread the continent allotted by Providence."[44] Often used as a catchall phrase reflecting the process of moving west, the term's popularity does not reflect the myriad of meanings it embodied. O'Sullivan's phrase epitomized older sentiments regarding westward expansion, land acquisition, freedom, and citizenship dating back to the American Revolutionary era. In the late eighteenth and early nineteenth centuries, the Jeffersonian vision of a "rising empire for liberty" based on private landownership, citizenship, and economic development filled Americans' minds with thoughts of controlling the entire North American continent, and fulfilling their destiny "to be the greatest power on earth."[45] Framed within a racialized agrarian vision, the Jeffersonian ideal viewed territorial expansion, private land ownership, and the white yeoman farmer-citizen as the bases for the growth of the American nation. Between the late 1780s and the early nineteenth century, these ideals fueled Americans' movement west and supported U.S. acquisition of French, Spanish, and Indigenous lands as well as the expansion of slavery.[46]

In the 1840s, Manifest Destiny encapsulated the Jeffersonian agrarian vision during a time of political, social, and economic change. This ideal sustained the notion that because American Anglo-Saxons were racially pure they were destined to rule over inferior groups. American Anglo-Saxon superiority not only ensured racial dominance over inferior groups but also predicted the latter groups' subordination and eventual extinction, thereby ensuring Anglo-Saxons permanent racial superiority.[47]

Armed with this belief in Providence and racial superiority, Americans continued their move westward, believing that their journey symbolized "the domination of civilization over nature, Christianity over heathenism, progress over backwardness."[48] In 1830, after Congress enacted the Indian Removal Act, the government confiscated Indigenous lands in Georgia and Alabama to meet the country's growing population and expanding cotton trade; as part of this search for land, some Americans moved farther west into Mexican territory. Articulated within the context of the territorial conquest of Mexico, Manifest Destiny supplemented the agrarian vision by constructing and emphasizing racialized ideas about Mexicans and other non-white groups.[49] American migration into Tejas y Coahuila, the area of present-day Texas and the Mexican state of Cohuila, gave rise to territorial conflict that culminated in the U.S.-Mexico War and Mexico's loss of one-third of its territory.[50]

Throughout the 1840s, Americans perceived Mexicans as a mongrel race, a lazy, shiftless and ignorant people resulting from intermarriage with Indians.[51] Basing their ideas on 1830s accounts by travelers such as Richard Henry Dana and Lansford Hastings, many believed Mexicans too ignorant to develop the rich soil of the Southwest and emphasized Americans' duty to dispossess these shiftless people of their lands.[52] For instance, in his 1830s description of California's Mexican population, traveler Lansford Hastings stated

> Many of the lower order of them [Mexicans], have intermarried with the various tribes, and have resided with them so long, and lived in a manner so entirely similar, that it has become almost impossible, to trace the least distinctions between them, either in reference to intelligence, or complexion. There is another class,

> which is, if possible, of a lower order still, than those just alluded to, and which consists of the aborigines themselves, who have been slightly civilized, or rather domesticated. These two classes constitute almost the entire Mexican population, of California, and among them almost every varicty and shade of complexion may be found, from the African black, to the tawny brown of our southern Indians.[53]

Statements such as Hastings' were quite common and created a negative image of Mexicans in the American Anglo-Saxon mind. Americans' racialization of Mexicans as black or Native American inserted Mexicans into the nation's dialogue about race. Americans, both those migrating to the West and those in the East, familiar with the racial rhetoric regarding slavery and Indian removal, utilized these racialized models to create an understanding about Mexicans in the Southwest.

In the narrative of Manifest Destiny, Mexicans became the racialized "other." These negative racial perceptions, compounded by growing social and political tensions with Mexico after 1835, contributed to the rise of white supremacy in Texas and the Southwest. White Americans' perceptions of Mexicans as lazy, backward, and ignorant paralleled similar beliefs about Amerindians and African Americans in other parts of the country and rationalized territorial conquest and economic exploitation.

CALIFORNIOS AND THE WORKINGS OF WHITE SUPREMACY

Manifest Destiny's link between racialized ideas about local populations and land use was not unique to American and Mexican interactions. Americans, similar to the Spanish and Mexicans who came before them, held ideals about what constituted optimal land use and utilized these beliefs to racialize Alta California's inhabitants. Euro-American agrarian visions of optimal land use depended on the opportunity and ability to produce viable agricultural crops.[54] Within the narratives of territorial expansion, Manifest Destiny, and white supremacy, American settlers were the only people capable of improving land they believed was mismanaged by racially inferior people.[55]

In California, attitudes about white supremacy and land development took a bit more time to evolve than in other parts of the Southwest because Euro-Americans remained in the minority until 1849. During the 1830s, Americans who had migrated to the region had successfully integrated themselves into the elite ranchero class. Amongst the elite, most of whom considered themselves Spaniards, a racialized class structure obscured Americans' idea of white supremacy through class distinctions. During the Mexican Period, Americans who sought to separate themselves from the lower landless class did so by utilizing Californio ideals that embraced Europeanness and built on Californios' practice of identifying themselves as blancos or españoles. These identities provided them with the privileges of the landed elite, placed them at the top of the socioeconomic hierarchy, and distinguished them from the inferior non-European Indian working class.

The ranchero elite's emphasis on Spanish identity and European bloodlines constructed an ideal comparable to white racial identity that temporarily helped suppress the rise of Anglo white supremacy in the region. By naming themselves gente de razón, Californios claimed a Spanish fantasy heritage and culture as a means of masking their mixed heritage.[56] Californios' claims to some European-based identity paralleled Anglos' ideas about white supremacy. Americans found Californios' social stratification and class distinctions friendly to their ideas of white superiority because they reflected a racially based binary that separated white from non-white mestizo, Indian, and mulatto peoples. During the Spanish and Mexican periods, these ideas of whiteness and Europeanness legitimated landed elites' treatment of lower racialized populations. Later, at the end of the nineteenth century, the American Conquest relegated Californios to a similarly inferior racial status.

The increased Euro-American population after 1850 contributed to the rise of American white supremacy and the implementation of a structure that defined Californios as racially inferior. Landed elites, many of whom had held political power prior to the war, were labeled as racially inferior, primarily as a result of American attempts to establish political and economic control in the region.[57] Euro-Americans' redefinition of Californios' racial status paralleled the region's social and political conquest. As the war approached, Americans racialized Californios as an inferior and backward people to legitimize the takeover of their lands. This racial rhetoric continued into the early American Period because the Californio elite still held significant portions of land, wealth, and political power. Interested in obtaining what these wealthy men had, Americans utilized legal and extralegal means grounded in the racialized rhetoric of Manifest Destiny to obtain the spoils of war. Amid these changes, elite Californios, many of whose daughters had intermarried with Anglos, redefined their social position within a changing racial and economic structure in the attempt to maintain their social, political, and economic status.[58]

California's ethnic and racial diversity required that Americans amend the simplistic racial binary of white and nonwhite to account for the variety of racial/ethnic groups, including the diverse Euro-Americans who flooded the region after 1849. Despite the racial designation of *Anglo*, which implied English descent, the Americans who entered California after the conquest consisted of Euro-Americans and foreigners of German, Irish, French, and Italian descent.[59] The term *Anglo-Saxon* and its connection to English identity are rooted in the American colonial past. It was brought to the colonies in the sixteenth and seventeenth centuries as part of the early colonists' religious and historical legacies.[60] Historically rooted in Anglo-Saxon England, English colonists and later American revolutionaries emphasized Anglo-Saxon superiority in establishing freedom, liberty, and popular government.[61]

Beginning in the 1830s the term *Anglo-Saxon* was used to assert superiority over Native Americans and justify Indian removal and westward expansion.[62] In the 1840s and 1850s the term *Anglo* began to replace the word *white* as a way to classify the variety of white ethnic groups, especially the Irish.[63] In the West, the fact that Euro-Americans were largely outnumbered by a diverse minority population resulted in the reconceptualization of racial categories.[64] Despite animosities in other areas of the country, ethnic white people entered into a racial project that redefined the meaning of white and black to suit their specific contextual needs.[65] Euro-Americans fabricated a collective racial identity that differentiated them from the Mexican, Indian, and Chinese populations they encountered.[66] Increasingly, white Americans celebrated their entrance into the region and denigrated local populations, including wealthy Californios, as a way of differentiating themselves from the minority populations they had overtaken through war. As critical race theorist and legal scholar Kimberlé Crenshaw argued, white Americans constructed their racial identity relationally against people of color they deemed inferior in order to delineate a "common identity of non-stigmatized parties—whose identity and interest are defined in opposition to the other."[67] In postconquest California, Mexicans became the racial other, the antithesis of whiteness, used to replicate the racial hierarchy that existed in other areas of the United States in a slightly different form.[68]

The construction of white racial identity and citizenship during the first half of the nineteenth century affected Mexicans in the newly attained regions by emphasizing the difference between rich Mexicans and poor Mexicans within the American racial structure. At the end of the U.S.-Mexico War, provisions in the Treaty of Guadalupe Hidalgo guaranteed Mexicans living in the former Mexican territory American citizenship and land rights.[69] In the antebellum era, the Naturalization Act of 1790 gave citizenship to free white persons and excluded all other groups, thereby creating race-based access to the privileges of citizenship and economic development.[70] By granting Mexicans (specifically wealthy Californios) citizenship, the federal government designated them as racially and legally white, making them eligible for the political, social, and economic status of white people.[71] In contrast to Californios' almost immediate racialization in the north, rancheros in Southern California were able to better access the American racial hierarchy by claiming a white racial identity or at the very least an identity that emphasized their Europeanness.[72] This negotiation of identity reflected the social construction of race and indicated that a variety of processes, institutions, and persons were involved in creating racial categories.[73] This designation was not unlike the one Californios utilized during the Mexican Period to create, deconstruct, and recreate the meanings of racial categories for personal gain.

In the American Period, Californios exploited the pliability of white racial identity within the new American racial structure by redeploying ideas about Spanish identity rooted in the white/European cultural supremacy and class privilege. In the south, Californios' identification with and accommodation of Americans' notions of Europeanness helped them to briefly maintain political and social power in the immediate postwar period and to maintain their class interests and social standing.[74] It provided them the necessary franchise rights to keep political and social influence in places such as Los Angeles and Santa Barbara well into the 1870s.[75]

As in the Spanish Colonial and Mexican eras, land ownership and control of labor were crucial to the maintenance of power and status. In the American Period, the lower landless classes did not receive the same treatment afforded to their wealthier landed compatriots. Americans racialized landless dark-skinned Mexicans as Mexican Indians. They considered them racially inferior to white people and unassimilable, and they denied them the social and political privileges of American citizenship.[76] This view often resulted in the passage of legislation that sought to control this population.[77] Americans' dichotomous perception of Mexicans as either white or Mexican Indian indicates the link between race and class.

Elite Californios' constructed racial status as white or Spanish European was contingent on their owning land. As Americans dispossessed them of their lands through unscrupulous business practices and legal maneuvers, Californio elites lost their political, social, and economic status.[78] In this context, the distinction between the wealthy ranchero elite and landless classes was of great importance in maintaining broader racial privilege as well as social and political power. Californios were placed into a racial structure that defined them in relation to Euro-Americans rather than their lower-class brethren.[79]

LAND LOSS AND POLITICAL POWER

In 1850, many prominent Californios with deep roots in the region served in local and state political office. In April 1850, after the first California legislature divided California into counties, Los Angeles County held an election for officers, electing landed Californios such as Antonio F. Coronel as county assessor, Agustín Olvera as county judge, and Manuel Garfias as the county's first treasurer.[80] In addition to Mexican Californios, assimilated Americans who had lived in the region since before the war also served as elected county officials. The most prominent assimilated American elected to county office in 1850 was Benjamin Davis Wilson. The fact that Wilson served alongside Californios as an elected official in the period immediately following the war indicates that the transition from Californio to American leadership was not immediate. In many ways, it shows a level of continuity that existed in the region after the war.

In the years immediately following the American Conquest, Los Angeles's social and political elites were the same people who were in power prior to the war. Assimilated Americans continued to participate in the region's social, cultural, political, and economic life as they had for decades before. The demographic changes in the Los Angeles area were unlike those prompted by the gold rush in Northern California. Americans remained a minority in the Los Angeles region for years after the war. This relative stability allowed Los Angeles's Californio elites to maintain their political power longer than those in California's central and northern regions.[81] For example, Californio Antonio F. Coronel served in a variety of political capacities ranging from county assessor to mayor to city councilman.

In Los Angeles, Californios' political participation continued well into the 1870s, until the expansion of the railroad prompted an increase in the Anglo population and a decline in Californios' political power. For example, the last Mexican mayor of Los Angeles, José Cristóbal Aguilar, lost his reelection campaign in 1872 after his Euro-American opponent, James R. Toberman, emphasized Aguilar's poor command of spoken English.[82] Toberman's emphasis on Aguilar's English skills indicates that there was a growing Euro-American population in Los Angeles that would accept this racialist critique.[83] Toberman's subsequent overwhelming defeat of Aguilar marked the beginning of a Euro-American-controlled mayoral office.[84] The increasing anti-Mexican attitude displayed in the 1872 election supports the general contention that the 1870s was the beginning of Californios' social and political declension; however, there is evidence that challenges this idea.[85]

Narratives of decline identify the 1870s and 1880s as the decades when Californios lost their political power. While the 1870s and 1880s point to a broader loss of political power for Californios, I contend that the seeds of their social decline began decades earlier in the late 1840s and 1850s. By changing this time frame, the present work focuses not only on the loss of political power but also on the decline of social power and cooperation between Californios and assimilated Euro-Americans and immigrants in the 1840s and 1850s.[86]

Californios' awareness of early anti-Mexican and anti-Californio attitudes as early as the 1850s is clearly illustrated in the editorials of the first Spanish language newspaper in California. *El Clamor Público*, published in Los Angeles in 1855 by precocious young journalist Francisco P. Ramírez, was a newspaper "devoted exclusively to the service and interests of native Californians."[87] Although only seventeen at the time he began publishing *El Clamor*, Ramírez had worked for several newspapers throughout California, including the *Los Angeles Star*, where at the age of fifteen he served as the editor for *La Estrella*, the English daily's one-page Spanish appendage.[88] Highly regarded in the industry, Ramírez also worked at the *Catholic Standard* and the *Weekly California Express*, small newspapers located in central and northern California. When the first edition of *El Clamor* debuted on June 19, 1855, leading American newspapers the *Los Angeles Star* and the San Francisco-based *Daily Alta California* enthusiastically endorsed it.[89] Ramírez, influenced by ethnic newspapers circulating in San Francisco in the early 1850s, saw *El Clamor* as a means for social change, with editorials seeking to raise readers' consciousness about issues pertaining to their community.[90] Although Ramírez sought to inspire political and social change, his efforts were often at odds with the Los Angeles ranchero class, especially during the early years of American rule.

In Los Angeles during late 1840s and early 1850s, a small group of wealthy southern Californios, about 3 percent of the population, expressed ideals aligned with those of the American Southerners who steadily migrated into the region.[91] This group sought to further their political and social alliances to the Americans, mostly Southerners, who touted a Democratic, proslavery agenda.[92] As elites cultivated these relationships, lower-class landless Mexicans endured the race-based violence caused by the imposition of American control.[93] As violence against the lower classes escalated, the Californio landed elites sided with the incoming Anglo population as a means to preserve their political power and wealth. Although Ramirez's editorials were often met with opposition from the Californio class, they are valuable in illustrating how American racial concepts considered Californios and Mexicans as alike. Often these articles reflected the complexity of the Californios' attempts to negotiate the newly imposed American system.

In *El Clamor Público*'s first publication, Ramírez published editorials detailing the negative economic and social consequences prompted by the American Conquest and colonization. Speaking of the region's economic decline, an October 1855 article stated that the "expected ruin of bankers and merchants and agriculture had finally come as a result of the extravagant speculations and importation of foreign products into the region."[94] The anonymous author cited the diminishing condition of la clase española:

> It must be understood that the major part the Hispano-American population, comprised of Mexicans, Chileans, Peruvians, etc., have dedicated themselves to agricultural production, and because of the complete paralyzing of the of the industry due to a lack of appreciation for these native products, have been obligated to abandon their jobs and find themselves ruined without a means of making a living. And being the only industry to which the Spanish class [Españoles] can dedicate themselves to, and because they lack knowledge of any other industry, they find themselves in an even sadder situation, without any hope for the future.[95]

This statement shows the tenuous basis of the class solidarity formed between Californios and Anglos during the American Period. As few as seven years after the war ended, Californios had experienced a loss in their economic standing and the decline of their prominence in the agricultural and pastoral economy due to the bust of the cattle boom. Because Californios' wealth and success are what allowed for their racialization as Europeans and non-Indians, the decline in their status left them susceptible to the racial prejudice encountered by their lower- class counterparts.

By 1857, *El Clamor Público* published articles that pointed to Anglos' continued racial prejudice and mistreatment of Californios. In an article titled "Americanos! Californios!" from February 1857, the anonymous author spoke to Americans' racial bias against Californios:

> It is very difficult in writing or in conversation to use these two words [Americanos and Californios] without leaving room to form bad ideas for those who are not familiar with our local relations. We desire with all our hearts to abolish the last vestiges of distinction implicit in this expression. When will the time come that the inhabitants [of California] will speak and treat each other under the same title, like brothers from the same family? Do we not exist under the same republic? Do we not have the same rights and protection under the law?[96]

The author points to the continued social and judicial inequity between Anglos and Californios. The quote indicates an awareness that, despite the guarantees made in the Treaty of Guadalupe Hidaglo, Californios did not receive equitable treatment. The author called many of the older respected "ciudadanos de California," such as the Picos, Domínguezes, and Olveras to meet and candidly discuss ideas about how to unify the two races.[97] As shown earlier in this book, Euro-Americans and other immigrants prior to 1840 followed social, cultural, and economic protocol as a means of assimilating into upper-class rancho society. Calling on these older residents to bridge the differences between these groups was significant because they had successfully created strong cultural bonds with Anglos who migrated into the area during the Mexican period.

After the American Conquest, Californios attempted to recreate bonds with incoming Americans by identifying with Anglos as brothers and citizens. Californios called on Anglos to allow them the opportunity to assimilate into the new social order. They asked Anglos to recount the instances in which "Californios had not followed through with their responsibilities as citizens to the best of their abilities" so that "their faults . . . [could] be clearly related" and "rectified" in the interest of "securing the prosperity of the community."[98]

Californios' calling on previous sentiments of class-based unity provides an interesting insight into the implicit racial project of American assimilation in the late Mexican Period. Assimilation and integration into Californio society and culture during the late 1830s allowed Americans to gain a foothold in the region prior to large-scale Anglo migration. These important class-based relationships carried over into the early American Period of the late 1840s and 1850s and allowed wealth to "dissolve many differences" based on both Californios' and Euro-Americans' common goal of obtaining wealth and social status through land ownership.[99] The links between these groups began to change as the Euro-American presence increased and ideas of class solidarity were replaced with social and cultural legitimation of Anglo-American ideas of white supremacy.[100]

Despite Californios' desire to assimilate and their calls for equality, an article republished in *El Clamor* from the *San Francisco Herald* in July 1859 declared that Mexicans were a "degraded race . . . [some] are so dark that it takes much effort to distinguish them from the Indians, for the small difference that there is between them and the African race."[101] Published on *El Clamor's* first page in bold capital letters, this statement shows Anglos' continued racialization of Californios and lower-class Mexicans. Erasing the racialized class line that distinguished the landed Californio elite from the poor clearly shows that the racial rhetoric of white supremacy had pierced the strategic solidarity of the earlier era. The decline of Californios' social status and wealth did not occur in the 1870s with the massive influx of Euro-American migrants.[102] Rather, the seeds of this decline were planted in the late 1830s and 1840s with the welcoming of Americans into Californios' social circles. The slow but deliberate imposition of the Euro-American racial, class, and cultural systems under the guise of class solidarity allowed Americans who held political power prior to the war to maintain their power during the transition into the American system in the 1850s. It is here that the decline of Californio power is rooted.

CHANGING LANDSCAPE: RANCHO SAN PASCUAL IN THE AMERICAN VISION

After his attempts at improving the land, Manuel Garfias's sale of San Pascual to Benjamin Davis Wilson and his business partner, John S. Griffin, ushered in the rancho's American Period. Wilson's tenure as owner of San Pascual brought many developments to the rancho and to the region. The broader significance of his development of San Pascual lay in his ability to use the land as a means of embodying the changing needs and visions of optimal land use.

Prior to the war, as an American immigrant in Mexican territory, Wilson negotiated cultural expectations and participated in a variety of business ventures; he very quickly became a very well-respected member the Californio community. His use of land to build his reputation and status was well in line with wealthy Californios' beliefs about what constituted an honorable ranchero and vecino. Wilson's marriage into the Yorba family gained him access to some of the region's most valuable land. By the time of the American Conquest, Wilson enjoyed a great deal of social privilege and wealth. Conversely, within the American system, land ownership still determined a man's status but was reliant on racialized ideals propelled through Manifest Destiny. Wilson, although having assimilated into Californio culture, epitomized the possibilities available to incoming Anglo-Americans after the U.S.-Mexico War. In many ways his successful ownership of some of Southern California's best lands, his ability to run a successful vineyard and winery, and his involvement in regional politics represented the triumph of Manifest Destiny and Anglo-American white supremacy. The manner in which Wilson approached his acquisition of San Pascual indicated his knowledge of both Californio and American visions of land use and socioeconomic and cultural ideals about land ownership and status.

Wilson knew the value of land ownership, and when Garfias offered San Pascual in exchange for zeroing out his debt, he wanted to assure himself that Garfias's land was productive and could bring him profit. Prior to signing the deed in January of 1859, Griffin sent Benjamin Eaton, a noted surveyor, to assess San Pascual's value.[103] Trusting Eaton's positive report regarding the land's premium condition, Griffin met with Garfias and his wife, Luisa Avila, to accept the land.[104] Griffin immediately wrote to Wilson and stated that he was confident that they had made "a good purchase" from which they would "receive full value for [their] money."[105] Wilson and Griffin quickly began to see how they could make money from their investment.

Most of Wilson's and Griffin's dealings with San Pascual consisted of selling off land parcels for a variety of uses. Water rights were of major importance in the region because the cultivation of grapes and the raising of livestock depended on the availability of water. One of the earliest deals connected to Wilson's sale of San Pascual dealt with issuing water rights.

In 1860, one year after they had obtained the land, Wilson made a deal with John Keever because of Keever's ability to obtain water that flowed thorough San Pascual.[106] Interestingly, the agreement did not contain any monetary fee for the use of the water but rather delineated San Pascual's boundaries and reaffirmed Wilson's sole ownership of the property. Although this agreement does not appear fiscally beneficial, Wilson's involvement in water rights issues was a crucial part of the development of the region's infrastructure during the 1860s and 1870s. Water, often a theme in the history of the West, is important to the discussion of how the West developed.[107] The control of water is what supported the optimal visions of land use. In San Pascual, the cultivation of grapes and other crops necessitated access to a consistent reliable water source. Recognizing the need for water, Wilson worked to create an intricate system that brought water to region. Later in the nineteenth century, Wilson's harnessing of the water supply solidified his legacy as the Father of Pasadena because it provided the crucial element necessary to facilitate the Indiana Colony's expansion.

Wilson's ability to dominate San Pascual and by extension many of the surrounding areas' water supplies speaks to a larger process regarding ideas about race and land use. The fact that Wilson, an American, was the first to divert water via an aqueduct from the origins of the Arroyo Seco in the San Gabriel Mountains symbolized the materialization of Manifest Destiny and Anglo-American white supremacy. Wilson had accomplished what Californios, especially Garfias, had failed to do; he made the land viable and productive. His distinction as the Father of Pasadena recognized his success and contributions to the region.[108] His positive reputation speaks to the way some Americans negotiated white and Californio society after the U.S.-Mexico War. Wilson navigated the transitional period quite well. His title Don Benito indicated his respected status and acculturation into Californio society during the Mexican Period.

After the war, although his first wife Ramona Yorba had died in 1849, Wilson kept in contact with his former brother-in-law, Raymundo. A short letter from Raymundo Yorba dated October 4, 1859 illustrated how the class relationship between Californios and Americans remained amicable. Yorba greeted Wilson as his "highly esteemed brother" and requested payment of a debt for a third party. After asking the favor, Yorba ended the letter with a warm salutation to Wilson's wife Margarita [Margaret] and the entire family.[109] Interestingly, Wilson's private papers are full of invitations and calling cards from noted Californios such as the Picos and the Sepúlvedas, indicating that Wilson and certain landed Californios maintained communication, albeit professional, during the early American Period.[110] Read one way, this communication indicates the mutual respect that existed between Wilson and Yorba. Conversely, in the context of a negotiation of power, Yorba's letter and the various invitations to social events may have been a way of maintaining a connection with Wilson at a class level. Even though Wilson had deep roots in Californio society and successfully participated in the regional economy of the Mexican Period, history remembers Wilson as an American *not* a Californio.

While Wilson's accomplishments fill the historical record, the physical landscape and historical memory represent Americans' triumph. The legacy of Don Manual Garfias, the last Mexican owner of San Pascual, represents Mexican Californios' inability to hold on to their lands. In April of 1857, Garfias advertised the sale of his home in Los Angeles:

> For sale in exchange for cash or livestock, the famous and elegant house situated in the Main Street of this city, owned by the person writing this ad; whose property, due to its very spacious rooms, fine construction and decoration offers all the comfort that good taste can provide. In addition it has a beautiful garden at the front of the house, and plot suitable for development in the back; both plots contain some fruit trees with plenty of land remaining for the same purpose. Interested persons come to the store of Twist y Aguilar, for more details. [The land is also] available for lease.[111]

This advertisement tells us several things about Garfias's home, social status, financial situation, and most importantly his land's value. First, Garfias described the home as elegant and having all of the upper-class comforts. By doing this, he employed a common practice among Californios; he used his property to distinguish himself as a member of the upper class. Secondly, aside from his description of the home, Garfias detailed the property's abundant land, describing its beauty and productivity and stressing its value, real and potential, for the growth of fruit trees and crops. Lastly, Garfias's advertisement implicitly spoke to his financial situation. Offering to sell his city home, a mark of wealth and distinction, for cash or exchange of livestock, indicated his attempt to obtain capital. Although this advertisement might simply be part of regular business transactions for the landed classes, the sale indicated that he was dealing with the rising debt that had arisen out of his dealings with Wilson and Griffin over San Pascual. Garfias's sale of his city home, his deeding of San Pascual to Wilson and Griffin in 1857, and his 1860 land patent signed by President Abraham Lincoln marked the last few times that Garfias was mentioned in relation to Rancho San Pascual. Garfias's experiences became part of a narrative in which racially inferior Californios lost their lands due to mismanagement and bad financial decisions. In this story, Garfias, like countless other Californios, disappeared into history, leaving the present to men such as Wilson.

The 1850s transition of Rancho San Pascual from Mexican to American hands shows how Californios lost their lands to American men who had assimilated into Mexican society in the period prior to the U.S.-Mexico War. Garfias's loss of San Pascual was quite different from the loss of land through economic denouncement during the Spanish and Mexican Periods because it occurred within a new political and economic context, fueled by the rhetoric of Manifest Destiny and Anglo-Saxon racial superiority. When Garfias denounced San Pascual's previous owners, he did so through his utilization of a well-established system used by Californios to take control of former mission lands. Not unlike other Californios, Garfias supported his claim to land by emphasizing his Spanish cultural identity and his financial status. This protocol provided a much-needed support system for the Californio elite. By the time of the U.S.-Mexico War, immigrant Americans who had entered Californio society through marriage had managed to attain a level of prestige, respectability, and wealth among the Californio elite. In the case of Wilson and Garfias, both men held a similar status, belonged to the same social circles, and were respected landed men.

The political and social consequences of the U.S.-Mexico War changed the structure of the system in which these men lived. Although they remained at a similar social level for a brief period, Wilson quickly surpassed Garfias in wealth and status. This was not unlike what occurred after Garfias's economic denouncement of Sepúlveda's right to San Pascual. Although similar in process, the difference can be seen in terms of what the loss represented. When Garfias took over San Pascual, he did so based on the idea that Sepúlveda and his heirs had failed to develop it in a meaningful way. This land acquisition was not a means of making wealth but rather a way of displaying wealth and social standing. In the Mexican Period, the land itself was wealth. One's status depended on the ability to have the land, develop a homestead, and make enough profit from it to maintain one's lavish lifestyle.

In the case of Wilson's takeover of San Pascual years later, there was a different vision of land use within the incoming American system: a vision in which the land represented not only wealth, but also a means of making more wealth.[112] This vision of land speculation had fueled westward expansion from as early as the late American Colonial Period and had prompted a variety of conflicts between Anglo-Americans and Indigenous peoples.[113] The end of the

U.S.-Mexico War and influx of Anglo settlers led to the growth of land speculation in the American Southwest during the second half of the nineteenth century.

Wilson's loan to Garfias in the early 1850s was part of a larger trend in which American financiers, land speculators, lawyers, and others provided high-interest loans to Mexican landowners using their lands as collateral; when the landowner defaulted, the loan guarantor confiscated their lands. Historian Deena J. González identified these and other practices as part of an unofficial policy of outright swindles and land grabs, in which Anglos gained land at the expense of Indigenous and Mexican peoples.[114] Framing her understanding of land loss within the power dynamics of colonization, she argued that the actions are not as important as the implications of those actions.[115] In other words, the importance lies in what those actions represented in terms of imposition of control over the conquered population.

The establishment of American hegemony after the war changed the dynamics that existed between men who had shared a similar status as landowners during the Mexican Period. After the war, Garfias's position in American society took on a racialized element that placed him beneath Wilson in the social hierarchy. Wilson's acceptance of San Pascual from Garfias as payment on a defaulted personal loan happened within a political, economic, and racialized context that matched the tenets of Manifest Destiny. The power dynamics involved in this transaction represented larger societal and cultural ideals about land use and race. Unlike Garfias's economic denouncement that changed only Sepúlveda's economic status, Wilson's appropriation of San Pascual changed Garfias's racial status from a that of a Californio blanco to that of a lower-class landless Mexican Indian.

The interactions between visions of land use and ideas of race are evident in the transaction related to San Pascual in 1859. When Wilson and Griffin took over San Pascual, their primary concern was whether the land could cover Garfias's defaulted loan. Wilson and Griffin did not indicate any desire to establish a homestead, raise cattle, or grow crops. From the beginning, their interest in this land came from their desire to parcel it out, take full advantage of it, and become wealthier in the process.[116] As businessmen dealing in land, Wilson and Griffin functioned as land speculators. They worked to get the most money back from the land. Despite his acculturation into Californio society and first-hand knowledge of how land ownership determined social status, Wilson now employed American visions of land use within an American economic and racial structure to gain the most he could from San Pascual. The end of San Pascual's Mexican Period represented the transition to the American Anglo-Saxon vision of land use.[117] As a direct consequence, the era of the small American farmer soon replaced the era of the rancho.[118]

THE AGE OF THE AMERICAN FARMER

The rise of Southern California agriculture in the 1860s and 1870s was the consequence of several changes set in motion by the gold rush. Massive migration into the northern mining districts strengthened the ranching economy by increasing demand for cattle and further expanding the need for pastoral land. The beginning of the bust of the cattle boom in the mid-1850s was completed by the decimation of the remaining cattle herds by drought in the 1860s, the slowing of the gold rush, and Californios' increased dispossession of their lands due to debt spelled the end of pastoral dominance and the rise of American agriculture in the region.[119]

The completion of the railroad led to the dramatic influx of settlers into the Los Angeles region in the 1860s and 1870s, producing a region that many observers such as New York author Charles Nordhoff regarded as violent and chaotic.[120] Stories of danger, violence, and hardship made their way back east and permeated the popular imagination.[121] The image of unruly Los Angeles, framed within the narrative of the Manifest Destiny, was a necessary part of the story as it provided the opportunity for Anglo-Americans to bring order and civility into the region. The completion of the transcontinental railroad and its links to the rail lines that ran from Los Angeles toward San Pascual positively changed the region's image in the popular imagination. More accessible to people and products, Los Angeles and its surrounding areas became a beautiful and more comfortable place. Increased travel and trade to and from the region during this period prompted an economic shift inextricably tied to the land's use. Slowly agriculture displaced the grazing of cattle.

The 1870s proved to be a vibrant period for California's agriculture. By this time, wheat had become California's most valuable crop, especially in the north.[122] Many settlers in the areas of Los Angeles and San Pascual found their attempts to grow wheat unsuccessful but began growing other crops. San

Pascual's climate facilitated the growth of apricots, figs, prunes, nectarines, plums, and cherries.[123] Additionally, similar to the San Gabriel Mission padres a century earlier, these settlers found that the area's soil and climate facilitated the growth of grapes, olives, and most importantly citrus fruit.[124] The foundation of the greater Los Angeles's citrus production began as early as 1841 when William Wolfskill, an American living in Los Angeles, successfully planted a plot of citrus trees.[125] Throughout the 1860s, the demand for citrus grew steadily. By 1870 oranges quickly became the region's chief export, boasting approximately 45,000 citrus trees throughout southern California alone. Wolfskill and other citrus farmers in the region sent their crops to San Francisco via ship.[126] By the 1880s citrus was at the center of the economies of communities such as Pasadena, Pomona, San Bernardino, and Riverside.[127] Farmers throughout Southern California grew oranges on tracts of land as far south as San Diego and exported large shipments eastward on the newly completed Southern Pacific railroad.[128] As in other areas throughout Southern California, cattle grazing at San Pascual (see fig. 12) had been replaced with orange groves (fig. 13).

The success of orange cultivation was crucial to regional development. It prompted migration into the area, brought tremendous wealth to farmers who successfully cultivated the crop, and came to represent the image of post-1860s California.[129] As the citrus industry grew during the latter part of the nineteenth

FIGURE 12 Cattle grazing on Raymond Hill ca. 1875. Courtesy of the University of Southern California, Libraries and California Historical Society. Digitally reproduced by the USC Digital Library; from the California Historical Society Collection at the University of Southern California, http://digitallibrary.usc.edu/cdm/singleitem/collection/p15799coll65/id/6752/rec/1.

FIGURE 13 Panoramic view of the orange groves of the first settlers of the Indiana Colony ca. 1874. On the right side of the photo, in the distance, are Colorado Boulevard and Fair Oaks Avenue. Courtesy of the University of Southern California, Libraries and California Historical Society. Digitally reproduced by the USC Digital Library; from the California Historical Society Collection at the University of Southern California, http://digitallibrary.usc.edu/cdm/singleitem/collection/p15799coll65/id/5999/rec/1.

century, the image of sun-kissed oranges adorned the colorful labels on the crates that carried the fruit eastward, sending with it the image of a tropical, Edenic place that could produce such sweet, delectable fruit.[130]

During these years, Southern California's image, including San Pascual, was rooted in the land. Americans cultivated the image of California as an Edenic place by highlighting its magnificent orange crops grown in a place that a mere twenty-five years earlier had been a sleepy region of "shiftless Mexicans" who had failed to develop to its full potential.[131] Within a racialized rhetoric, Californios' rancho era became a remnant of a failed endeavor, in which everything non-Anglo was relegated to a romantic yet doomed past. Locations such as San Pascual were places of promise and Anglo success. More importantly, they represented an Anglo future. Gradually, the landscape began to change; saplings of citrus trees filled the once wide-open range coloring the region's future in a bright orange hue.

The creation of the citrus culture in the latter part of the nineteenth century embodied the agricultural vision of Manifest Destiny and marked the land as a place of progress and modernity created by Anglo-American hands. The citrus industry was a pervasive imperial force that affected political, social, and cultural control in California.[132] The Los Angeles Basin's natural landscape nestled between the San Gabriel and San Bernardino Mountains, an excellent Mediterranean climate influenced by the Pacific Ocean and three watersheds, helped grow the orange empire.[133] The land provided the canvas for the new Anglo-American nation with limitless potential for wealth. Not unlike the way in which overseas trade facilitated the expansion of the tallow and hide economy and changed the landscape during the Spanish and Mexican eras, the railroad facilitated a lucrative agricultural trade through which American California "became infused with market force and bound up in a web of economic and political" growth.[134] Combining nature with Anglo-Americans' scientific ingenuity, technology, and quickly expanding markets, the orange empire changed the landscape and people's relation to the land while simultaneously creating an Edenic vision of place and solidifying a racial hierarchy reflective of Manifest Destiny and Anglo-Saxon racial superiority.[135]

Caught in the whirlwind of change, San Pascual's landowners used the physical land to create a regional future framed within Anglo-American ideals of optimal land use. Knowing that the land was not suitable for grazing cattle when they bought it, Benjamin Wilson and J. S. Griffin began looking to sell portions of San Pascual to interested individuals.[136] The first plot of land was sold in December of 1862 to Eliza Johnston, sister of J. S. Griffin and widow of General Albert Sidney Johnston, a Confederate Army surgeon killed at the Battle of Shiloh in 1862.[137] The documents pertaining to the sale indicate that, although Johnston was Griffin's sister, Wilson alone conducted the land transaction. Wilson sold Johnston six hundred and forty acres of land for $1,000. The land contained a number of oak trees and green bushes; it was close to the southwest bank of the Arroyo Seco and was near the *zanja* or trench used to bring water into area.[138] With this prime land in her control, Johnston quickly built a home that she named Fair Oaks Ranch after her childhood home in Virginia.[139]

Johnston's Fair Oaks Ranch, described by contemporaries as a "large tract of choice land, in the heart of the orange tracts," became a shining example of San Pascual's viability.[140] Shortly after establishing the homestead, Johnston encountered personal tragedy when her son Albert died in a steamship explosion off the coast of San Pedro in April 1863.[141] After her son's death, Johnston returned to Virginia. Her departure left the question of who would take control of the Fair Oaks homestead. Unofficially, it is most likely that J. S. Griffin took care of the property after his sister's departure. Over the next three years, Johnston slowly gave Griffin legal control over the property. In 1865, Johnston granted Griffin power of attorney, ceding all power over the property to him.[142] One year later, documents indicate that she sold Griffin a portion of the 260-acre property for $2,500.[143] The sale of Fair Oaks to Griffin ended Johnston's control of the property and allowed her brother to sell off the remaining parcels of the land.

Two years after his purchase of the estate, Griffin sold the homestead to his brother-in-law, Judge Benjamin Eaton.[144] Eaton was no stranger to San Pascual, having evaluated the land a decade earlier, prior to Wilson's purchase of it from Manuel Garfias.[145] Prior to his purchase of the Fair Oaks estate in 1868, with his wife, Helena Hayes, in bad health, Eaton tired of living in Los Angeles and moved his family into the Garfias adobe. Beginning in 1858, Eaton served as San Pascual's caretaker. When Helena died in 1859, Eaton took his family and returned east.[146] He returned to San Pascual six years later in 1865 and lived in the Fair Oaks estate. Interested in buying the land, Eaton purchased the eastern portion of Wilson's share of San Pascual for $500 in November of 1868.[147] One month later, Eaton purchased the rest of the land, including the Johnston home for $1,000.[148] This was end of a long sequence of transactions created from Manuel Garfias's loss of the land.

After the U.S.-Mexico War, land ownership that had been sustained through social, cultural, and familial networks was maintained through court systems and bureaucracy.[149] The passage of the Federal Land Act of 1851 required Californios and other Mexicans throughout the Southwest to produce legal title to their lands.[150] The costly process of defending the title and the high-interest loans extended by more than willing American speculators proved economically disastrous to Californios, often leaving them indebted, penniless, and landless.[151]

Wilson and Griffin utilized the new system to force Garfias into a situation in which he had no choice but to give up his land to resolve his debt. Within Californio culture Garfias's experience would represent an economic denouncement, but within the context of American colonization, it was a delegitimization of Garfias' rightful land ownership. In the former instance, Garfias had failed because he was economically unfit by Californio standards. In the latter situation, following the logic of Anglo white supremacy, Garfias failed because he was racially unfit.

Agricultural development, specifically the establishment of private farms and small homesteads on which to grow wheat, oranges, and other crops, was the main impetus for development in California. Americans' desires to establish these homesteads reflected long-held Euro-American views premised on the

Jeffersonian ideals of the yeoman farmer. More importantly, the entrance of the American farmer, regardless of the region, exemplified the civilizing of the backward savage society he replaced.[152] In the San Gabriel Valley, of which San Pascual was a part, the middle-class white gentleman farmer was the foundation of American settlement.[153] As land speculators, Wilson and Griffin held designs for San Pascual that reflected long-held racialized ideas about land use and coalesced with the emerging export markets of the late nineteenth century.

6

THE INDIANA COLONY

Becoming the Crown of the Valley, 1873–1890

Knowest thou land where the citrus and olive is fairest of fruit and the voice of the meadowlands never is mute . . . it is Pasadena.

THOMAS BALCH ELLIOTT

THE SUCCESS OF THE CITRUS industry in the Los Angeles and San Gabriel Valleys during the 1870s created an appealing image of the region's landscape. As the region's Edenic reputation traveled east on the colorful labels of orange crates shipped on the railways, Midwesterners suffering through bitter winters and disillusioned with the decline of their financial options looked west toward sunny California.

The rise of industrialization and the expansion of the railroad during the late nineteenth century prompted a broad economic reorganization that led to the growth of urbanization and the decline of rural areas. The fast-paced large-scale farming that emerged because of industrialization led many Midwestern farmers to feel disconnected from the Jeffersonian yeoman vision of individual ownership and small-scale production. These changes created a financial situation marked by rural population decline, falling crop prices, foreclosures, and farmers' exploitation in corporate markets.[1] Economic hardship in rural areas and increasing disinterest in farming prompted many, especially the children of farmers, to avoid farming altogether. While some moved to cities, those who remained in their rural communities undertook vocations that provided a middle-class existence.[2] Many middle-class Midwesterners saw California and its emerging gentleman farming model of small-scale suburban agriculture as the way to achieve financial stability and maintain their middle-class social status.[3] They looked to build a new life for themselves based on a "rural urbanism that combined the best of rural and urban lifestyles."[4] California promised Midwestern immigrants a chance to live culturally sophisticated lives while enjoying the fruits of agrarian life.[5]

Rancho San Pascual's rich soil, variety of crops, and beautiful landscape enchanted many, including Daniel Berry and the Indiana Colony, to seek opportunity in Southern California.[6] The colony's expansion throughout the 1870s gave rise to a bustling agricultural community. It manifested the agricultural vision of the nineteenth century and exemplified the opportunities that lay in the West. However, the rise of the railroad and the expansion of markets in the region during the mid-1880s altered the colony's vision of land use. The subsequent land boom, influx of migrants, and growth of tourism led to the colony's incorporation as Pasadena but also brought an end to the age of the gentleman farmer.

FINDING THE CROWN OF THE VALLEY

The epigraph, included in the "History of the San Gabriel Orange Growers Association" by Thomas Balch Elliot, a former army surgeon, well-respected Indianapolis businessman and president of the association, reflected the attitude of San Pascual's first Midwestern colonists. One year after the Indiana colonists had moved to San Pascual from Indianapolis, Elliot, shown in fig. 14, sat down to record their story. Putting his pen to paper, still quite unsure of the colony's future, Elliot wrote of the decision to move west in search of land and a new way of life. The idea for a colony had emerged in late 1872–1873, when Elliott and a group of friends spoke about moving to a warmer climate. As Elliott related in his narrative,

> In May of 1872, a few warm blooded and adventurous persons could not endure the frigid cold Northern winter, gathered in Indiana and formed a society for removal to some more equable climate.[7]

The men quickly organized the California Colony of Indiana and drafted an agreement delineating the colony's rules and addressing issues about purchase price and land appropriation.[8] The agreement stipulated that members set up a committee whose approval was necessary for all expenditures related to the search and purchase of land. Each member's payment was not to exceed $12.50

FIGURE 14 Portrait of Thomas B. Elliot, president of the Indiana Colony, who was credited with giving Pasadena its name. Courtesy of the University of Southern California, Libraries and California Historical Society. Digitally reproduced by the USC Digital Library; from the California Historical Society Collection at the University of Southern California, http://digitallibrary.usc.edu/cdm/singleitem/collection/p15799coll65/id/13098/rec.1.

per month.[9] In addition to determining how the group would raise money and sustain itself, the agreement also limited members' minimum and maximum land ownership to 40 and 160 acres, respectively.[10] The colony set up these guidelines to keep the overall endeavor economical and to personalize land ownership based on individual economic circumstances. By setting limits on the amount of land a member could own they sought to discourage large-scale agricultural production, create more equitable social relations, and allow working of the land without outside or hired labor.[11] These provisions were consistent with larger federal practices regarding land distribution and racialized ideas of land use.

As part of American expansion into the West, the U.S. government appropriated millions of acres of Indigenous lands and distributed them to Euro-American settlers.[12] In 1862 Congress passed the Homestead Act distributing private 160-acre land allotments to homesteaders in areas of the West. Premised on a vision of populating the West with small-scale white farmers and extending the idea of private land ownership, the federal government indirectly attempted to eradicate what they saw as a flaw of the Mexicano/Californio land system: too much land owned by one person was not productive and allowed for blurred boundaries of ownership.[13] The Indiana Colony's restriction on land ownership indicates that broader societal ideals of land use and purpose informed the colony's actions. The colony held that their purpose in Southern California was to establish a small agricultural community comprising "persons of good moral character."[14] After setting up the colony, Elliott and ten others committed themselves to purchasing an allotment of land there.[15] This began their search for land that met their needs: land with an agreeable climate, opportunity to own a homestead, and the potential for improvement.

In contemplating where to establish their new colony, members spoke of settling in Texas, Florida, or Louisiana, sites that fit their desire to escape the harsh winters. Health was another motivating factor for the Indiana Colony. Having been in weather-induced ill health for some time, Mrs. Helen Elliott strongly pressed her husband to find a warmer place to live. With these factors in mind, the colony quickly decided that Southern California provided the best options, stating that the place represented "the tropics without the heat."[16] Elliott wasted no time and contracted his brother-in-law, Daniel M. Berry (fig. 15), a former schoolteacher and journalist, to go west and find land.

The completion of the first transcontinental railroad in 1869 created a flurry of interest in the western regions of the United States. Completion of additional railroad lines in the 1870s, including the Atchison-Topeka and Santa Fe railways connecting the San Gabriel Valley to Los Angeles, further heightened people's interest in the Greater Los Angeles area.[17] Railroad promoters, land speculators, and local boosters seeking to increase profits by attracting tourists and potential settlers began publicity campaigns consisting of touring agencies, colorful images of Edenic landscapes, guidebooks, and travel journals.[18] Each of these helped sell the region to outsiders and acquaint them with all its offerings.[19] In the broader context of expansion they were essential in organizing or scripting the region's physical and social world by accentuating specific aspects of its landscape, people, and history.[20]

The language and images used in the process of scripting space reflected racialized ideas connected to westward expansion. Travel accounts often contained discourses that reinforced ideas of Manifest Destiny and white supremacy by reinscribing a racial order that subordinated racialized groups.[21] These

FIGURE 15 Portrait of Daniel M. Berry, land scout and first secretary of the Indiana Colony, ca. 1873. Berry arrived in Pasadena in November 1873. Courtesy of the University of Southern California, Libraries and California Historical Society. Digitally reproduced by the USC Digital Library; from the California Historical Society Collection at the University of Southern California, http://digitallibrary.usc.edu/cdm/singleitem/collection/p15799coll65/id/5853/rec/1.

discourses were fundamental in shaping how Euro-Americans viewed themselves in relation to the region and its people. By marginalizing people of color in the West, these writers, boosters, and land speculators presented the physical land as exclusively Euro-American.[22] The land and its possibilities were endless. The region was waiting for Euro-American tourists and settlers to make it theirs.

Travel accounts and observations played a major role in peoples' decisions to permanently settle in the region. In the 1873 as interest in Southern California increased, traveler and journalist Charles Nordhoff published his guidebook *California For Health, Pleasure and Residence*.[23] Basing his book on his 1871 travels throughout Southern California, he provided descriptions of travel routes, famous sites, climate, cost of living, and inhabitants. Similarly, Daniel M. Berry, as land scout for the Indiana Colony, provided his detailed observations of

Southern California to Thomas and Helen Balch to help determine where to establish their settlement.

Charles Nordhoff and Daniel Berry were contemporaries. Both recorded their observations and impressions of Southern California. Although their audiences were different in scale, they both set out to convince people of Southern California's premier lands. Both Nordhoff's work, which became a well-known guidebook credited for attracting many tourists and permanent settlers, and Berry's letters encouraging the colony's migration reflected the racialized ideas about the region's lands and its minority populations.[24] Both presented the lands as fertile ground for the growth of the white gentleman farmer.

A major feature highlighted to attract tourists and permanent settlers was the health benefits provided by Southern California's climate. Travel writers, boosters, and doctors alike claimed that region's climate provided an escape for those looking to leave the cold damp areas of the East and Midwest. They emphasized the range of health benefits, from easing and alleviating consumption and asthma to providing much needed relaxation.[25] Charles Nordhoff's account, in addition to highlighting Southern California's health benefits, included the variety of pleasures a traveler could enjoy:

> Certainly in no part of the continent is pleasure traveling so exquisite and unalloyed a pleasure as California. Not only are the sights grand and wonderful, and surprising in the highest degree, but the climate is exhilarating and favorable to an active life; the weather is so certain that you do not lose a day.[26]

Implicit in Nordhoff's account is the productivity made possible by the climate, a point that was not lost to Daniel Berry.

In the fall of 1873, Berry made his way to California. Upon his arrival in San Diego, he entered a world of land speculators, men who sold land by creating visions of its potential uses. Berry's frequent letters to T. B. Elliott (as many as two per day over the course of a few months) indicated the visions of land use presented by land speculators throughout Southern California during this period.[27] More importantly, they reflected ideas about the land the Indiana Colony desired to purchase. Berry's reports on his travels throughout Southern California confirmed what Nordhoff described in his travel accounts.

Berry's letters discussed a variety of topics pertaining to the different places he considered for the colony. Arriving at Cajón Ranch in San Diego in late August of 1873, Berry reported that the "ranch contains 25,000 acres of the most beautiful bottom land, much of it cultivated for grain."[28] Aside from the acres of tillable land, he very early on described the quality of the fruit he found in California. After four days of visiting farms and gardens, he related that "I am now eating big peaches, pears and grapes that I picked with my own hand and all I have to say is that they are as good as the best and finest I ever saw."[29] His interest in the region's agricultural production and its potential for cultivating more fruits and grains continued throughout his visit. A week after his visit to San Diego, Berry arrived in Los Angeles and scheduled a visit to Rancho Santa Anita, located east of the city's center, bordering Rancho San Pascual. His description of Santa Anita focused on the region's accessibility to water and characterized the land as kingly. He referred to the land's expansive orange groves, pointing out that the "orange trees produce as much as $1,500 per acre, with a potential of increasing to $2,000."[30] He added that the income from the fruit cultivation could supply "two cities like Indianapolis with fruit and food."[31] This letter, although focused on Santa Anita's agricultural potential, hinted at the increase in land value resulting from the presence of the railroad:

> [A] very important fact has just come to light. The Southern Pacific Railway from Bakersfield via Los Angeles to San Bernardino is located throughout the San Gabriel Valley. You have the map in our office. This of course puts an increased value on the place.[32]

This letter is significant because it provides a glimpse of Berry's transition from private land agent to land speculator. From this point onward, Berry looked at the land through a slightly different lens. He focused on profit from agricultural production, not simply subsistence and small-scale farming.[33] Very impressed with the land, Berry reluctantly stated that, without the committee's unanimous approval, the colony could not purchase this land because it cost twenty dollars an acre. Disappointed with the fixed price, Berry continued his trek.

Berry continued northward toward the San Fernando Valley. He was not struck with this location because it lacked an easy source of water. He stated that, although the purchase price of two dollars per acre was well below the colony's limit, it was not a feasible option because it would "cost a great deal to build reservoirs to hold water for irrigating trees."[34] Although he stated that it would be possible to produce a profitable crop of wheat and rye on the land during the rainy season, he quickly brought the conversation back to citrus cultivation. His focus on the need for available water to grow oranges revealed that the colony's main vision for their newly acquired land was to grow oranges, not wheat or grain. Berry recognized that, to produce the crop it wanted, the colony needed to funnel in money that they did not have; he stated that, if a larger company bought the land and established an irrigation system, the colonists could then afford to purchase several tracts to subdivide.[35] Berry did not provide a positive description of this place, indicating that it might be better to "get consent of the colonist to pay $10.00 per acre where water was plenty." Berry left the San Fernando Valley bound for Los Angeles in the hope of finding land that fulfilled the colony's desire for a warm climate, easy access to water, tillable land, and access to a railroad. The next place that Berry visited would be the crown gem he was looking for.

On September 12, 1873, Berry wrote to Elliott about his stay at a ranch in the "heart of the orange tract," the former home of Eliza Johnston, the Fair Oaks Ranch. By the time of Berry's arrival, Judge Benjamin Eaton was the owner of the ranch. Immediately captivated by the land, Berry gave an inventory of the trees on the property. He enthusiastically described the growth of "30,000 grape vines, 260 walnut trees, 150 lemon trees, 700 orange trees," as well as an "old orchard of pears, peaches, apples, apricots, and olives." Additionally, he noted that the remaining 2,800 acres of San Pascual had a "heavenly climate and scenery."[36] Impressed by the land, Berry worked hard to get the colony to authorize paying ten dollars per acre. His letters to the Indiana Colony over the course of the next couple of months illustrate his attempts at convincing Elliott of the land's potential. By this point, Berry had become a land speculator who utilized a variety of tactics to sell Elliott on San Pascual.[37]

In his letters, Berry focused on San Pascual's rich soil, its variety of crops, and the volume of its production. Aside from emphasizing its potential agricultural value, he also touted the health benefits of the region's climate. Others such as Nordhoff had written about Southern California's health benefits, but Berry focused on San Pascual and distinguished it from Los Angeles. Nordhoff had contended that the area around the "Mission San Gabriel had a better climate for consumptives than the city itself."[38] Similarly, Berry wrote,

> The climate in the city is sometimes bad. Some nights the fog gathers thick and pestiferous and the air is heavy with slow but sure coming death. I have seen some such and want to get out of this dead level spot with its decaying vegetation and motionless air, and thousand provoking stenches.[39]

He noted that at San Pascual the "unvaporous air of the elevated land up nearer to God and the mountains" provided him the "sweetest sleep of years," and he "awoke to the music of a thousand linnets and blackbirds in the evergreen oaks."[40] Berry was struck by San Pascual's crisp air because as a severe asthmatic he rarely slept the whole night through, often wakening in the middle of the night and sleep sitting up to breathe better. The detailed description of his restful sleep and San Pascual's clean air was crucial to his account because he aimed to show Elliott that San Pascual could provide a healthy and beneficial place for Elliott's wife, Helen. Berry's choice of words when describing San Pascual placed it ahead of all the other areas he had visited in California. This made San Pascual, with its vast acreage of viable land, succulent fruits, and unparalleled climate, the standard by which he judged other possible locations.

Berry knew that describing the land's viability alone would not be enough to prompt Elliott and the Indiana Colony to purchase the land so he began to look at social and economic opportunities available in San Pascual. In several letters, he described the life of the gentleman farmer, often emphasizing the potential for social mobility in the region in comparison to that of the East and Midwest. In a letter dated September 18, 1873, Berry stated that "fruit growers here [in the Los Angeles area] are a much more prosperous class than the commercial men. The same time and labor devoted to fruit here that we give at home to business would make us happy and rich in a short time."[41] At one level, Berry's statement indicated an interest in augmenting colonists' personal wealth, but within the larger national context of the 1870s, his statement illustrated his shift in perspective about agriculture.

As established earlier, urbanization and industrialization prompted the reorganization of agricultural production and led to the disruption of the Midwestern economy. For many Midwestern farmers the introduction of large-scale agricultural production had resulted in a significant decline in their financial stability, causing many second-generation Midwesterners to avoid farming as an occupation.[42] Through his letters, Berry discussed San Pascual's agricultural possibilities and emphasized the benefits agricultural production presented for the colonists. By detailing California's prosperous agriculture as a means of social mobility, he supported boosters' and land speculators' contention that Southern California provided opportunities for white middle-class gentleman farmers to create civilized lives of urban luxuries and rural values.[43]

The emphasis on the West as a place for economic and personal improvement fits within westward expansion's broader ideologies and values. In the Turnerian sense, moving west represented the opportunity for Americans to create the characteristics of individualism and hard work and the image of the self-made man, who regardless of his lineage had a chance to be successful.[44] Within this narrative, the West provided opportunity that the East and Midwest did not, a chance to create oneself anew. The challenge to creating the new gentleman farmers was that most Midwestern transplants were not experienced professional farmers but "usually [came] after having made a success in some other vocation."[45] Many of the migrants were not prepared to for the hardships that small-scale agriculture posed.

Contrary to the utopian images of wealth and prosperity painted by land agents and boosters, the creation of this new rural urbanism required migrants to work very hard to establish themselves as self-sufficient gentlemen farmers.[46] In a letter to his sister Helen, Berry discussed the land's potential for effecting change in a person's identity and class status, as well as the hard work required to establish oneself in Southern California. In referring to the changes that San Pascual could engender in her husband, Thomas, he stated:

> You will have to re-construct the Doctor [Thomas Elliot], he will have to do as others here and go to work, burn up his newspaper, get out of schools and public life and live for himself and family. The aristocracy here work and raise fruit. People who come here expecting to have a social status and good living from their antecedents in the East will find that they are d— fooled and have to [make] their way by work.[47]

Berry described that moving west required breaking the notions of propriety afforded by one's middle-class status. To illustrate his point, he described how the West had changed several of the affluent Easterners he had met during his travels in the region:

> Sunday night as I was coming from San Pascual the damned wagon wheel . . . [document torn] in the dark and the foothills. The chap who was driving the wagon was a lawyer once in Boston and a graduate of Harvard with the consumption and rich besides. He runs a vineyard. The chap who went for a wrench at a ranch was nephew of Edward Atkinson, the great free trader, a graduate of Harvard and keeps sheep for a living. The chap who owned the wagon is an ex-judge, and was a student of Judge Storey and Parsons at Harvard Law School, once an editor in Missouri, now runs a vineyard. The chap who lifted the wagon was a senator for Nebraska. The chap who fixed the wheel and killed a tarantula was myself.[48]

His story told how each had left a well-established career in the East to remake himself as a rugged man in the West. What is implied is that Eastern notions of commercial and professional success did not immediately translate into a high social status; affluence in the West had to earned. This was something that many migrants had not considered when moving into the area. For example, Elliott, an Indianapolis doctor and well-known businessman, would need to change his entire way of life in order to succeed in the region. Although Berry was responsible for reporting his travel experiences and observations regarding the region, this topic was something that he shared only with his sister, Helen. Berry's correspondence with Thomas Elliott always focused on economic matters.

Through the 1860s and 1880s, due to the efforts of boosters and real estate agents, white people became Southern California's majority population.[49] In the San Gabriel Valley inclusive of San Pascual, promoters specifically targeted middle-class white people from the Midwest and East.[50] In detailed letters about his travels, Berry provided observations about the region's racial and ethnic landscape. He wrote of specific white ethnic groups who purchased land in the region. For example, he remarked that Germans comprised a significant portion of the white population and that they had "recently purchased Rancho Santa Margarita near San Diego" and were quickly developing the settlement.[51] The racialized aspect of boosters' settlement efforts affected the region's racial composition and race relations, a fact reflected in Berry's correspondence.

On various occasions, Berry provided descriptions of the diverse nonwhite groups that lived in the Greater Los Angeles region. He referred to them in a racialized manner and described their appearance, social position, and contribution to the growth of California's agricultural economy. He described nonwhite people as being dark skinned, "utterly and completely different" with an "average color of the people [as] that of 10-cent sugar, with invariably black hair," in comparison to white people.[52] Interestingly, he differentiated among the diverse Spanish-speaking populations by identifying them as "Mexicans, Peruvians, Chileans, Spaniards, Chinese, Kanakas, and every kind of southern Indian that is left."[53] His use of the term *Spaniard* here is important because it is a clear racialization of the region's Mexican population.[54] By including both *Mexican* and *Spanish* as identifiers he indicated that the perceived racial distinction between Spanish Californios and Mexican Indians had not yet completely faded.

Census data for the decades from 1850s to the 1890s show Los Angeles county's racial composition. In Table 1 the racial designation of *white* refers to both white Euro-American and white Mexicans. It shows that most of the

TABLE 1 Race in Los Angeles County, 1850–1890

	1850	1860	1870	1880	1890
White	3,456	9,221	14,720	31,707	47,205
Black	12	87	134	188	1,258
Indian	62	2,014	219	316	35
Chinese	—	11	236	1,170	1,871
Japanese	—	—	2	0	26
Total	3,530	11,333	15,311	33,381	50,395

Sources: 1850–1890 U.S. Federal Census, Population Reports, and Census Schedules.

county's population consisted of these two groups. Table 2 shows that close examination of persons classified as white revealed that about half had Spanish surnames, indicating that they were of Mexican descent.[55] This is important in showing that Mexicans still comprised a significant portion of the region's population during the latter part of the nineteenth century. It is also important in critiquing how ideas of race were used to create the image of communities such as Pasadena.

The racialized ideas of nineteenth century rural urbanism were premised on the success of white gentlemen farmers who could build self-sufficient agricultural homesteads without outside labor.[56] Despite these ideals and within the broader context of white supremacy, Southern California's racialized populations of Mexican, Chinese, Japanese, African Americans, and Native Americans comprised the major source of the region's labor force (see table 3).[57] In Berry's discussion of labor in his letters, he refers to only two groups as laborers. The first group are identified as Kanakas, a term used to describe the Polynesians that arrived in California during the mid- to late-nineteenth century. In California, under both the Mexican and American systems, the Kanaka or Rapanui people were contracted as agricultural workers, seamen, fur trappers, herders, and domestics.[58] After their three-year contracts ended, they often married into the local Mexican and Indigenous populations.[59]

The second group of laborers to which Berry referred is the Chinese. Migrating to the California as part of the gold rush, the Chinese, a decade later, comprised a significant portion of California's labor force.[60] By the mid-nineteenth century, journalists and anti-Chinese groups referred to Chinese workers with the epithet *John* or *John Chinaman* to portray them as part of an anonymous undifferentiated mass of workers.[61] Many worked as miners, railroad laborers,

TABLE 2 Spanish surname and Indian population in Los Angeles, 1860–1880*

	1860	1870	1880
Spanish surname	2,565	2,131	2,231
Indian population	2,104	219	316

Sources: 1850–1890 U.S. Federal Census, Population Reports, and Census Schedules.
*Data regarding Spanish surnamed persons is from Griswold del Castillo's "La Raza Hispano Americana," 66 (as cited by Camarillo, *Chicanos in a Changing Society*, 117).

TABLE 3 Occupations in Los Angeles County by nativity, 1870 and 1880

	1870			1880		
OCCUPATION	TOTAL	NATIVE WHITE	CHINESE/ JAPANESE	TOTAL	NATIVE WHITE	CHINESE/ JAPANESE
Agricultural labor	16,231	10,203	1,637	23,856	14,597	5,657
Farmers/planters	24,061	16,734	346	43,489	29,133	4,424
Stock Raisers/herders	3,790	2577	33	4,967	2,988	1,245
Domestic Servants	15,472	3,872	4,343	22,858	5,896	10,990
Laborers	37,586	14,305	7,800	57,510	23,751	19,459
Launderers	4,043	441	2,593	7,013	687	5,734

Sources: 1870 and 1880 U.S. Federal Census, Population Reports, and Schedules.

domestic servants, and agricultural workers.[62] Large-scale employers such as the railroads regarded them as cheap, reliable, and easily exploitable labor.[63] By 1870 they comprised one-tenth of all agricultural laborers, and by the 1880s they accounted for one-third of California's agricultural labor force.[64] In his letter to Elliot he addressed the economic benefits of Chinese labor:

> The number of Chinamen here is great. One reason of the great prosperity of California is the cheap labor of John. He has done great work here for little pay and his employers have gotten rich. Here the labor is cheap.[65]

Berry recognized Chinese laborers' contribution to regional prosperity, but he also was conscious of how their exploitation allowed for the growth of individual wealth. In a letter to his sister, Berry remarked that "with one Chinaman, doctor [T. B. Elliott] could do all the work and make a handsome living."[66] Berry was not alone in looking at the Chinese as a necessary and reliable labor force; a few years earlier, traveler Charles Nordhoff dedicated an entire chapter of his book to the role of Chinese workers in California.

Nordhoff described Chinese workers as *Johns* he stated that they were the perfect laborers because "they were [the] best trained and [the] quickest witted servant[s] in the world, who have made housekeeping a pleasure and after cooking, . . . [did] not object to washing and ironing." As servants, they were "economical and . . . [did] not make a fuss." They made every Anglo "wish that their life could be comforted by such a John."[67] He stated that what made the Chinese such great workers was their docile passive character. Furthermore, he argued that they made more efficient workers because, as "heathens," they did not observe the Sabbath, allowing them to work every day, including Sundays.[68] Both Berry's and Nordhoff's statements about Chinese laborers reflected racialized ideas about the Chinese rooted in the ideologies of white supremacy. They were not perceived as equal to Euro-Americans but rather were used to provide labor that would enrich their employers, whether large-scale industries or gentlemen farmers.

Despite Berry's and Nordhoff's discussions of labor in their writings, they both failed to make any explicit reference to Mexican workers. However, Nordhoff provided a chapter describing the labor of California Indians. Within the racial thinking of the time it was common for landless Mexicans to be racially categorized as Indians due to skin color.[69] For example, the occupations Nordhoff listed for this group show that he may have merged the two groups:

> The farmers are chiefly Indians. These people, of whom California still has several thousands, are a very useful class. They trim the vines; they plough; they do household chores; they are shepherds, vaqueros, and helpers.[70]

He categorized the nonwhite people as docile workers, a population that had been subdued by white men. He described Indians as "harmless" and continued that, "being white, and of the superior race, you [Anglos] have the privilege of entering any Indian's house and you will be kindly received."[71] This statement reified white superiority over the entire nonwhite population. It was a way of assuring white middle-class tourists and potential settlers, the targets of his travel account, that they would be secure in this region.[72]

Despite his failure to directly discuss landless Mexicans, Nordhoff included the "old Spanish Californians" in his account. His privileging of whiteness or

Europeanness by emphasizing the perceived differences between the Indian and the Spaniard reflected his racialized and class-based understanding of labor and social status.[73] For example, in describing the regional homes, he praised the Spaniards' civilized adobe houses and disparaged Indians' homes made of "reeds and laced barley straws."[74] Furthermore, he referenced the influence of Spanish culture among the Indians by citing the continuation of fandangos, where Indians claimed themselves civilized because they danced only in the Spanish style.[75] Yet, while temporarily uplifting Californios by praising their efforts at civilizing Indigenous populations, he quickly reasserted white supremacy by claiming that the Spanish Californians never succeeded in creating men that reached the "men of our [American] century," determining that the remnant culture of "old Spanish Californians" was unable to compete with Anglo civilization.[76]

In an account quite different from Nordhoff's, Berry avoided the Californio Period, reflecting the privileging of whites over non-Anglo populations. Although Berry's letters very overtly excluded elite Californio rancheros and landless Mexicans, he mentioned Dons Benjamin [Benito] Wilson and John [Juan] Forster, Anglo landowners who had at one time assimilated into the elite Californio society.[77] Berry's mention of these rich American men supported the idea of Manifest Destiny by showing that it took white Americans to make the land productive. Additionally, the fact that Berry did not refer to Californio landowners showed that by the 1870s Anglos had taken control of most of greater Los Angeles area including San Pascual, reiterating that, despite their continued political power, Californios had experienced significant land loss.

Through their personal letters and travel books, both Berry and Nordhoff produced a racialized image of the region and its people. To those who read their observations, whether T. B. Elliott and the Indiana Colony or tourists interested in coming to California, these men perpetuated the ideas of Manifest Destiny and Anglo-Saxon racial superiority. Those who believed their words came into California with the belief that they, white middle-class men, were the region's future. For Daniel M. Berry, after he set foot on San Pascual, the future became clear. San Pascual would be the Indiana Colony's new home.

THE INDIANA COLONY ARRIVES

After having spent a crisp September night at the Fair Oaks estate in 1873, Daniel M. Berry knew that this was the perfect land parcel for the Indiana Colony. The day after he began writing about the land's beauty and endless possibilities, he frantically wrote to the Elliotts as well as to other potential buyers about the opportunities at San Pascual. He demanded that the colony send the necessary capital to secure the land purchase, often stating that Griffin would readily sell the land to another buyer if the colony did not act fast. Elliott, taken by Berry's argument, authorized him to pay fifteen dollars per acre, more than what the colony had originally intended. Berry prepared to make the offer, but Griffin's and Wilson's land manager was out of town. Unable to proceed, Berry waited for the land manager to return and worked to collect the necessary monies. One day after Elliot authorized the offer, the U.S. economy collapsed, plunging the country into the Panic of 1873.[78] After the collapse, Berry worried about the panic's effect on the Indiana Colony, specifically the colonists' sale of their homes to finance the purchase of the land. A letter written to T. B. Elliott two days after the collapse conveyed those fears:

> I fear the financial crash in New York will stop movement in real estate in Indianapolis. I hope to hear that you have sold, but fear you have not.[79]

On October 8, lacking a reliable source for the money, Berry told Wilson and Griffin that his group would purchase the available lands. He arranged to pay a $200 deposit on the following day. He wired Elliott to request the funds, stating that "if he did not secure the land for the Indiana people it will probably be too late."[80] Despite the urgency of his request, Berry did not hear from the Indiana Colony for one week. Angry with the lack of response, he wrote a frantic letter to Elliott requesting remittance for San Pascual as well as for his services.[81] Four days later, Berry requested $1,000 for a deposit on the land. By October 19, after having received only $200 of the expected $500 deposit, Berry angrily wrote:

> People here will think I represent a d—— small set of capitalists who can't raise $500 on a trade of $20,000. Isn't it very thin? I am ashamed, I am. I have spent two months hard work and worn out clothes, boots, and cash for $300 more than I charged the colony, equal to at least $600.00 to me. I want to get some land and go to work and be free from doubt and distrust and financial earthquakes. . . . I shall hunt no more for land for the colony, unless I am paid for it.[82]

Despite his disillusionment with the colony, Berry's personal view about San Pascual shone through. His statement indicated that he wanted freedom and a security that he, as an individual, could produce for himself. This is quite significant for this period. In an age in which industrial capitalism had constructed a new masculinity that made men dependent on factory owners and markets for survival, the return to land ownership and farming could restore men's power and control over their lives.[83] By shifting the discussion away from citrus groves and climate, Berry candidly expressed his desire to control his own future and stability. His desires were not unlike those of the Californio men before him who during the 1820s and 1830s called for mission secularization as a way of obtaining land and controlling their own futures. Here, in the American Period, Berry wanted to escape the bonds of the industrial capitalist order that often kept people from controlling their own financial futures.

As October dragged on, Berry waited for word from the colony. By November 8, it became clear that the Indiana Colony could not produce the money to purchase San Pascual. Berry wrote Elliot that he had stalled the surveyors as much as he could but that they needed to raise the money somehow.[84] Refusing to give up on his vision, Berry organized a group of local investors interested in purchasing land in the region. Together, Calvin Fletcher, Thomas Croft, Judge Benjamin Eaton, W. T. Clap, and A. O. Bristol raised the additional monies needed for the Indiana Colony to purchase San Pascual. Daniel Berry and the contingent of Western investors formed the San Gabriel Orange Grove Association (SGOGA), establishing 100 shares of capital stock at $250 each for a total sum of $25,000.[85] Rather than relying solely on the Indiana Colony to purchase the land, Berry pooled money from all the interested men he could find and then invited T. B. Elliott and the remaining Indiana Colonists to be part of the SGOGA. Ten days after the formation of the SGOGA, Berry received a $3,000 draft from Indianapolis. The SGOGA spent the rest of November and early December making the purchase.

On December 18, Wilson deeded 3,962 acres of land to John S. Griffin; this acreage included the 2,516 acres in the heart of San Pascual as well as 1,386 acres in the upper area.[86] Upon reaching the agreement, Berry sent Elliott a newspaper clipping of the deal:

> The San Gabriel Orange Grove Association have purchased from Dr. Griffin 2,500 acres of land lying four to six miles north of the city, which is to be divided among the members of the association (mostly eastern families) and settled and improved immediately. The Doctor [John Griffin] sold the land to the colonists at a very low figure in order to encourage the settlement, and by thus uniting they will be able to bring water on the tract at a mere nominal cost to each, and secure

> many other advantages not enjoyed by parties purchasing and settling alone. We expect to see a thriving and prosperous community.[87]

This newspaper clipping, taken from an unidentified newspaper and included with Berry's letter, reflected the local region's ideas and expectations regarding the colony. On December 26, Thomas Croft, a wealthier member of SGOGA, secured the down payment on San Pascual and received the deed to the land.[88] A few days later, the association reimbursed him and he transferred the title to the SGOGA. The Indiana Colonists finally had their land. The land that Elliott later described as the "paradise of Southern California, the gem of the world as to climate, health, productions, and air"[89] was finally theirs. During the mid-1870s members of the first Anglo-American colonists in the region, the Indiana Colony, were enticed by the possibilities that the land held for them. Within the next year prompted by visions of land use rooted in the cultivation of citrus and other crops, they migrated to their new home. Finding the land "new and unfinished," settlers quickly began claiming their land parcels and building their new homes and their new colony.[90]

WATER

Almost immediately, Calvin Fletcher became the person responsible for planning the colony's layout. With an eye toward aesthetics, Fletcher designated a 1,500-acre area between the Arroyo Seco at the west and present-day Fair Oaks Boulevard on the east. This land was one mile north of the now famous Colorado Boulevard. Fletcher chose what he considered to be San Pascual's most beautiful land as the place for residential development and worked to divide the land into one hundred plots of fifteen acres each.[91] Within a little over a month, on January 27, 1874, members, and nonmembers of the association, as well as friends and families of the colonists, came to participate in the designation and distribution of lots. As organizers called out names, people indicated what plot they wanted. In about twenty minutes the colonists in attendance received their desired land allotments and officially founded the Indiana Colony of California.[92]

The first crops the settlement cultivated were wheat and barley; citrus trees and grapes followed shortly thereafter. Mostly middle-class professionals, the new gentlemen farmers encountered obstacles that made it difficult for them to grow their crops. First, unaware of planting cycles, they planted the seeds for the wheat and barley too late in the season, not allowing time for the crops to flourish. Secondly, in June 1874, a plague of grasshoppers attacked the fruit trees and grape vines, destroying their efforts but not their will.[93] The obstacles presented by nature, compounded by their inexperience, complicated the colony's initial growth. Despite these setbacks, colonists continued to work and improve their lands. The Indiana Colony's aspiring small agriculturalists came in search of a place that could provide aesthetically pleasing surroundings, viable land, and a secure future. One crucial element in the creation of the American landscape was the control of water.

During his search for a place to settle, Berry disqualified San Diego and San Bernardino because getting reliable access to drinking and irrigation water would prove to be expensive.[94] At San Pascual, Berry found water to be in abundant supply, writing that in some areas there was "no need for irrigation because the water supply was only five feet beneath the surface."[95] In other places, zanjas brought water into the valley and kept the land moist.[96] When Berry showed serious interest in San Pascual, Griffin and Wilson offered to facilitate the colony's access to water by drawing the property's boundaries to include specific streams and helping to defray part of the cost of building a water system.[97] As the settlement took shape, colonists began planning their access to water.

Judge Benjamin Eaton, owner of the Fair Oaks Estate located on part of San Pascual, was no stranger to matters of water control. In 1865 upon settling in the area, he set up a rudimentary irrigation system that transported water from a nearby canyon to his property. This system helped supply water for his large crops of grapes, oranges, figs, and peaches.[98] Now, as an investor in the SGOGA and founding member of the Indiana Colony, he helped settlers plan a three-mile pipeline that would bring water from the Arroyo Seco into a small reservoir at the intersections of Orange Grove Avenue and Colorado Street in the heart of the Indiana Colony.[99] From February until May, colonists, including Eaton and Berry, worked to build the pipeline, finally completing it on May 15, 1874.[100] The completion of this water system was a landmark moment because this system brought water necessary to propel the colony toward achieving its agricultural vision for the land; however, this project was not without financial hardship that slowed the colony's development.

The colonists were responsible for paying most of the costs for the system, an expense they estimated at about $2,500, a 10-percent assessment on the $25,000 stock. The SGOGA expected Wilson to follow through with his initial commitment to pay half the cost. When the time came to pay, Wilson reneged on his commitment, instead allowing the colonists unlimited access to Arroyo Seco for three years.[101] Wilson's refusal to pay resulted in a 20-percent assessment, meaning that the colony would have to pay $5,000 for the system. The colony had only $2,862 on hand and was unable to pay for the water system. The financially better off members of the community (mainly Calvin Fletcher) paid for most of the remaining cost of the water system and waited for reimbursement from the community.[102] Other colonists found it difficult to raise the money for their part of the payment and opted to sell portions of their plots to recently arrived friends and relatives.[103]

After resolving the initial problem of funding its water system, the colony did not have any more difficulty with water access. The original organization of water distribution remained in place until early 1882, when the Pasadena Land and Water Company replaced the SGOGA.[104] Although its cost created a financial setback that caused many to sell portions of their lands, the water system contributed to the colony's growth and expansion during its first year by providing much needed water. By the end of 1874, the colony grew by more than a dozen families. Within the narrative of westward expansion and growth, the colonists had triumphed over nature. Their vision of an agricultural community was now a reality.

MUSCAT BECOMES PASADENA

As the colony grew (see fig. 16), many were concerned that the settlement did not have a formal name. In his correspondence with Elliot, Berry often referred to the colony by two names, the Indiana Colony and Muscat. The former referred directly to the loose organization of Midwesterners who wanted to migrate to California. The latter name, Muscat, referred to the Muscat grape that grew in Southern California. Since the time of the mission, Muscat grapes had grown in the region. Either black or white, the Muscat grape could be used to produce wine or be eaten as raisins and table grapes. In one of his early letters to T. B. Elliott, Berry noted his captivation with the Muscat, stating that that "[I would] not touch an eastern grape as long as I could get the white Muscat, the most delicious fruit my palate ever encountered."[105] In later letters, because the grape grew in the region of San Pascual, Berry began referring to the location as Muscat.[106] Despite his favorable opinion about the grape, Berry disliked the name because he believed it "sounded too much like muskrat" and hoped

FIGURE 16 Panoramic view of Mission Street and Orange Grove ca. 1874. The photograph, which shows only a handful of homesteads over a vast stretch of land, was taken at the time of the first colonists' purchase. Several fields appear to be arranged in crop rows at center. The mountains can be seen faintly in the background. Courtesy of the University of Southern California, Libraries and California Historical Society. Digitally reproduced by the USC Digital Library; from the California Historical Society Collection at the University of Southern California, http://digitallibrary.usc.edu/cdm/singleitem/collection/p15799coll65/id/25813/rec/1.

that Elliott could help think of a name that reflected the land's "beauty and fertility."[107] Elliot, in cooperation with a friend, a college professor who was familiar with the Chippewa dialect, suggested a variety of names from the Chippewa dialect.[108] Below is the list of the names considered for the colony, along with their meanings and an instruction about how to pronounce the word *Pasadena*:

> Weognan Pasadena: Crown of the Valley
> Gishkadena Pasadena: Peak of the Valley
> Tapekaegun Pasadena: Key of the Valley
> Peuadena Pasadena: Hill of the Valley
> Accent the last syllable of word.[109]

All of these names describe the area's landscape. The first Chippewa words in these phrases are topographical indicators referencing the low-lying San Gabriel Valley and one of the highest peaks on the San Gabriel Foothills, eventually known as Mount Wilson. The second word in each phrase, *Pasadena*, means valley. After much debate, the two men settled on Pasadena as the name for the settlement; however, there were additional elements in the process of naming the colony that were not included in Elliot's narrative. According to established folklore based on the work of local historian Hiram Reid, the decision to name the colony Pasadena resulted from more than a conversation between T. B. Elliot and his friend. Reid asserted that there were a variety of stories detailing the town's name ranging from the factual to the absurd.[110]

In his work, Reid began his response to stories that he called "idle misrepresentations and guesswork" by contesting a claim made by "Bancroft's Railway Guide," a periodical publication that provided time tables, train routes, fare information, descriptions of principal cities, and general advice for those travelling by train. Reid said that the railway guide misidentified *Pasadena* as a term "first used by the Spanish Padres" to mean *paso ha eden* (gateway of Eden), but Americans mispronounced it as Pasadena. He critiqued this story as the "climax of absurdity" and a "mongrel combination of Spanish words," reiterating that Pasadena was of Chippewa rather than Spanish origin, as evidenced in T. B Elliot's writings. Although Reid dismissed any connection between the colony's proposed name and the Spanish language, he interestingly added another piece to the story—an element that implies a link to the colony's Mexican past. Reid said that, while the colonists discussed names, one of the early members, Calvin Fletcher, "appealed to [him] to know if there [were] not some Spanish name that had been applied to the ranch, descriptive of its location and general characteristics," thinking that a name that "smacked a little of the language of the country would sound better than any name imported from the Eastern states . . . something a little less common." Reid, in his attempt to help Fletcher, recalled his conversation with Manuel Garfias, Rancho San Pascual's former owner. He recounted Garfias's response of "por que es la llave del rancho" (because it is the key to the rancho) to his inquiry about why he had located his rancho home on such an "impractical place" that did not allow him a panoramic view of his vast domain and herds. Garfias's response to the inquiry centered on the rancho's physical landscape and topography. His reference to *la llave del rancho* illustrated how he placed his home at the entrance of the rancho as a way to control access to his property. Upon hearing Reid's recommendation, Fletcher replied, "Yavvy what? Well, what does it mean? Give it to us in English."[111] Reid translated and explained, and Fletcher brought the meaning, but not the phrase itself, to Elliot and other colonists for consideration. At this point Reid's history circled back to Elliot's story about Pasadena's origin.

According to Reid, Elliot appealed to his missionary friend to help him find an "Indian word of pleasant sound" that would mean "the key of the rancho" or upper valley.[112] His friend replied with several words, one of which was Pasadena. These narratives, the Spanish origin detailed by the rail guide, Elliot's version, and Reid's memory of his conversation with Garfías all point to how each party involved conceived of the land. Although it is significant that each version described the land's characteristics—the Edenic ideal, beautiful valley, or logistical layout—what is more intriguing is the decision to pursue a pleasant sounding Indian word rather than a Spanish phrase. Was it because, as Reid stated, "no Yankee would ever try to pronounce a name that commenced with two consonants" or was it something else?

Through the critical lens of imperialist nostalgia, the process of (re)naming the Indiana colony provides insight into why colonists chose to use the language of one vanquished group to (re)name its new home. As defined by scholar Renato Rosaldo, *imperialist nostalgia* refers to the practice in which "agents of colonization mourn the passing of what they themselves have transformed."[113] Within the process of westward expansion and the ideology of Manifest Destiny, Native peoples, both Indians and Mexicans, were dispossessed of their lands; their ways of life and societies were replaced as part of a mission of civilization and uplift.[114] While the underlying racialized ideas of expansion and progress manifested themselves on the physical landscape through the American homestead or farm in this case, the act of naming a place represents an ideological process of imperialist nostalgia that helps justify and rationalize Native peoples' displacement on a subconscious level. In this case, using an Indigenous language, albeit the language of the Midwestern region from which the colonists originated, to name their new home in the West, implies a recognition of the land's previous history and people. This naming process helped colonists to reassert their successful domination of the land and by extension its people. By mid-1874, the colony adopted its new name. As Page indicates, colonists who liked the name used it; those who did not simply continued calling it Muscat.[115]

The colony's success and growth throughout the 1870s solidified Berry's and Elliott's vision of Pasadena as the crown of the valley. In January 1876, Benjamin Wilson and his son-in-law, J. DeBarth Shorb, opened a new tract of land in the region. The Lake Vineyard Land and Water Association settlement was located to the east of the Indiana Colony tract and sold for seventy-five dollars an acre.[116] Although distinct from the Indiana Colony tract, Wilson's subdivision was often seen as part of Pasadena. The combination of these two tracts created Pasadena's present-day boundaries.

Over the next few years, the settlement grew, gaining a store, a church, a school, mail service, and a stagecoach service.[117] In addition to its infrastructural growth, the settlement planted and cultivated citrus groves and grape vineyards.[118] To publicize its fruit, the community held its first citrus fair on March 24, 1880. The festival's success soon gained Pasadena a reputation for its citrus and it became known as one of California's best fruit-growing districts.[119] The community's rapid growth and its successful cultivation of oranges defined Pasadena as a success. In a speech given at the citrus festival, prominent Pasadenan Donald M. Graham stated that the community had "ceased to be an experiment" and was "an acknowledged success."[120] Settlers' successful pursuit of gentleman farming, control of a reliable water source, and rapid regional growth signified the foundation of white middle-class society.

The Pasadena of the 1870s and the early 1880s reflected the strengths of Manifest Destiny and white racial supremacy and the triumph of the small farmer over the burgeoning industrial capitalism of the time. Whereas farmers in the Midwestern areas of the country experienced overall financial difficulty, gentlemen farmers in places such as Pasadena "domesticated the Wild West and created a civilized and productive society" on their own terms (see fig. 17).[121]

By the late nineteenth century Pasadena was a manifestation of Euro-American visions of land use. It had become a viable productive settlement, the physical materialization of rural urbanism and gentleman farming. During the mid-1880s, Pasadena settlers' growing affluence and need for services and conveniences combined with the expansion of the colony to create a dynamic that forever changed Pasadena's development and vision of land use. Slowly, over the course of fifteen years, Pasadena's thriving agriculture helped transform the settlement into a city that embraced a more urban vision of land use. Ironically, the railroad, the technology that allowed citrus farmers to increase their wealth and reputation by shipping their crops to markets throughout the country, is what spelled the death knell for the gentleman farmer's way of life.

RAILROAD AND TOURISM

During the nineteenth century, the completion of the transcontinental railroad influenced the expansion of the Western settlements. It opened markets that

FIGURE 17 Landscape of Pasadena on Orange Grove Avenue looking north ca. 1875. "This was Pasadena to the Indiana Colonists of about 1875. The photograph looks from a point near Arroyo Seco northeast, with winding Orange Grove Avenue at right and Bellefountain Avenue in the foreground. The house at left belonged to H. G. Bennet, a founder of Pasadena's first school, is under the trees at the center." (*Los Angeles Times*, January 24, 1954). Courtesy of the University of Southern California, Libraries and California Historical Society. Digitally reproduced by the USC Digital Library; from the California Historical Society Collection at the University of Southern California, http://digitallibrary.usc.edu/cdm/singleitem/collection/p15799coll65/id/6297/rec/1.

facilitated trade, allowed for the construction of towns and the launching of businesses, and brought both tourists and potential settlers into the Southwest.[122] These consequences affected places throughout the West and most certainly Pasadena. Part of San Pascual's appeal was the fact that land speculators mapped a route through the San Gabriel Valley for the Southern Pacific Railroad (see fig. 18).

In December of 1865 the Southern Pacific Railroad was incorporated and sought a way to bring lines into the great Los Angeles area.[123] In 1872, after years of opposition to the rail line and facing bureaucratic hurdles, Los Angeles voted to allow a route into the city. Three years later, in 1875, the Southern Pacific Railroad connected Los Angeles with its transcontinental rail line.[124] Over the next several years, other railroad lines such as the Atchison Topeka and Santa Fe Railroads entered Los Angeles from the east. The railroad proved crucial to the development the San Gabriel Valley by providing rail for the Los Angeles-San Gabriel Railroad.[125]

FIGURE 18 Los Angeles and San Gabriel railroad train. Photograph of a Los Angeles and San Gabriel railroad train on the bridge at Garvanza, the first trestle across the Arroyo Seco, approaching Highland Park from South Pasadena ca.1885. Courtesy of the University of Southern California, Libraries and California Historical Society. Digitally reproduced by the USC Digital Library; from the California Historical Society Collection at the University of Southern California, http://digitallibrary.usc.edu/cdm/singleitem/collection/p15799coll65/id/2979/rec/2.

Benjamin Wilson was aware of the railroad's desire to construct a railway in the region as early as 1868 when two Pacific Railroad surveyor parties appealed to him for support.[126] Four years later, in 1872, Wilson's wife, Margaret, recorded in her diary that Benjamin and his son-in-law had attended a railroad meeting in Los Angeles.[127] This meeting, held one year before Berry offered to purchase San Pascual, promised to make the region's land more valuable than it already was. Berry's knowledge of the coming of the railroad may explain his urgent letters about the purchase of San Pascual. Regardless, despite their intention to establish an agricultural settlement, Indiana Colony's founders clearly knew of the possible benefits of having a railroad nearby.

Prior to the 1885 completion of the Los Angeles and San Gabriel Valley Railroad connecting Pasadena to Los Angeles, travel between the two places took an hour and a half by stage if weather conditions permitted. The rough road and long trip did not stop settlers from conducting business in Los Angeles, nor did it dissuade people from visiting Pasadena.[128] As Pasadena grew in reputation, people traveled to the area to get a look at its beautiful landscape. Increased travel to the town prompted newly affluent settlers with money to spare to establish boarding houses and later hotels to host visitors. The first two hotels established in Pasadena during the early 1880s were the Pasadena House and the Lake Vineyard House. Both early hotels were small-scale two-floor dwellings that offered visitors a quaint place to stay while in Pasadena.

The railroad's completion in 1885 created a need for commercial and recreational spaces to accommodate incoming tourists. By the mid-1880s, larger scale resort-like hotels such as the Raymond Hotel were established by wealthy Boston businessman Walter Raymond. When completed in 1886 the Raymond Hotel (fig. 19) was the first grand hotel in Pasadena, with an estimated worth of $200,000.[129] Raymond built the hotel to provide a place for wealthy Easterners to stay while they visited the area in the winter months.[130] His success came at a time when Pasadena's local community flourished. Many local residents took the money they had made from their citrus cultivation and established businesses that benefited tourists and locals alike. By 1886 they had established shops, restaurants, banks, and the town's first billiard hall and saloon.[131] The establishment of these hotels and the growth of local businesses targeting tourists slowly altered visions about proper land use. At this point, Pasadena began its transition from an agricultural community to a tourist and commercial district.

FIGURE 19 Exterior view of Raymond Hotel ca. 1887. The elegant six-story hotel was situated at the top of a hill. Mountains are visible in the distance. Courtesy of the University of Southern California, Libraries and California Historical Society. Digitally reproduced by the USC Digital Library; from the California Historical Society Collection at the University of Southern California, http://digitallibrary.usc.edu/cdm/singleitem/collection/p15799coll65/id/6769/rec/1.

The completion of the railroad and the opening of the Raymond Hotel prompted a subsequent land boom. Land speculators A. O. Porter, H. G. Bennet, P. M. Green, F. M. Ward, W. E. Ward, C. S. Martin, and B. W. Bates enthusiastically bought twenty acres of land for $15,000.[132] They then subdivided the land into eighty-four lots that they intended to sell at auction. On February 23, 1886, potential bidders from Los Angeles were brought in to participate in the auction. They were treated to lunch and entertainment at the palatial Raymond Hotel. Bidders quickly bought up the land, netting land speculators an estimated total of $22,140.[133] The frenzy with which people bought land that day indicated that Pasadena had viable land with endless possibilities for development, a vision not lost to the bidders, who paid prices ranging from $180 to $520 for their plots.[134] The man who paid $520, the highest price for a plot that day, was J. W. Wood, a local druggist turned land speculator. In his memoir, *Pasadena California, Historical and Personal*, he discussed how the land boom affected people's attitudes about land:

> It was a strange overturning that began in 1886 and drove hitherto placid minded, contented citizens to acts of frenzy and drew to the village of Pasadena thousands of boomers and speculators, turning the ordinary conditions topsy-turvy and firing the imagination of the most phlegmatic. It was a rabid procession of men—and women, too, for women participated—that crossed the horizon and for a brief period filled it to the exclusion of all normal affairs and transactions. The professional left his office, the mechanic his shop, the merchant his counter and the farmer abandoned his plough, all to engage in that mad quest for quick wealth which obsessed them and was for a time their ruling passion.[135]

For two years, from 1886 to 1888, land speculation—the possibility of wealth and land development—engulfed people. Wood stated that for many "the song of the robin in the Arroyo was forgotten and the orchestration of the mockingbirds was unheeded, because the siren cry of the dealer in lots and the flubdub of speculators on the street corners drowned out those sweet carols in more unusual and now attractive strains."[136]

The success of the early 1880s permeated the dreams of many and contributed to the city's rapid growth. As more people came to Pasadena to become land owners, the city's population swelled from 391 in 1880 to 7,222 by 1890.[137] The incoming population did not share the Indiana Colony's values of and emphasis on gentleman farming. Despite the colony's short fourteen-year existence and its success as an agricultural society, the age of the orchard and grove had passed.

Pasadena slowly moved away from its agricultural roots and became a commercial tourist destination; the buying and selling of land became commonplace. Like the Spanish missionaries, pobladores, and Californios before them, the aspiring gentlemen farmers from Indiana who settled the region were relegated to a pioneer past, considered historical remnants and casualties of progress.

In late 1887, despite the promises of wealth, the land boom collapsed because of overspeculation. Many of the new landowners, unable to afford the payments on their lands, defaulted on their loans. Many "putative 'millionaires' [became] financial wrecks—dazed and amazed at the sudden tragic conclusion of their dreams."[138] The physical landscape bore the marks of the financial collapse. Slowdown in construction left subdivisions overgrown with weeds, orchards lay dry and abandoned, and once prosperous groves lay "neglected with fruit rotting on the ground."[139] Storefronts were vacant and the streets, no longer bustling with activity, grew up in weeds, indicating "that the pace was reverting to the slow and unhurried times known before the boom."[140] The financial panic and collapsed land boom of the late 1880s tarnished Pasadena's Edenic self-image. Residents saw that the promises of land speculation—mainly wealth and larger scale development—had distanced them from the Indian Colony's original goal of creating a strong stable community of personal homesteads that would engender more equitable relations. Many spent the last year of the 1880s trying to rebuild their homesteads. They planted orange trees, wheat, and barley and worked toward regaining their freedom and security. By 1890, the region's citrus production had recuperated, and Pasadena once again became the main exporter of oranges in Los Angeles County.[141]

Despite renewed success, Pasadena would not remain an agricultural community for long. The 1890s introduced a new land boom that saw the influx of wealthy Easterners looking for land on which to build their winter vacation homes and an increase in tourism. With the rise of the tourist industry during the late nineteenth century, Pasadena needed to highlight and share the majestic landscape and beauty that had called the original Indiana colonists to leave the cold harsh winters in exchange for the beauty of the Crown of the Valley.

In February 1887, Pasadena became an incorporated city, providing for the election of local government officials and development of the city's civic organization. By establishing a local democratically elected city council, Pasadena's citizens paved the way for the improvement of the city's infrastructure, including the construction of roads, schools, post offices, and a central library. Pasadena's incorporation gave the town legitimacy and indicated a higher level of Euro-American civilization.

FIGURE 20 Rear quarter view of a flower-decorated horse-drawn float in the Tournament of Roses Parade 1891. Courtesy of the University of Southern California, Libraries and California Historical Society. Digitally reproduced by the USC Digital Library; from the California Historical Society Collection at the University of Southern California, http://digitallibrary.usc.edu/cdm/singleitem/collection/p15799coll65/id/19823/rec/1.

As Pasadena entered the 1890s, it began a new epoch in which the agricultural past was framed by the idea that gentleman farming was the city's heritage. In January 1891, Pasadena held the first Tournament of Roses Parade to highlight the natural and physical beauty of the land and its products (see fig. 20). In his memoir, Los Angeles businessman and resident Harris Newmark captured the uniqueness of the Pasadena Rose Parade:

> There were [ostrich] chariot races and other sports, but the principal event was a parade of vehicles of every description which, moving along under the graceful burden of their beautiful floral decoration, presented a magnificent and typically Southern California winter sight.[142]

Although the roses, fruits, and animals reflected the beauty of the land and natural resources, the city's inhabitants looked forward to the growth brought by tourism. Unlike the previous boom of the 1880s, Pasadenans entered this boom more cautiously and did not forget their pioneer antecedents, recognizing that their influence was crucial to achieving their descendants' distinctive vision of optimal land use. This event, not the collapse of the 1880s, would define Pasadena; it would reflect the foundation of rural urbanism—a modern sophisticated lifestyle combined with the fruits of agrarian life. The races, the sports, the oranges, and most importantly the parade of stunning colorful flowers—breathtakingly arranged and showcased for all to see—would help define Pasadena as it entered the twentieth century.

Today, Pasadena is known around the world for its grandiose Tournament of Roses Parade, its annual Rose Bowl Game, its luxurious five-star resort hotels, its host of cultural attractions, and its first-class shopping district. A stroll down Colorado Boulevard in the Old Town District gives presence to Pasadena's pioneers, the settlers of the Indiana Colony. As shown in fig. 21, a look to the northeast presents a view of the Mount Wilson, named after the Father of Pasadena, Benjamin Wilson. However, Pasadena's natural beauty, its storefronts, and its tourist attractions reveal only one layer of what came *before the roses*.

FIGURE 21 Pasadena panoramic view looking northeast toward mountains ca.1898–1900. Courtesy of the University of Southern California, Libraries and California Historical Society. Digitally reproduced by the USC Digital Library; from the California Historical Society Collection at the University of Southern California, http://digitallibrary.usc.edu/cdm/singleitem/collection/p15799coll65/id/6008/rec/1. o

CONCLUSION

COMPETING VISIONS AND DYNAMIC CONTINUITIES

Father Sánchez gave me two ranches, that is land for one rancho and land for an orchard.

EULALIA PÉREZ

EVERY SUMMER PASADENA'S BIRTHDAY is celebrated with special exhibits, newspaper articles, and Old Town walking tours to highlight the city's origins in the Indiana Colony. Every January the world comes to Pasadena to witness the spectacle that is the Pasadena Tournament of Roses Parade. A caravan of intricately fashioned floats makes its way down Colorado Boulevard while commentators relate stories of Pasadena's pioneer past. The ostrich races, foot races, and a parade to highlight the abundance of fresh flowers, even in winter—all to tell the world about this piece of paradise.[1]

These commemorations tell the history of Pasadena's pioneer past. They highlight the period of the late 1870s when Euro-American gentlemen farmers from Indiana established their homesteads and overcame all odds to create the foundation of what is now a bustling city. Through street names, building façades, placenames, and a variety of other reminders, there are physical traces of the history and the experiences of the Indiana Colony.

The epigraph above is a quotation from the 1870s testimonio of former San Gabriel Mission llavera Eulalia Pérez in which she described mission priests granting her ownership of Rancho San Pascual, consisting of the San Gabriel Mission lands, in 1826. Aside from Pérez's testimonio, no other official record of this transaction exists, and the story is now part of Pasadena folklore. It, along with a brief mention of the Hahamog'na Tongva, San Gabriel Mission, and the

Mexican Period, are contained in blurbs and mentioned in passing as part of the region's heritage from 1771–1859.[2]

Historical narratives such as these fuel the many commemorative celebrations, parades, social rituals, and even the physical landscape. However, not every narrative is remembered, and some are privileged more than others. Although the Indiana Colony is an important part of the region's history and identity, it is one of many histories that displaces those that came before it, privileging one history while burying the multiple others that comprise part of the region's identity.

CYCLES OF HISTORICAL DISPLACEMENT

Over the course of 120 years from 1771 to the 1890, the land comprising present-day Pasadena and its surrounding areas changed hands several times. During each historical moment groups such as the Tongva people, Spanish missionaries and pobladores, Californios, and American colonists used the land in diverse ways that represented their ideas of what optimal land use meant. What remained constant was their belief that their vision of land use was superior to those of previous groups.

Pasadena Before the Roses began as a project of historical recuperation. It was a means of recovering the region's Indigenous, Spanish, and Mexican history and disrupting a narrative that focused solely on Pasadena's Euro-American pioneer history. By shifting the spatio-temporal boundaries of Pasadena's history to include broader Los Angeles and San Gabriel regions beginning in the late eighteenth century, the region's multiple and layered histories, presently obscured by the shadows of Pasadena's Euro-American historical narrative, came to the surface. These are the histories that have been buried by the continuous and multifaceted legacy of colonialism and the (re)defining of culture during the Spanish, Californio, and American Periods. Looking across the region's different historical eras, one can see that the physical land is what unified the Spaniards, Mexicans, and Americans who entered the area. Each group entered the region with their its articulation of optimal land use. The land itself consistently served as the crux of each moment of colonization and influenced the social behavior, cultural construction, and economic systems of the people who owned and controlled it.

Within the distinct social and historical reality, broader themes emerged that allowed for the interrogation of how power materialized and the visualization of the dynamic continuity of this power over time.[3] During each era the land began to tell the stories of the people who inhabited it. Stories of the creation of wealth, the assertion of dominance, and the subsequent dispossession illustrate that regardless of who was at the top of social hierarchy—Spanish missionaries, wealthy Californios, or Euro-Americans—each utilized specific ideologies to create privilege, legitimize their power, and displace those who came before them.

Specific historical moments and ideologies spanning the early 1770s to the late nineteenth century demarcate this dynamic continuity. The establishment of Spanish colonialism and the mission system, Mexican liberalism, secularization and the rise of the rancho, the U.S.-Mexico War, Manifest Destiny, the gentleman farmer, and the land booms of the late nineteenth century each prompted significant shifts in the way regional inhabitants defined optimal land use and influenced the construction of their socioeconomic and cultural identities.

DYNAMIC CONTINUITIES: MISSIONARIES, RANCHEROS, AND GENTLEMEN FARMERS

In 1771, as part of Spain's colonizing process in Alta California, Franciscan missionaries established the San Gabriel Mission among the local Tongva populations in what became the San Gabriel region. Utilizing a program of religious indoctrination linked to a strict labor regiment, missionaries sought to eradicate Indians' culture by instilling the tenets of Catholicism and a Spanish work ethic. Aside from its purpose of conversion, the mission institution played a crucial role in the development of the regional economy. As one of the wealthiest missions, San Gabriel's connection to the land is an important part of Pasadena's and the San Gabriel Valley's overall economic growth because it provided the main source for goods and products during late eighteenth and early nineteenth centuries. Defining a vision of optimal land use based on the cultivation of a variety of crops and the grazing of cattle, San Gabriel's Franciscans controlled thousands of acres of land and used Indian labor to establish it as the center of the regional economy.[4] As missionaries successfully controlled mission lands and Indian labor, the mission helped shape the contours of Spanish society and culture in this region.

As the representation of Spanish society throughout California, missionaries, pobladores, and soldiers increasingly defined themselves using the identities produced through the mission project. Structuring their identities within the language of colonialism, Alta California's Spanish inhabitants distinguished themselves from Tongva Indians through colonial binaries of Christian and heathen and de razón and indio. As the region's population grew, these distinctions became increasingly important and ultimately solidified the sociocultural and economic boundaries between Spanish and Indian.

During the early nineteenth century, the Mexican War for Independence and the emergence of Mexican liberalism gave rise to localized critiques and resentment of the San Gabriel Mission's control of the region's premier lands. After independence in 1821, aspiring elites who regarded land as the key to social status, mobility, and wealth increasingly pressed for governmental secularization of mission lands. Mission secularization in 1833 allowed for the distribution of former mission lands, giving rise to a private rancho system controlled by a landed oligarchy. Calling themselves Californios, these men linked their identities to their lands and ushered in California's Rancho Period. Rancho San Pascual's multiple changes in ownership during this period reflected the innerworkings of a racialized class system that used land to affirm its social and cultural status.

Californios whitened their casta origins and created a narrative in which they were the dominant class. They used their land ownership and wealth to create a material culture that distinguished them from the lower landless classes consisting of mestizos and Indians. Their exertion of patriarchal authority, the upkeep of their ranchos, their control of labor, and their other displays of wealth helped define them as part of society's upper echelon.

Despite Californios' emphasis on distinguishing themselves from the lower classes, they still maintained a level of social cohesiveness. Through community fiestas framed in ritual and paternalism and fictive familial relationships, elites attempted to maintain the loyalty and labor of the landless classes. These social rituals and relationship helped connect the distinct classes and offered social legitimation for elites while simultaneously maintaining social distinctions.

During the 1830s and early 1840s, the availability of land and fast-paced economic growth through ranching and the tallow and hide trade encouraged immigrants to make their way to California in the hope of finding wealth. A small number of Americans were among the immigrants who came into California in the Mexican Period. These Americans assimilated into Californio culture, converted to Catholicism, became naturalized Mexicans, and married the daughters of the Californios as a way to gain status and land in Mexican California. Californios' racialized class structure allowed many to mask the ideal of American Anglo-Saxon superiority. As members of the elite class, they gained large amounts of land and political influence in the region—power that slowly altered Californio elites' interactions with the lower classes.

After the U.S.-Mexico War, changes in the government and land policies resulted in the disintegration of class ties between Californios and Americans. Seeing their social and political status decline, Californios attempted to integrate themselves into the new race-based structure. Slowly, Californios realized that the new Anglo elite did not welcome them into its circles and that their land ownership bought limited tolerance but not acceptance. As Californios lost their lands through policies such as the Land Act of 1851, they also experienced a loss of economic wealth and political control.

By the 1860s, California's American population had increased. For Americans, their settlement in the region fulfilled ideals of Manifest Destiny and racial progress. In addition to Anglos who aspired to own large acreages of land, many small-scale farmers enticed by the model of the gentleman farmer sought a future rooted in agricultural pursuits in less rural areas of Southern California, such as Pasadena. Due to Pasadena's short distance from the developing city of Los Angeles and its position within the emerging national economy created by the railroad and the growing citrus industry in the 1870s, the ideal of the gentleman farmer was realized by the Midwestern settlers of the Indiana Colony, who quickly established their thriving agricultural colony on San Pascual's former lands.

The late 1870s and the 1880s marked a shift in land use among Pasadena's Euro-American population. A widespread land boom and speculation changed the structure of land ownership and brought people into the region who saw land as a commodity to be bought and sold for profit. Among these new populations, land ownership provided an opportunity for social mobility and increased social status.

In the larger frame of Manifest Destiny, the actions of this new land-owning class reflected the linking of the Anglo-American ideals of racial progress and the physical land. The link between land and status in the American period was not unlike the Californio elites' relationship to the land. Both groups wanted to develop the land as a means of obtaining and maintaining social status and wealth. By interweaving ideas of race and cultural identity with ideals of land use, Californios racialized land ownership. Similarly, Americans included a racial structure in their policies of land ownership and exclusion. What differed between these two groups were the specifics produced through two different national projects. The racial dynamics of Mexican independence created distinctions among the classes based on economics, which was reflected through land ownership. Because the area's regional identity emerged from the intermixing of various groups, societal divisions were based on perceptions of culture and class. In the period following the U.S.-Mexico War, a conflict based on Americans' perceptions of Mexicans as racially inferior, Californios' economic and political power in the region began a slow decline.

By the end of the nineteenth century, Anglos controlled California's land and developed it according to their visions of optimal land use. In the 1880s and 1890s, the American racial structure based on white Anglo-Saxon superiority combined with economic development to whiten land ownership. Racial difference subsumed the class cooperation enjoyed by Californios and early American settlers during the era immediately before and after the U.S.-Mexico War. Within this new exclusively racial structure and narrative, the land's development was tied to the white Americans who settled and developed it, not to the previous groups who simply inhabited the region. Political changes, the solidification of Anglo control, and the development of Pasadena's lands relegated the region's Indigenous, Spanish, and Californio people to a distant past. These groups, the region's original settlers, were seen as a people who had failed to properly develop the land and were subsequently overtaken by progress and a much superior group. With the dawn of industrialization and the large-scale expansion of a capitalist market economy facilitated by the railroad, the physical landscape bore the marks of modernity. Through hotels established for leisure and rails built for traveling into these newly developed regions, the pioneer heritage of the Indiana Colony became a quaint memory of a place that developed into a symbol of American progress.

PRIVILEGED NARRATIVES: UNTOLD STORIES AND PASADENA'S PRESENT

In 2010 as part of its bicentennial celebration, the Mexican government sponsored a float in the 121st Annual Tournament of Roses Parade. The Mexico Bicentennial float featured several key symbols and moments from Mexican history. The front of the float contained a replica of the Ángel de la Independencia and portraits of revolutionaries Padre Miguel Hidalgo and Francisco Madero.[5] Aside from highlighting Mexico's war for independence and the 1910 Mexican Revolution, the float also emphasized Mexico's Indigenous roots by including a sculpture of an eagle perched on a nopal cactus with a serpent in its mouth and a large replica of an Aztec pyramid and codex.[6] At the center of the fifty-five-foot-long float, "50,000 roses spelled out Mexico–2010 under red, white, and green pennants."[7] On the day of the parade, Mexican immigrants, Mexican Americans, and their families who had helped build the float, stood together on the float while thirty-six Aztec and *baile folklórico* dancers performed to traditional music as the float traveled down Colorado Boulevard.

Historically, the bright and vibrant float was not out of place, but rather a step toward recognizing the region's Mexican past. However, within the contemporary context of anti-Mexican and anti-immigrant sentiment, the float prompted a flurry of nativist responses. The most vocal responses came from anti-illegal-immigration organizations such as the Americans for Legal Immigration PAC (ALIPAC) and the California Coalition for Immigration Reform (CCIR). For example, members of ALIPAC referred to the float as an underhanded way for the Mexican government to "put its stamp on their invasion."[8] Barbara Coe, leader of CCIR, worried that due to the massive discontent over the float, based on the "few emails and some calls" she had received, "high tensions associated with the escalating immigration debate . . . [might] spill over onto the parade and create problems."[9] Reponses such as these reflect the anti-immigrant sentiments that have permeated the United States for several years now.[10] What is also troubling is that, aside from targeting immigrants, these statements have broader implications about American's perceptions of Mexican Americans. For instance, one ALIPAC member stated that the float was "not really a gift to any other culture in California. Just an in-your-face flaunt about overwhelming the rest of us with their [Mexican/Latino] numbers."[11] What is particularly problematic about this statement is that it makes no distinction between Mexican immigrants and Mexican Americans. I highlight this lack of distinction not to support the stigmatization of Mexican immigrants nor to legitimize xenophobic and nativist attitudes against them, but rather to show the consequences of the privileging of some narratives over others.

The protests against the 2010 Mexico float illustrate how untold narratives of place produce specific knowledge about the present. Framed within the pioneer trope, Pasadena's history privileges a Euro-American-based narrative that does not credit the pivotal roles played by the region's minority population, both historically and in the contemporary era. Over the course of Pasadena's 130-year history, countless Indigenous people, Mexican Americans, and Mexican immigrants labored to build the region—from its waterways, its citrus groves, and railways to its definitive buildings, bridges, and roads, including the now world-famous Colorado Boulevard on which the Tournament of Roses travels every New Year's Day. Despite their essential part in building the region and the city's history their stories remain largely untold and displaced.

In Pasadena's past, each group's vision for the land led to the exploitation, exclusion, and subsuming of groups who did not espouse majority beliefs about land use. The continued combination of land use and racial identity over one hundred years served to establish and (re)create a specific regional identity and reputation for the Pasadena region. Continuously reconceptualizing identity through competing visions of land use and economics fashioned regional and social identities and shaped social interactions, power dynamics, and historical narratives. Through *Pasadena Before the Roses* I hope to provide an understanding of how the past, regardless of how distant, still affects the way we remember our spaces and places, as well as how we view ourselves within them.

NOTES

INTRODUCTION

Epigraph: Laura Barraclough, *Making the San Fernando Valley: Rural Landscapes, Urban Development, and White Privilege* (Athens: University of Georgia Press, 2011), 17.

1. Frieda Knobloch, *Culture of Wilderness: Agriculture as Colonization in the American West* (Chapel Hill: University of North Carolina, 1996), 1–2; Stephen Pitti, *The Devil in Silicon Valley: Northern California, Race, and Mexican Americans* (Princeton, NJ: Princeton University Press, 2003), 35–36.
2. In her work on the San Fernando Valley, Barraclough defined the term gentleman farming as small-scale agriculture. Barraclough, *Making the San Fernando Valley*, 29.
3. Imposed agricultural mission labor was a crucial element in the "civilizing process." See James Sandos, *Converting California: Indians and Franciscans in the Missions* (New Haven: Yale University Press, 2004), 9–10.
4. Lisbeth Haas, *Conquests and Historical Identities in California, 1769–1936* (Berkeley: University of California Press, 1995), 37.
5. Pitti, *The Devil in Silicon Valley*, 29.
6. Haas, *Conquests and Historical Identities*, 57. For a discussion of the classification of Mexicans as Indians in the U.S. racial system, see Martha Menchaca, "Chicano Indianism: A Historical Account of Racial Repression in the United States," *American Ethnologist* 20, no. 3 (August 1993): 583–603.
7. Tómas Almaguer, *Racial Fault Lines: The Historical Origins of White Supremacy in California* (Berkeley: University of California Press, 1994), 63–65.

8. María Raqúel Casas, *Married to a Daughter of the Land: Spanish-Mexican Women and Interethnic Marriage in California, 1820–1880* (Reno: University of Nevada Press, 2007), 148–49.
9. Almaguer, *Racial Fault Lines*, 79, 90; Leonard Pitt, *The Decline of the Californios: A Social History of the Spanish-Speaking Californians, 1846–1890* (Berkeley: University of California Press, 1966), 13–16, 269. Pitti, *The Devil in Silicon Valley*, 36–37.
10. Barraclough, *Making the San Fernando Valley*, 25.
11. These understandings of space are based in the field of geography and spatial theory. See Denis Cosgrove, *Social Formation and Symbolic Landscape* (Madison: University of Wisconsin Press, 1984), 13–14; Michael Dear and Jennifer Wolch, "How Territory Shapes Social Life," in *The Power of Geography: How Territory Shapes Social Life,* ed. Michael Dear and Jennifer Wolch (Boston: Unwin Hyman, 1989), 10; Edward Soja, *Postmodern Geographies: The Reassertion of Space in Critical Social Theory* (London: Verso, 1989), 6.
12. Soja, *Postmodern Geographies*, 6.
13. Dear and Wolch, "How Territory Shapes Social Life," 9.
14. Emma Pérez, *The Decolonial Imaginary: Writing Chicanas into History* (Bloomington: Indiana University Press, 1999), 4; Linda Heidenreich, *This Land Was Mexican Once: Histories of Resistance from Northern California* (Austin: University of Texas, 2007), 2.
15. Leonard Pitt, *The Decline of the Californios*; Albert Camarillo, *Chicanos in a Changing Society: From Mexican Pueblos to American Barrios in Santa Barbara and Southern California, 1848–1930* (Cambridge: Harvard University Press), 1979; Douglas Monroy, *Thrown Among Strangers: The Making of Mexican Culture in Frontier California* (Berkeley: University of California Press, 1990); Richard Griswold del Castillo, *The Treaty of Guadalupe Hidalgo: Legacy of Conflict* (Norman: University of Oklahoma Press, 1990); Almaguer, *Racial Fault Lines.*
16. See Camarillo, *Chicanos in a Changing Society.*
17. Genevieve Carpio, "From Citrus Belt to Inland Empire: Race, Place, and Mobility in Southern California 1880–2000" (PhD diss., University of Southern California, 2013), http://digitallibrary.usc.edu/cdm/ref/collection/p15799coll3/id/323141; Matt García, *A World of Its Own: Race, Labor, and Citrus in the Making of Greater Los Angeles, 1900–1970* (Chapel Hill: University of North Carolina Press, 2001); Pitti, *Devil in the Silicon Valley*; Ricardo Romo, *East Los Angeles: History of a Barrio* (Austin: University of Texas Press, 1983).
18. See Haas, *Conquests and Historical Identities.*
19. See Barraclough, *Making the San Fernando Valley.*
20. Robert Fogleson, *The Fragmented Metropolis: Los Angeles, 1850–1930* (Cambridge: MIT Press, 1967).
21. David Torres-Rouff, *Before L.A.: Race, Space, and Municipal Power in Los Angeles, 1781–1894* (New Haven, Conn.: Yale University Press, 2013).
22. Casas, *Married to a Daughter of the Land*; Antonia Castañeda, "Presidarias y Pobladoras: The Journey North and Life in Frontier California," in *En Aquel Entonces: Readings in Mexican American History*, eds. Manuel G. Gonzales and Cynthia M.

Gonzales (Bloomington: Indiana University Press, 2000); Miroslava Chávez-García, *Negotiating Conquest: Gender and Power in California, 1770s to 1880s* (Tucson: University of Arizona Press, 2004); Deena J. González, *Refusing the Favor: The Spanish Mexican Women of Santa Fe, 1820–1880* (New York: Oxford University Press, 1999); Haas, *Conquests and Historical Identities*; Linda Heidenreich, *"This Land Was Mexican Once": Histories of Resistance from Northern California* (Austin: University of Texas Press, 2007); Angelina Veyna, "'It Is My Last Wish That . . .': A Look at Colonial Nuevo Mexicanas Through their Testaments," in *Building With Our Hands: New Directions in Chicana History*, eds. Adela de la Torre and Beatríz Pesquera (Berkeley: University of California Press, 1990).

23. Louise Pubols, *The Father of All: The de la Guerra Family, Power, and Patriarchy in Mexican California*. Western Histories 1 (Berkeley: University of California Press, 2009). Pubols's study focused on Santa Barbara's de la Guerra family and its very wealthy patriarch, José de la Guerra.

CHAPTER 1

1. David J. Weber, *The Spanish Frontier in North America*, The Lamar Series in Western History (New Haven, Conn.: Yale University Press, 1992), 94.
2. Both the Franciscan and Jesuit orders were involved in the conversion of Indigenous populations throughout the newly acquired Spanish territories. Although Jesuits were also present in Florida and Texas, their presence was stronger in Antigua or Baja California. In these areas, the Jesuits established various missions that helped solidify Spanish control. In the 1760s the Spanish Crown expelled the Jesuits from its American colonies. The remainder of this project focuses on the role of the Franciscan Order, as it was responsible for the missionizing of the Alta California's Indigenous peoples. For a discussion of the Jesuits' role in missionizing Indians, see Weber, *The Spanish Frontier*, 241.
3. Weber, *The Spanish Frontier*, 95.
4. Weber, *The Spanish Frontier*, 105–11.
5. Weber, *The Spanish Frontier*, 241.
6. Weber, *The Spanish Frontier*, 242.
7. Weber, *The Spanish Frontier*, 242. In his capacity as visitador general, Gálvez was put in charge of implementing the 1767 Jesuit expulsion as part of the Bourbon Reforms.
8. Presidios were well-established components of empire throughout the northern frontier, dating back to the mid to late 1500s. By 1730 Spain's northern borderlands counted eighteen presidios. See Max Moorehead, *The Presidio: Bastion of the Spanish Borderlands* (Norman: University of Oklahoma Press, 1975), 7.
9. Weber, *The Spanish Frontier*, 217.
10. Weber, *The Spanish Frontier*, 213.
11. Pekka Hämäläinem, "The Shapes of Power: Indians, Europeans, and North American Worlds from Seventeenth to Nineteenth Centuries," in *Contested Spaces of*

Early America, eds. Juliana Barr and Edward Countryman (Philadelphia: University of Pennsylvania, 2014), 38.

12. Don Carlos II, *Recopilación de Leyes de Los Reynos De Las Indias*, vol. 4, title xii, law xix (Madrid:: Julián de Paredes, 1681. Reprint. Madrid: Ediciones Cultura Hispánica, 1973).
13. James Sandos, *Converting California*, 177–78.
14. Sandos, *Converting California*, 177.
15. R. Louis Gentilcore, "Missions and Mission Lands of Alta California," *Annals of the Association of American Geographers* 51, no. 1 (March 1961): 46.
16. Sandos, *Converting California*, 3.
17. Sandos, *Converting California*, xvi.
18. Sandos, *Converting California*, 67; "Tongva Language," Keepers of Our Indigenous Ways, Inc., accessed June 3, 2011, http://www.keepersofindigenousways.org/id9.html. This study speaks specifically to the villages in the immediate areas of Pasadena and San Gabriel: Hahamongna (Pasadena) and Sibanga (San Gabriel).
19. Edward D. Castillo, "Gender Status Decline, Resistance, and Accommodation Among Female Neophytes in the Missions of California: A San Gabriel Case Study," *American Indian Cultures and Research Journal* 18, no. 1 (1994): 68.
20. Rosanna Welch, *A Brief History of the Tongva Tribe: The Native Inhabitants of the Lands of the Puente Hills Reserve* (Claremont, Calif.: Claremont Graduate University, 2006) 7–8.
21. Welch, *Brief History of the Tongva*, 8–9.
22. William McCawley, *The First Angelinos: The Gabrielino Indians of Los Angeles* (Novato, Calif.: Ballena Press, 1996), 27.
23. Castillo, "Gender Status Decline, Resistance, and Accommodation," 68.
24. Castillo, "Gender Status Decline, Resistance, and Accommodation," 69.
25. There are many different theories about the origins of the Chengiichngech religion. Some are classified as foreign influence theories that argue the religion was a reactionary religion fueled by Spanish presence; other theories argue for its Indigenous nature, citing evidence of its existence dating back to as early as 1602, the year of the Vizcaíno expedition. For a discussion on Tongva religion and practices, see McCawley, *The First Angelinos*, 143–69.
26. Castillo, "Gender Status Decline, Resistance, and Accommodation," 68.
27. McCawley, *The First Angelinos*, 144.
28. Castillo, "Gender Status Decline, Resistance, and Accommodation," 68.
29. Bernice Johnston, *California's Gabrielino Indians* (Los Angeles: Southwest Museum, 1962), 33–34; Bruce Miller, *The Gabrielinos* (Los Osos, Calif.: San River Press, 1991), 64; McCawley, *The First Angelinos*, 148.
30. Franciscan missionary Gerónimo Boscana documented many Tongva religious beliefs and practices. Boscana's *Chinigchinich: A Historical Account of the Origin, Customs, and Traditions of the Indians at the Missionary Establishment of St. Juan Capistrano, Alta California Called the Acagchemem Nation* (New York: Wiley and Putnam, 1846) provided an in-depth ethnographic study of Alta California's Native

peoples. This text was translated from Spanish by American businessman Alfred Robinson, who quickly became part of the economic elite after the American conquest of California. The full citation for the book is *Fray Gerónimo Boscana, Chinigchinich (Chi-ñićh-ñich): a Revised and Annotated Version of Alfred Robinson's Translation of Father Geronimo Boscana's Historical Account of the Belief, Usages, Customs and Extravagencies of the Indians of This Mission of San Juan Capistrano, Called the Acagchemem Tribe* (Santa Ana, Calif.: Fine Arts Press, 1933).

31. Johnston, *California's Gabrielino Indians*, 32.
32. Francisco Lasuén to Antonio Nogueyra, 21 January 1797, in *Writings of Fermín Francisco Lasuén*, vol. II, ed. and trans. Finbar Kenneally (Washington, D.C.: Academy of American Franciscan History, 1965), 6.
33. Sandos, *Converting California*, 12.
34. Francisco Lasuén to Guardian de Colegio de San Fernando de México, letter, April 23, 1774, Misión San Gabriel, Documentos Relativos a las Misiones de California, 1768–1802, vol. 7, box 1, folder 55, Bancroft Library, University of California Berkeley.
35. Robert H. Jackson, "The Formation of Frontier Indigenous Communities: Missions in California and Texas," in *New Views of Borderlands History*, ed. Robert H. Jackson (Albuquerque: University of New Mexico Press, 1998), 134.
36. Sandos, *Converting California*, 9–10.
37. Ramón Gutiérrez, *When Jesus Came, the Corn Mothers Went Away: Marriage, Sexuality, and Power in New Mexico, 1500–1848* (Stanford, Calif.: Stanford University Press, 1991), 105–6.
38. Opponents of the system, such as Dominican Friar Bartolomé de Las Casas, called for the end of the system, citing that as free persons Indians deserved the same treatment as others. In 1542, after extensive debate, Las Nuevas Leyes outlawed the encomienda system. Fearing colonists' revolt, the king scaled back the ban and allowed *encomenderos* to retain their rights to Indian tribute, but limited their right to Indian labor. See Amy Butler Greenfield, *A Perfect Red: Empire, Espionage, and the Quest for the Color of Desire* (New York: Harper Collins, 2005), 64.
39. Although making links between seventeenth and eighteenth century encounters between missionaries and Indian borders is an extreme generalization with no regard for social/historical context, it is clear that there are several foundational ideas that continued to frame this colonial relationship well into the late eighteenth century in Alta California.
40. David Sweet, "The Ibero-American Frontier Mission in Native American History," in *The New Latin American Mission History*, ed. Erick Langer and Robert H. Jackson (Lincoln: University of Nebraska Press, 1995), 4.
41. Herbert E. Bolton, "The Mission as a Frontier Institution in the Spanish-American Colonies," *American Historical Review*, 23, no. 1 (October 1917): 43–44.
42. David J. Weber, *Bárbaros: Spaniards and Their Savages in the Age of Enlightenment* (New Haven: Yale University Press, 2005), 14–15.
43. Weber, *Bárbaros*, 17.

44. Steven W. Hackel, *Children of Coyote, Missionaries of Saint Francis: Indian-Spanish Relations in Colonial California, 1769–1850* (Chapel Hill: University of North Carolina Press, 2005),140.
45. Hackel, *Children of Coyote*, 141.
46. Hackel, *Children of Coyote*, 131.
47. Sherburne F. Cook, *Conflict Between the California Indian and White Civilization* (Berkeley: University of California Press, 1976), 94.
48. Randall Milliken, *A Time of Little Choice: The Disintegration of Tribal Culture in the San Francisco Bay Area*, 1769–1810 (Banning, Calif.: Ballena Press, 1995), 85.
49. Milliken, *A Time of Little Choice*, 86.
50. Zephyrin Engelhardt, *San Fernando Rey: The Mission of the Valley* (Chicago: Franciscan Herald Press, 1927), 88–89; Milliken, *A Time of Little Choice*, 85.
51. Charles C. Noel, "Missionary Preachers in Spain: Teaching Social Virtue in the Eighteenth Century," *American Historical Review*, 90, no. 4 (October 1985): 877.
52. Noel, "Missionary Preachers in Spain," 877.
53. Lasuén to Antonio Nogueyra, 21 January 1797, 205.
54. Noel, "Missionary Preachers in Spain," 877; Hackel, *Children of Coyote*, 280.
55. José de Gálvez to Junípero Serra, 15 September 1768, letter, Real de Santa Anna, Junípero Serra Collection, folder 124, Santa Barbara Mission Archive Library (Santa Barbara, CA).
56. Cook, *Conflict Between the California Indian and White Civilization*, 99.
57. Hackel, *Children of Coyote*, 281.
58. Hackel, *Children of Coyote*, 281.
59. Sandos, *Converting California*, 9.
60. Sandos, *Converting California*, 9. Although Sandos lists several other occupations, I included only jobs related to the activities at the San Gabriel Mission. Occupations at San Gabriel were connected to the cattle industry—primarily the tallow and hide trade.
61. Sandos, *Converting California*, 9.
62. Sandos, *Converting California*, 9.
63. Milliken, *A Time of Little Choice*, 89, 195; Hackel, *Children of Coyote*, 283–84.
64. Milliken, *A Time of Little Choice*, 86–87; Hackel, *Children of Coyote*, 285; Sandos, *Converting California*, 8.
65. Hackel, *Children of Coyote*, 281.
66. Finbar Kenneally, ed. and trans., *Writings of Fermín Francisco de Lasuén*, II (Washington, D.C.: Academy of American Franciscan History, 1965), 220.
67. Hackel, *Children of Coyote*, 281; Sweet, "The Ibero-American Frontier Mission in Native American History," 22.
68. Milliken, *A Time of Little Choice*, 89.
69. Francis F. Guest, "Cultural Perspectives on California Mission Life," *Southern California Quarterly* 65, no. 1 (Spring 1983): 20; Milliken, *A Time of Little Choice*, 89.
70. Haas, *Conquests and Historical Identities*, 26.
71. Casas, *Married to a Daughter of the Land*, 64.

72. Casas, *Married to a Daughter of the Land*, 64; Chávez-García, *Negotiating Conquest*, 21; Haas, *Conquests and Historical Identities*, 26.
73. Sarapes, frazadas, sillas de montar, frenos, botas, zapatos y demás aviós de ese ramo. Eulalia Pérez, "Una vieja y sus recuerdos dictados . . . a la edad avanzada de 139 años, 1877," BANC MSS C-D 116, Collection of the Bancroft Library, University of California Berkeley. Unless otherwise noted, all translations are by the author.
74. Pérez, "Una vieja y sus recuerdos dictados."
75. Pérez, "Una vieja y sus recuerdos dictados."
76. The term *indios ya de razón*, literally translated, means Indians already of reason; it indicates that these Indians had already converted to Christianity. In her testimonio Pérez stated, "Yo, Eulalia Pérez, naci en el presidio de Loreto en la Baja Califonia. Mi padre se llamaba Diego Pérez . . . ; mi madre se llamaba Antonia Rosalía Cota; ambos eran blancos puros. (I Eulalia Pérez, was born at the presidio of Loreto in Baja California. My father was named Diego Pérez . . . ; my mother was named Antonia Rosalía Cota, both were pure whites.)" Peréz, "Una vieja y sus recuerdos dictados."
77. Susan Kellogg, "From Parallel and Equivalent to Separate but Unequal: Tenocha Mexica Women, 1500–1700," in *Indian Women of Colonial Mexico*, eds. Susan Schroeder, Stephanie Wood, and Robert Haskett (Norman: University of Oklahoma Press, 1999), 132.
78. Castillo, "Gender Status Decline, Resistance, and Accommodation," 68.
79. Castillo, "Gender Status Decline, Resistance, and Accommodation," 74.
80. Antonia I. Castañeda, "Engendering the History of Alta California, 1769–1848: Gender, Sexuality, and the Family," in *Contested Eden: California Before the Gold Rush*, eds. Ramón Gutiérrez and Richard Orsi (Berkeley: University of California Press, 1998), 232; Gerda Lerner, *The Creation of Patriarchy* (New York: Oxford University Press, 1986), 238–39.
81. Antonia I. Castañeda, "Sexual Violence in the Politics and Policies of Conquest: Amerindian Women and the Spanish Conquest of California," in *Building with Our Hands: New Directions in Chicana Studies*, eds. Adela de la Torre and Beatríz Pescuera (Berkley: University of California Press, 1993), 27; see also Gutiérrez, *When Jesus Came, the Corn Mothers Went Away*, 176–206.
82. Castañeda, "Engendering the History of Alta California," 231; Castillo, "Gender Status Decline, Resistance, and Accommodation," 70.
83. Castañeda, "Sexual Violence in the Politics and Policies of Conquest," 25–27.
84. Boscana. *Chinigchinich*, 87; Sandos, *Converting California*, 22–23; Patricia Seed, *To Love, Honor, and Obey in Colonial Mexico: Conflicts over Marriage Choice, 1574–1821* (Stanford, Calif.: Stanford University Press, 1988), 87.
85. Edith Wallace, "Sexual Status and Role Differences," in *California*, ed. Robert F. Heizer, 683; *Handbook of North American Indians*, ed. William Sturtevant, vol. 8 (Washington, D.C.: Smithsonian Press, 1978).
86. Many historians have looked at gender parallelism among many Native American groups in pre-Columbian MesoAmerican groups, the Peruvian Incas, and other Indigenous populations in North America. For a discussion of gender parallelism

in Peru, Mexico, and the present-day United States, respectively, see Irene Silverblatt, *Moon, Sun and Witches: Gender Ideologies and Class in Inca and Colonial Peru* (Princeton, N.J.: Princeton University Press, 1987); Susan Kellogg, "From Parallel and Equivalent to Separate but Unequal," 123–43; Paula Gunn Allen, *The Sacred Hoop: Recovering the Feminine in the American Indian Tradition* (Boston: Beacon Press, 1985); Antonia I. Castañeda, "Malinche, Calafia, y Toypurina," in *Three Decades of Engendering History: Selected Works of Antonia I. Castañeda*, eds. Linda Heidenreich and Antonia Castañeda (Denton: University of North Texas Press, 2014), 71.

87. McCawley, *The First Angelinos*, 155–58.
88. Castillo, "Gender Status Decline, Resistance, and Accommodation," 75; Milliken, *A Time of Little Choice*, 89–90.
89. Chávez-García, *Negotiating Conquest*, 21.
90. Eulalia Pérez, "Una vieja y sus recuerdos dictados," 17.
91. Castañeda, "Malinche, Calafia, y Toypurina," 71.
92. Chávez-Garcia, *Negotiating Conquest*, 21.
93. These ranchos were later referred to as San Pascual, Santa Anita, Asuza, Los Coyotes, Los Alamitos, and Los Cerritos. See *The Indians of Los Angeles County: Hugo Reid's Letters of 1852*, ed. Robert F. Heizer (Los Angeles: Southwest Museum, 1968), 84.
94. New mission history scholarship identifies the negative changes or constraints as disease, malnutrition, regimentation, discipline and punishment, deculturation, infantilization, and alienation from nature. For this work, I focus specifically on regimentation, discipline, and punishment and their relationship to Indigenous resistance. For examples of new mission history scholarship, refer to *The New Latin American Mission History*, eds. Erick Langer and Robert H. Jackson (Lincoln: University of Nebraska Press, 1995).
95. Stephen Silliman, "Theoretical Perspectives on Labor and Colonialism: Reconsidering the California Missions," *Journal of Anthropological Archaeology* 20, no. 4 (December 2001): 382. For a discussion of action, social actors, and agency, see chapter 2 in Anthony Giddens, *Central Problems in Social Theory: Action, Structure, and Contradiction in Social Analysis* (Berkeley: University of California Press, 1979), 49–96.
96. Hackel, *Children of Coyote*, 281; see also Milliken, *Time of Little Choice*, 87–88.
97. Castillo, "Gender Status Decline, Resistance, and Accommodation," 78–79; Hackel, *Children of Coyote*, 264–65.
98. Castañeda, "Malinche, Calafia, y Toypurina," 75; Castillo, "Gender Status Decline, Resistance, and Accommodation," 79–80; Hackel, *Children of Coyote*, 266.
99. Castillo, "Gender Status Decline, Resistance, and Accommodation," 80.
100. Sweet, "The Ibero-American Frontier Mission in Native American History," 1–48.
101. Hackel, *Children of Coyote*, 283.
102. Table 19. Annual Indian Adult Communions, Alta California Missions, 1814–1819 in Hackel, *Children of Coyote*, 176.

103. For San Gabriel Mission productions for these years, refer to *Annual Mission Report, San Gabriel Mission, 1824*. Santa Barbara Mission Archive Library (Santa Barbara, CA).
104. Paul Farnsworth and Robert H. Jackson, "Cultural, Economic, and Demographic Change in the Missions of Alta California: The Case of Nuestra Señora de la Soledad," in *The New Latin American Mission History*, eds. Erick Langer and Robert H. Jackson (Lincoln: University of Nebraska Press, 1995), 118.
105. Farnsworth and Jackson, "Cultural, Economic, and Demographic Change," 118.
106. Hackel, *Children of Coyote*, 285.
107. Hackel, *Children of Coyote*, 287.
108. Hackel, *Children of Coyote*, 290.
109. Hackel, *Children of Coyote*, 287.
110. Hackel, *Children of Coyote*, 296.
111. Often contracts for Indian labor occurred between missions that had accompanying adjacent presidios. Although San Gabriel did not have an accompanying presidio, it provided laborers to the Santa Barbara and San Diego Presidios. See Hackel, *Children of Coyote*, 297.
112. Hackel, *Children of Coyote*, 309.
113. Hackel, *Children of Coyote*, 287.
114. Michael J. González, "Searching for the Feathered Serpent: Exploring the Origins of Mexican Culture in Los Angeles, 1830–1850" (Ph.D. diss., University of California, Berkeley, 1993), 35.
115. Hackel, *Children of Coyote*, 311.
116. Hackel, *Children of Coyote*, 311.
117. Lieutenant Francisco Ortega to Governor Pedro Fages, April 1784, letter, California Archive, folder 176, box 22; cited in William M. Mason, "*Fages' Code of Conduct Toward Indians, 1787*," *Journal of California Anthropology* 2, no. 1 (Summer 1975): 95.
118. Hackel, *Children of Coyote*, 311.
119. Hackel, *Children of Coyote*, 311.
120. Mason, "Fages' Code of Conduct Toward Indians," 90–100.
121. Mason, "Fages' Code of Conduct Toward Indians," 97.
122. Haas, *Conquests and Historical Identities*, 9.
123. Hackel, *Children of Coyote*, 311.
124. Nancy Van Deusen, *Between the Sacred and the Worldly: The Institutional and Cultural Practice of Recogimiento in Colonial Lima* (Stanford, Calif.: Stanford University Press, 2001), 12. For a discussion of transculturation, see Fernando Ortíz, *Contrapunteo Cubano del Tabaco y el Azúcar* [Cuban Counterpoint, Tobacco and Sugar] (Havana, Cuba: Jésus Montero, 1940).
125. Barbara L. Voss, "From Casta to Californio: Social Identity and the Archaeology of Culture Contact," *American Anthropologist*, 107, No. 3 (September 2005): 461–74.
126. The casta system was put into place in all of colonial Spain's holding. Here I specifically refer to the system within New Spain. R. Douglas Cope, *The Limits of*

Racial Domination: Plebeian Society in Colonial Mexico City, 1660-1720 (Madison: University of Wisconsin Press, 1994), 18–19.

127. Voss, "From Casta to Californio," 462.
128. New Spain refers to Spain's colonial holdings in North America. The interior of New Spain describes the areas comprising present-day Mexico. Cheryl Martin and Mark Wasserman, *Latin America and Its People* (New York: Pearson Longman, 2005), 169.
129. Voss, "From Casta to Californio," 462.
130. Haas, *Conquests and Historical Identities*, 31.
131. Haas, *Conquests and Historical Identities*, 31.
132. Haas, *Conquests and Historical Identities*, 32; Rosaura Sánchez, *Telling Identities: The Californio Testimonios* (Minneapolis: University of Minnesota Press, 1995), 57, 59; Barbara L. Voss, *The Archeology of Ethnogenesis: Race and Sexuality in Colonial San Francisco* (Gainesville: University Press of Florida, 2015), 2.
133. Patricia Seed, "Social Dimensions of Race: Mexico City, 1753," *Hispanic American Historical Review* 62, no. 4 (November 1982): 569.
134. Barbara L. Voss, "A Land of Ethnogenesis: Material Culture, Power, and Identity," in *Contemporary Issues in California Archaeology*, ed. Terry L. Jones, et al. (Walnut Creek, Calif.: Left Coast Press, 2012), 306.
135. R. Douglas Cope, *Limits of Racial Domination*, 19.
136. Cheryl E. Martin, *Governance and Society in Colonial Mexico: Chihuahua in the Eighteenth Century* (Stanford, Calif.: Stanford University Press, 1996), 44.
137. Haas, *Conquests and Historical Identities*, 25.
138. Voss, "A Land of Ethnogenesis," 306.
139. Steven Hackel, *Children of Coyote*, 294.
140. Martin, *Governance and Society in Colonial Mexico*, 39.
141. Haas, *Conquests and Historical Identities*, 31; Sánchez, *Telling Identities*, 57; Seed, "Social Dimensions of Race," 569.
142. Voss, "A Land of Ethnogenesis," 306. In his study on New Mexico. Gutierrez found that this resulted from the polarization of racial labels between 1760 and 1846 into español or indio (Gutierrez, *When Jesus Came, the Corm Mothers Went Away*, 193).
143. Heidenreich, *This Land Was Mexican Once*, 59–60; Martin, *Governance and Society*, 148; Voss, "A Land of Ethnogenesis," 306.
144. Stuart Hall, "Cultural Identity and Diaspora," in *Identity: Community, Culture, Difference*, ed. Jonathan Rutherford (London: Lawrence and Wishart, 1990), 225.
145. Matrimonial investigations were used to help uncover behaviors such as bigamy and familial desertion as well as to prohibit marriage between persons sharing close consanguine relations. San Gabriel Mission Matrimonial Investigation Records, McPherson Collection, Special Collections, Honnold Mudd Library, Claremont University Consortium (Claremont, CA).
146. Ross Frank, *From Settler to Citizen: New Mexico Development and the Creation of the Vecino Society* (Berkeley: University of California Press, 2001), 1.
147. Frank, *From Settler to Citizen*, 291.

148. The term was often used in missionaries' annual reports to refer to neophyte Indians residents within missions. In the San Gabriel Matrimonial Investigations, the term was used more broadly to describe the location in which a person lived: presidio or pueblo, for example. For early use of the term see, J. N. Bowman "The Neophyte Residents (Existentes) of the California Missions, 1769–1834," *Historical Society of Southern California Quarterly* 40, no. 2 (June 1958): 138–48.
149. Frank, *From Settler to Citizen*, 178.
150. Frank, *From Settler to Citizen*, 178–80.
151. Frank, *From Settler to Citizen*, 201–2; Omar Valerio-Jimenez, *River of Hope: Forging Identity and Nation in the Rio Grande Borderlands* (Durham, N.C.: Duke University Press, 2013), 23–27; 37.
152. The term was used throughout Spain's northern provinces. Vecino identity and culture, although similar, developed within the specifics of each region. For New Mexico, see Frank, *From Settler to Citizen*; for Texas, see Valerio-Jimenez, *River of Hope*; and for Sonora, see Cynthia Radding, *Wandering Peoples: Colonialism, Ethnic Spaces, and Ecological Frontiers in Northwestern Mexico, 1700–1850* (Durham, N.C.: Duke University Press, 2007).
153. "Juan José Duarte, soltero, hijo de José Duarte y Juana Gertrudis originantes del Real de Los Alamos y dijo que de su propio voluntad quería contraer matrimonio según el orden de Nuestra Iglesia . . . con una Gertrudis Moreno, hija de José Moreno y María Guadalupe vecinos del Pueblo de la Reyna de Los Angeles." Matrimonial Investigation of Juan José Duarte and María Gertrudis Moreno, 11 November 1798, San Gabriel Mission Matrimonial Investigation Records, McPherson Collection, Special Collections, Honnold Mudd Library, Claremont University Consortium (Claremont, CA).
154. The Huntington Library, Early California Population Project Database, 2006. Marriage Register Data, Juan José Duarte and Gertrudis Moreno, http://missions.huntington.org/MarriageData.aspx?ID=1992.
155. Padrón de 1781, cited in Antonio Ríos-Bustmante, *Mexican Los Angeles: A Narrative and Pictorial History* (Moorpark, Calif.: Floricanto Press, 1992), 42–43.
156. As cited in the Los Angeles Census of 1790 contained in William M. Mason's *The Census of 1790: A Demographic History of Colonial California* (Banning, Calif.: Ballena Press, 1998), 84.
157. The Picos were one of the most prominent families in California. Different branches of the family intermarried with other well-known families such as the Alvarado and Avila clans. See the Pio Pico Genealogy, Pio Pico Inc., accessed March 18, 2018, http://web.archive.org/web/20110718232021/http://www.piopico.org/The_Family_Genealogy_of_Pio_Pico.htm.
158. Se presento a fin de contarer matrimonio según el orden de nuestra iglesia José Miguel Pico, soltero, originario de la villa de Sinaloa, hijo de Santiago Pico de la Cruz, y de María Jacinta Bastidos, y soldado de Santa Barbara; y dijo que de su libre espontánea voluntad quería casarse con María Casilda de la Cruz, soltera, habitante de el Pueblo de los Angeles, originantes de la Mission de Santa Clara de

esta N. [Nueva] California, hija de [José] Francisco Sinoba, y de María Gertrudis Bojoya, vecinos del mensionado pueblo. Matrimonial Investigation of José Miguel Pico and María Casilda de la Cruz Sinova, 31 October 1794, San Gabriel Mission Matrimonial Investigation Records, McPherson Collection, Special Collections, Honnold Mudd Library, Claremont University Consortium (Claremont, CA).

159. Mason, *The Census of 1790*, 85, 90.
160. Martin, *Governance and Society in Colonial Mexico*, 128.
161. Matrimonial Investigation of José Miguel Pico and María Casilda de la Cruz Sinova, 31 October 1794, San Gabriel Mission Matrimonial Investigation Records, McPherson Collection, Special Collections, Honnold Mudd Library, Claremont University Consortium (Claremont, Calif.).
162. Frank, *From Settler to Citizen*, 180.
163. Frank, *From Settler to Citizen*, 179; Kent G. Lightfoot, Indians, Missionaries, and Merchants: *The Legacy of Colonial Encounters on the California Frontiers* (Berkeley: University of California Press, 2006), 68.

CHAPTER 2

1. Bolton, "The Mission as a Frontier Institution," 46–47.
2. Oakah Jones, *Los Paisanos: Spanish Settlers on the Northern Frontier of New Spain* (Norman: University of Oklahoma Press, 1996), 207–8.
3. *Annual Mission Report, San Gabriel Mission, 1824*, Santa Barbara Mission Archive Library (Santa Barbara, CA); Robert H. Jackson, "The Changing Economic Structure of the Alta California Missions: A Reinterpretation," *Pacific Historical Review* 61, no. 4 (May 1992): 406. The production of corn during this year was also low, but it was higher than the amount of wheat produced. Missionaries attempted to grow barley but the number of fanegas for the entire period was 757.
4. Jackson, "The Changing Economic Structure," 412.
5. Robert Archibald, *Economic Aspects of the California Missions* (Berkeley, Calif.: Academy of American Franciscan History, 1978), 104–5; Julia G. Costello, "Purchasing Patterns of the California Missions," *Historical Archaeology* 26, no. 1 (1992): 59–63. For a discussion about Los Angeles' reliance on the mission for these products, see Michael J. González, "Searching for the Feathered Serpent," 35–75.
6. José de Gálvez, Reglamentos acordados y contenidos con el Padre Presidente de las Misiónes [Agreed upon regulations and contents with the father president of the missions], 30 November 1768, La Paz, Junípero Serra Collection, Folder 151, Santa Barbara Mission Archive Library (Santa Barbara, CA).
7. Rafael Verger to Manuel Lans de Casafonda, Mexico, June 30, 1771, Archivo General Naciónal, Coleción de Documentos para la Historia de Mexico, Segunda Serie, Bol. 15 (cited in Archibald, *Economic Aspects of the California Missions*).
8. Junipero Serra to Bucareli to Don Fray Antonio María Bucareli y Ursúa, Representación, 30 March 1773, Junípero Serra Collection, Folder 327, Santa Barbara Mission Archive Library (Santa Barbara, CA).

9. Castañeda, "Sexual Violence in the Policies and Politics of Conquest," 15–33.
10. Rose Marie Beebe and Robert M. Senkewicz, *Junípero Serra: California, Indians, and the Transformation of a Missionary* (Norman: University of Oklahoma, 2015), 238–40.
11. The Echeveste Reglamento, May 19, 1773, reprinted in Francisco Palou, *Historical Memoirs of New California*, trans. and ed. Herbert E. Bolton, 4 vols. (Berkeley: University of California Press, 1926), 1: 58–77.
12. Archibald, *Economic Aspects of the California Missions*, 10.
13. "Sowings and harvest at San Gabriel," J. N. Bowman Papers Regarding California History, BANC MSS C-R 18, Spanish Archives, Bancroft Library, University of California, Berkeley.
14. Jackson, "The Formation of Frontier Indigenous Communities," 132.
15. In the late 1780s, the Spanish government reluctantly agreed to allow Spanish merchants to enter into the Sea otter trade as a way to limit the Russian and English presence in the region. For more on the Spanish establishment of the sea otter trade, see Adele Ogden's classic work, *The California Sea Otter Trade, 1784–1848* (Berkeley: University of California Press, 1941), 15–31.
16. During the late eighteenth century, the Bourbon Reforms changed Spain's mercantilist policies. The Crown attempted to strengthen colonial defenses, improve administration, and limit spending while simultaneously producing revenue for Spain. See Edward Castillo and Robert H. Jackson, *Indians, Franciscans, and Spanish Colonization: The Impact of the Mission System on California Indians* (Albuquerque: University of New Mexico Press, 1995), 26.
17. Archibald, *Economic Aspects of the California Missions*, 13.
18. Farnsworth and Jackson, "Cultural, Economic, and Demographic Change," 110.
19. Archibald, *Economic Aspects of the California Missions*, 14.
20. Archibald, *Economic Aspects of the California Missions*, 17.
21. Lasuén to Ugarte, Monterey, 12 October 1787, letter, California Mission Documents, folder 69, Santa Barbara Mission Archive Library (Santa Barbara, CA).
22. Archibald, *Economic Aspects of the California Missions*, 18.
23. Alta California's place in the Spanish borderlands replicated economic and social conditions present in other borderland regions, mainly in terms of the need to create community and negotiate for survival despite differences. For Texas, see Jesús de la Teja, "Discovering the Tejano Community in 'Early' Texas," *Journal of the Early Republic* 18, no. 1 (Spring 1998), 73–98, and Armando Alonzo, *Tejano Legacy: Rancheros and Settlers in South Texas, 1734–1900* (Albuquerque: University of New Mexico Press, 1998). For Sonora, see Miguel Tinker-Salas, *In the Shadow of the Eagle: Sonora and the Transformation of the Border During the Porfiriato* (Berkeley: University of California Press, 1997); Thomas E. Sheridan, *Los Tucsonenses: The Mexican Community in Tucson, 1854–1941* (Tucson: University of Arizona Press, 1986); and Cynthia Radding, *Wandering Peoples*. For New Mexico, see Charles Montgomery, *The Spanish Redemption: Heritage, Power, and Loss on New Mexico's Upper Rio Grande* (Berkeley: University of California Press, 2002). For a general

collection pertaining to borderland negotiation, see Donna Guy and Thomas Sheridan, *Contested Ground: Comparative Frontiers on the Northern and Southern Edges of the Spanish Empire* (Tucson: University of Arizona Press, 1998).

24. Ogden, *The California Sea Otter Trade*, 116–18.
25. Archibald, *Economic Aspects of the California Missions*, 117–18; Hackel, *Children of Coyote*, 278.
26. Although the official policy made the otter trade illegal, it was quite profitable, and officials quite likely knew that the trade continued despite the official end. This clandestine trade was made possible through a network of military and mission personnel, as well as civilians.
27. Costello, "Purchasing Patterns of the California Missions," 62.
28. Costello, "Purchasing Patterns of the California Missions," 62. The amounts detailed in the ship's ledger reflect the total received at each mission as well as the total amounts netted throughout the region. Costello posited that the totals are an indication of the population of each mission.
29. Costello, "Purchasing Patterns of the California Missions," 62.
30. Ogden, *The California Sea Otter Trade*, 20–24.
31. "Periodization of the History of California Agriculture," J. N. Bowman Papers Regarding California History, BANC MSS C-R18, carton 3, folder 17. Spanish Archives, Bancroft Library, University of California, Berkeley.
32. The decade-long war devastated both mining and agriculture. The mining industry, on which the Mexican economy relied, collapsed due to lack of workers, many of whom left to join the war effort. Agricultural and livestock production declined because crops were destroyed, and livestock were slaughtered.
33. El Pueblo de Los Angeles was second to the San Gabriel Mission in wheat production. Many of Pueblo's inhabitants were not interested in farming; therefore, settlers obtained their wheat from the mission. For discussion on this topic, see González, "Searching for the Feathered Serpent," 35–75.
34. Archibald, *Economic Aspects of the California Missions*, 95.
35. Archibald, *Economic Aspects of the California Missions*, 7; David J. Weber, *The Mexican Frontier, 1821–1846: The American Southwest Under Mexico* (Albuquerque: University of New Mexico Press, 1982), 11.
36. Archibald, *Economic Aspects of the California Missions*, 97.
37. California State Archives, Provincial State Papers, Benicia, Vol 1XXIX, 653. Cited in Zephyrin Engelhardt, *San Gabriel Mission and the Beginnings of Los Angeles* (Chicago: Franciscan Herald Press, 1927), 134: Archibald, *Economic Aspects of the California Missions*, 104–5.
38. Archibald, *Economic Aspects of the California Missions*, 62.
39. Archibald, *Economic Aspects of the California Missions*, 124.
40. Archibald, *Economic Aspects of the California Missions*, 125.
41. J. N. Bowman Papers Regarding California History, BANC MSS C-R18, item 70, Spanish Archives, Bancroft Library, University of California, Berkeley. Used to measure the volume of dry goods as well as land size, the fanega was not a stan-

dardized measurement and often reflected regional conditions, but it was generally about 1.5 bushels. The term *fanega de sembradura* indicated the area of land that could be sown with a fanega of grain. See J. N. Bowman, "Weights and Measurements of Provincial California," *California Historical Quarterly* 30, no. 4 (December 1951): 318–19, 323.

42. Bowman, "Weights and Measurements of Provincial California," 323. For a discussion on weights and measurements in other areas of New Spain throughout the colonial period, see Manuel Carrera Stampa, "Evolution of Weights and Measurements in New Spain," *Hispanic: American Historical Review* 29, no. 1 (February 1949): 2–24.
43. Archibald, *Economic Aspects of the California Missions*, 121–22.
44. Pubols, *The Father of All*, 44.
45. Pubols, *The Father of All*, 45.
46. Pubols, *The Father of All*, 45.
47. "Angustias de la Guerra Ord: Occurrences in Hispanic California," in *Nineteenth Century Testimonials*, eds. Rosaura Sánchez, Beatrice Pita, and Bárbara Reyes (La Jolla: University of California, San Diego, 1994), 235.
48. Eugene P. Moehring, *Urbanism and Empire in the Far West, 1840–1890* (Reno: University of Nevada Press. 2004), 62.
49. William Hartnell was able to establish a successful relationship with Fr. Payéras, who then gave him permission to enter into three-year contracts with individual missions. See Weber, *The Mexican Frontier*, 138, and Casas, *Married to a Daughter of the Land*, 54.
50. José María Zalvidea, carta a Hartnell, San Gabriel, 7 April 1823, folder 130, Spanish Archives, Bancroft Library, University of California, Berkeley.
51. José María Zalvidea, carta a Hartnell, San Gabriel, 15 April 1823, Archivo de las Misiónes, BANC C-C4–5, folder 131, Spanish Archives, Bancroft Library, University of California, Berkeley.
52. This was not unique to Hartnell or to Alta California. Anglos were easily incorporated into the social structure in this early period because their numbers were so low that they did not threaten existing social structures.
53. For details of this courtship see Casas, *Married to a Daughter of the Land*, 54–61.
54. Pubols, *The Father of All*, 118.
55. Archibald, *Economic Aspects of the California Missions*, 185.
56. Teresa De La Guerra Hartnell's father was José de la Guerra, large land owner and former purchasing agent for the Santa Barbara Mission. He owned more than 35,000 acres of private land. She was married to former trader William Hartnell.
57. "I have heard many people that, without being current on how things have changed over time, use a thousand denigrating epithets towards the reverend missionaries." María Teresa de la Guerra Hartnell, *Narrativa de la distinguida matrona californiana*, BANC MSS C-E 67, 19, Bancroft Library, University of California, Berkeley.
58. Confío que gente de mi raza que han preciado la conducta de eso dignos ministros de Dios dejaran de reconocer que la civilización es deudora mas a ellos del

progreso que ha hecho esta, mi patria que el estranjero. Tal sin niguna excepción fue la Buena conducta que los padres misioneros observaron en la Alta California desde el dia 3 de 1770 hasta 1833. No tengo embarazo en hacer esta aserción pues mis abuelos y parientes, verdaderos fundadores de este pais, me han contado. Tengo referido, y yo misma he preciado, muchos actos meritorios de los reverendos padres misioneros cuyas virtudes he admirado cuando joven gozaba de los placeres de este mundo y que fui madre de viente varones y cinco hembras con un pie en la tumba recuerdo *con la mas* completa satisfacción. de la Guerra Hartnell, *Narrativa de la distinguida matrona californiana*, 20.

59. Antonio Rios-Bustamante, "Los Angeles, Pueblo and Region, 1781–1850: Continuation and Adaptation on the North Mexican Periphery" (Ph.D. diss., University of California, Los Angeles, 1985), 83.
60. After Mexican independence, nineteenth century Mexican liberal discourse reflected the social, economic, and political contours of classic liberalism that emphasized tenets of democracy, secularism, individual freedom, and property rights. These ideals that had fueled the end of colonial rule in Mexico became more widespread during the early years of the independent Mexican Republic. As the liberal discourse spread throughout the Mexican interior and into its borderland regions, liberal ideals often took shape according to the specific social, cultural, and economic contours of a given location. See Sánchez, *Telling Identities*, 99.
61. Sánchez, *Telling Identities*, 97.
62. Sánchez, *Telling Identities*, 97.
63. Sánchez, *Telling Identities*, 103.
64. Charles Hale, *The Transformation of Liberalism in Late Nineteenth-Century Mexico* (Princeton, N.J.: Princeton University Press, 1989), 4.
65. Brian Connaughton, "The Enemy Within: Catholics and Liberalism in Independent Mexico, 1821–1860," in *The Divine Charter: Constitutionalism and Liberalism in Nineteenth-Century Mexico*, ed. Jaime E. Rodríguez (Lanham, Md.: Rowman and Littlefield, 2005), 183–202.
66. Alison Lake, *Colonial Rosary: The Spanish and Indian Missions of California* (Athens: Ohio University Press, 2014), 92.
67. Connaughton, "The Enemy Within," 184–85.
68. Sánchez, *Telling Identities*, 101–3.
69. Sánchez, *Telling Identities*, 97.
70. Hale, *The Transformation of Liberalism*, 4.
71. Hale, *The Transformation of Liberalism*, 4.
72. Juan Bandini became one of the largest land owners in California. Under Governor Juan Bautista Alvarado, who served from 1836–1842, Bandini received the 40,569-acre Rancho Jurupa, and 4,431-acre Rancho El Rincón. See Juan Bandini, "A Statistical Description of Alta California," in Rose Marie Beebe and Robert M. Senkewicz, ed., *Land of Promise and Despair: Chronicles of Alta California, 1535–1846* (Santa Clara, Calif.: Santa Clara University: 2001), 380. Both these land case files can be found at Bancroft Library, BANC MSS Land Case Files 1852–1892, 263SD

and 297SD, respectively. Collection of the Bancroft Library, Documents Pertaining to the Adjudication of Private Land Claims in California, University of California Berkeley.

73. Bandini, "A Statistical Description of Alta California," 385.
74. David Hornbeck, "Land Tenure and Rancho Expansion in Alta California, 1784–1846," *Journal of Historical Geography* 4, no. 4 (October 1978): 379.
75. Hornbeck, "Land Tenure and Rancho Expansion in Alta California," 379.

CHAPTER 3

1. Jackson and Castillo, *Indians, Franciscans, and Spanish Colonization*, 88–89.
2. Gómez Farías, originally Santa Anna's vice president, assumed the presidential duties in Santa Ann's absence from Mexico City. For detail on his anticlerical platform, see Charles A. Hale, *Mexican Liberalism in the Age of Mora, 1821–1853* (New Haven, Conn.: Yale University, 1968), 160.
3. Jackson and Castillo, *Indians, Franciscans, and Spanish Colonization*, 89.
4. Jackson and Castillo, *Indians, Franciscans, and Spanish Colonization*; Casas, *Married to a Daughter of the Land*, 129.
5. Sánchez, *Telling Identities*, 64.
6. Sánchez, *Telling Identities*, 64.
7. Ray Allen Billington and Martin Ridge, *Westward Expansion: A History of the American Frontier*, 6th ed. (Albuquerque: University of New Mexico Press, 2001), 193–94; William Carey Jones, *On the Subject of Land Titles in California Made in Pursuance of Instruction from the Secretary of State and the Secretary of the Interior* (Washington, D.C.: Gideon, 1850), 4–5; Weber, *The Mexican Frontier*, 162–63.
8. Billington and Ridge, *Westward Expansion*, 194.
9. Paul W. Gates, *Land and Law in California: Essays on Land Policies* (Ames: Iowa State University Press, 1991), 6.
10. A detailed discussion of land grant procedures can be found in Hornbeck, "Land Tenure and Rancho Expansion in Alta California," 371–90.
11. Documents can be found in the Spanish Mexican Land Grants Index, California State Archives. File numbers are as follows: Pérez and Enrique Sépulveda and Garfías, vol. 3, 326, exp. 211; vol. 7, 321, unclass. exp. 77; vol. 7, 369, unclass. exp. 77; vol. 3, 20, exp. 157; vol. 3, 20, exp. 157; Gallardo and Villa, vol. 3, 596, exp. 258.
12. Haas, *Conquests and Historical Identities*, 34.
13. Haas, *Conquests and Historical Identities*, 34.
14. Haas, *Conquests and Historical Identities*, 34.
15. Hackel, *Children of Coyote*, 376; Covadonga Lamar Prieto, "Landownership as a Resources for Constructing Otherness in 19th Century California," in *Otherness in Hispanic Culture*, ed. Teresa Fernández Ulloa (Newcastle upon Tyne, England: Cambridge Scholars Publishing, 2014), 295.
16. Hackel, *Children of Coyote*, 376–77.

17. Hackel, *Children of Coyote*, 376.
18. Haas, *Conquests and Historical Identities*, 38.
19. Haas, *Conquests and Historical Identities*, 34; Hackel, *Children of Coyote*, 376–77.
20. Haas, *Conquests and Historical Identities*, 34; Hackel, *Children of Coyote*, 377, 381–82.
21. Eulalia Pérez, "Una vieja y sus recuerdos dictados,"14–18.
22. Pérez, "Una vieja y sus recuerdos dictados," 15.
23. Haas, *Conquests and Historical Identities*, 35.
24. Chávez-García, *Negotiating Conquest*, 19; Haas, *Conquests and Historical Identities*, 35; Sánchez, *Telling Identities*, 126–28. For more on the Híjar-Padrés colony, see C. Alan Hutchinson, *Frontier Settlement in Mexican California: The Híjar-Padrés Colony, and its Origins, 1769–1835*. Yale Western Americana Series 21. (New Haven, Conn.: Yale University Press, 1969).
25. Casas, *Married to a Daughter of the Land*, 128.
26. Haas, *Conquests and Historical Identities*, 35.
27. Haas, *Conquests and Historical Identities*, 35.
28. Sánchez, *Telling Identities*, 67.
29. Sánchez, *Telling Identities*, 66.
30. Sánchez, *Telling Identities*, 66–67.
31. Douglas Monroy, "The Creation and Re-Creation of Californio Society," in *Contested Eden: California Before the Gold Rush*, eds. Ramón A. Gutiérrez and Richard J. Orsi (Berkeley: University of California Press, 1998), 182.
32. Hackel, *Children of Coyote*, 389.
33. Antonio Ríos-Bustamante, *Mexican Los Angeles: A Narrative and Pictorial History* (Encino, Calif.: Floricanto Press, 1992),88.
34. Martha Menchaca, *Recovering History, Constructing Race: The Indian, Black and White Roots of Mexican Americans* (Austin: University of Texas Press, 2001), 206.
35. Haas, *Conquests and Historical Identities*, 39; Menchaca, *Recovering History*, 206–7.
36. Haas, *Conquests and Historical Identities*, 40–41.
37. Hackel, *Children of Coyote*, 398.
38. Haas, *Conquests and Historical Identities*, 35–37; Sánchez, *Telling Identities*, 131.
39. J. W. Wood, *Pasadena, California, Historical and Personal: A Complete History of the Indiana Colony* (Boston: Harvard University Press, 1917), 30.
40. J. M. Guinn, *A History of California and an Extended History of Its Southern Coast Counties*, (Los Angeles: Historic Record Company, 1907), 1: 384.
41. This connection to the mission was not uncommon; various Californios' testimonios discuss the importance of the mission and its work. See Sánchez, *Telling Identities*, 66–68.
42. Historical records contain several variations of Juan Mariné's last name, for example, Mariné, Marin, and Mariner.
43. Juan Mariner, Expediente sobre el paraje nombrado Rincon de San Pascual, Solicitado por Don Juan Mariner, Record on the place called Rincon de San Pascual, Solicited by Don Juan Mariner, vol. 2, 236, exp. 237. California State Archives, Spanish Mexican Land Grants.

44. Hiram Reid, *History of Pasadena* (Pasadena: Pasadena History Co., 1895), 62; Wood, *Pasadena, California*, 30–31.
45. Guinn, *A History of California*, 384.
46. Guinn, *A History of California*, 384.
47. Jack D. Forbes, *Native Americans of California and Nevada* (Happy Camp, Calif.: Naturegraph Publishers, 1969), 28.
48. Hubert Howe Bancroft, *History of California* (San Francisco: A.L. Bancroft and Co. Publishers, 1884), 1: 607; M. M. Livingston, "The Earliest Spanish Land Grants in California," *Annual Publication of the Historical Society of Southern California* 9, no. 3 (1914): 195–96; William Wood, "The Trajectory of Indian Country in California: Rancherias, Villages, Pueblos, Missions, Ranchos, Reservations, Colonies, and Rancherias," *Tulsa Law Review* 44 (2013): 317, 321–22.
49. Bancroft, *History of California*, 1: 607.
50. Wood, *Pasadena, California*, 30–32.
51. Pérez, "Una vieja y sus recuerdos dictados," 13; Wood, *Pasadena, California*, 30–32.
52. No me quería casar. Pérez, "Una vieja y sus recuerdos dictados," 13, 128.
53. William Wilcox Robinson, *Land in California: The Story of Mission Lands, Ranchos, Squatters, Mining Claims, Railroad Grants, Land Scrip and Homesteads* (Berkeley: University of California Press, 1948), 82.
54. Cuando Padre Sánchez me dio dos ranchos, más bien, tierra para un rancho y para una huerta; cuando me entregó la tierra [yo] ya estaba casada con Juan Mariné. Pérez, "Una vieja y sus recuerdos dictados," 28.
55. For discussion of women's rights in marriage in New Mexico, see González, *Refusing the Favor*; for women's rights in California, see Miroslava Chávez-García, *Negotiating Conquest*.
56. Después el [Mariné] no me entregó más que la mitad de la tierra y se quedó con la otra mitad. Pérez, "Una vieja y sus recuerdos dictados," 28.
57. González, *Refusing the Favor*, 22.
58. González, *Refusing the Favor*, 22, 93. González argued that, under the Spanish family laws established under the Laws of Toro in 1369, women were granted the right to defend their inheritances, property, and goods brought into or acquired during their marriage. Husbands were to keep, protect, and preserve women's estates.
59. Pérez, "Una vieja y sus recuerdos dictado," 13.
60. Para darmelos [tierra para un rancho y para una huerta], juntó toda la indiada en el Colegio el Padre Zalvidea les habló en su lengua, y les preguntó si quisiéran darme ese terreno para huerta y para rancho, por que yo los habia cuidado y atendido siempre que los que querian levantaran la mano. Toda la indiada a una levantó las manos, diciendo que sí querían. Pérez, "Una vieja y sus recuerdos dictado," 28.
61. "Juan Mariner teniente retirado de artillería de Departamento de Mejico en la Alta California, y avecindado en la Misión de San Gabriel y por haber tenido la desgracia de averme llevado la inundación que hubo en el año de 1831 una huerta que tenia en el pueblo de Los Angeles, pase a la Mision de San Gabriel con el Reverendo Padre Sánchez, para que me hiciera favor de darme un pedas[z]o de

tierra, para sembrar, y fabricar casa y un sitío, para tener, mi ganado. Lo cual se hizo una junta de los alcaldes . . . [en] la junta dijieron los alcaldes, que estaba bueno [y] que si me lo darían, y les dijo el padre que no era para un año o dos, sinó que para siempre, pues todos respondieron, que estaba bueno, pués luego tomaron providencia de medir las tierras y darme el sitío, para tener el ganado llamandose el Rincón de San Pascual, con tres leguas en contorno." (author's translation). Juan Mariner, Expediente sobre el paraje nombrado Rincón de San Pascual, Solicitado por Don Juan Mariner, vol. 2, 236. Spanish Mexican Land Grants, California State Archives.

62. Teniente retirado de artillería del Departamento de Méjico en Alta California y avecindado en la Misión de San Gabriel. Juan Mariner, 15 July 1833, Expediente sobre el paraje nombrado Rincón de San Pascual.
63. Juan Mariner, 28 December 1833, Expediente sobre el paraje nombrado Rincón de San Pascual, Solicitado por Don Juan Mariner, vol. 2, 236, Spanish Mexican Land Grants, California State Archives.
64. Juan Mariner, 28 December 1833, Expediente sobre el paraje nombrado Rincón de San Pascual.
65. This phrase was part of the official/formal format of petitions for land allotments. It is present at the beginning of Mexican expediente files relating to San Pascual.
66. Eulalia Pérez requested a portion of the land in 1840 after the land was granted to José Pérez.
67. Fruto Mariner, vol. A-1053–1058, Los Angeles County Prefecture Records, Huntington Library, San Marino, California; English translation.
68. Mariner, vol. A-1053–1058, Los Angeles County Prefecture Records.
69. Francisco Villa, vol. 3, 596–659, Spanish Mexican Land Grants, California State Archives. The Spanish *vara*, literally meaning rod, was the most commonly used lineal measurement in Alta California. *Cordeleros* (land surveyors) used it to determine the length of the *cordel* or land surveyor's chain when measuring land. In Alta California, the standard measurement for the vara was approximately thirty-three and one third inches. One thousand varas totaled 4,340.28 acres. For more on the vara and other Spanish measurements see J. N. Bowman, "Weights and Measures of Provincial California," *California Historical Society Quarterly* 30, no. 4 (December 1951): 315–38.
70. Francisco Villa to Governor Alvarado, 11 July 1838, vol. 3, 596, Spanish Mexican Land Grants, California State Archives.
71. Villa to Alvarado, 11 July 1838, 596.
72. Villa to Alvarado, 11 July 1838, 596.
73. Bandini to Governor Alvarado, 20 July 1838, vol. 3, 597, Spanish Mexican Land Grants, California State Archives.
74. Alvarado to Bandini, 27 July 1838, vol. 3, 597, Spanish Mexican Land Grants, California State Archives.
75. Sepúlveda to Prefect Manuel Dominguez, 3 August 1839, vol. 7, 322, Spanish Mexican Land Grants, California State Archives.

76. Sepúlveda to Dominguez, 3 August 1839, vol. 7, 321, Spanish Mexican Land Grants, California State Archives.
77. Comisión de Terrenos Válidos a Ayuntamiento, 24, 1839, vol. 7, 322–23, Spanish Mexican Land Grants California State Archives.
78. Sepúlveda to Governor Alvarado, 10 February 1840, vol. 7, 369–70, Spanish Mexican Land Grants, California State Archives.
79. Casas, *Married to a Daughter of the Land*, 9; Castañeda, "Engendering the History of Alta California," 230–59; Haas, *Conquests and Historical Identities*, 73–75; Pubols, *The Father of All*, 32; Torres-Rouff, *Before L.A*, 56.
80. Sepúlveda to Alvarado, 10 February 1840, vol. 7, 370, Spanish Mexican Land Grants, California State Archives.
81. Sepúlveda to Alvarado, 10 February 1840. The term *güilos* does not appear in contemporary Spanish dictionaries. The *Diccionario de la Real Academia Española* relates the word to the term *tullida*, which means a person who has lost all bodily movement or of one of his/her body parts, possibly someone who is fully or partially paralyzed. In the document "habian dos dementes ó guilos" suggests that *güilos* is synonymous with *dementes*, which means someone who is not in his or her right mind or considered "crazy." In some regions of Mexico, *güila* is a slang term used when referring to a promiscuous woman. In this case, it seems to most closely relate to a simple-minded person.
82. Sepúlveda to Alvarado, 10 February 1840.
83. Sepúlveda to Alvarado, 10 February 1840.
84. For example, in her 1843 statement renouncing her deceased husband's claim to San Pascual, the widow María Merced Lugo stated that "mis hermanos varones se han dedicado al ramo de agricultura [por que] no es a propósito para me sexo" (my brothers have dedicated themselves to agriculture [because] it is not appropriate to my sex.). María Merced Lugo, 8 July 1843, vol. 7, 325, Spanish Mexican Land Grants, California State Archives.
85. González, *Refusing the Favor*, 21.
86. Concession to Sepúlveda and Peréz, vol. 3, 326, Spanish Mexican Land Grants, California State Archives.
87. Manuel Garfias to Manuel Micheltorena, 10 June 1843, vol. 7, 321, Spanish Mexican Land Grants, California State Archives.
88. Pubols, *The Father of All*, 58.
89. For a discussion of marriage, see Almaguer, *Racial Fault Lines*; Casas, *Married to a Daughter of the Land*; Castañeda, "Engendering the History of Alta California," 230–59; Chávez-García, *Negotiating Conquest*; and González, *Refusing the Favor*.
90. Manuel Garfias and María Luisa Avila, Matrimonial Investigation, San Gabriel Mission Matrimonial Investigation Records, McPherson Collection, Honnold Mudd Library, Claremont University Consortium.
91. Garfias and Avila, Matrimonial Investigation, 1–3.

92. Garfias and Avila, Matrimonial Investigation, 13.
93. Manuel Micheltorena to Prefect Manuel Dominguez, 12 June 1843, vol. 7, 323, Spanish Mexican Land Grants, California State Archives.
94. Antonio José Coronel to Prefect Dominguez, 30 June 1843, vol. 7, 324, Spanish Mexican Land Grants, California State Archives.
95. Coronel to Dominguez, 30 June 1843.
96. Coronel to Dominguez, 30 June 1843.
97. Manuel Domínguez to Governor Manuel Micheltorena, 1 July 1843, vol. 7, 324, Spanish Mexican Land Grants, California State Archives.
98. Domínguez to Micheltorena, 1 July 1843.
99. Enrique Sepúlveda to Prefect Dominguez, 7 July 1843, vol. 7, 325, Spanish Mexican Land Grants, California State Archives.
100. Sepúlveda to Dominguez, 7 July 1843, vol. 7, 325.
101. Domínguez to Governor Micheltorena, 10 July 1843, vol.7, 324.
102. María Merced Lugo to Prefect Dominguez, 8 July 1843, vol. 7, 325–26, Spanish Mexican Land Grants, California State Archives.
103. Manuel Garfias to Governor Micheltorena, 12 July 1843, vol. 7, 326–27, Spanish Mexican Land Grants, California State Archives.
104. Antonio José Coronel to Prefect Manuel Dominguez, 14 August 1843, vol. 7, 327–28, Spanish Mexican Land Grants, California State Archives.
105. The office or department to whom the petition was directed depended on the size of the land applicants wanted. Petitions for small portions of land, mainly for use as space to build a house, small-scale cultivation, and livestock grazing were directed to the prefecture; appeals for ranchos were directed to the governor. In the claims for ranchos, the prefecture would conduct the governmental investigation of the land claim and offer a recommendation to the governor.
106. Discursive practices in the Foucauldian sense refer to the manner in which language produces, creates, maintains, and subverts systems and institutions of power. Michel Foucault, *The History of Sexuality* (New York: Pantheon, 1978).
107. Steve J. Stern, *The Secret History of Gender: Women, Men, and Power in Late Colonial Mexico* (Chapel Hill: University of North Carolina Press, 1995), 161.
108. Manuel Antonio to Pío Pico, letter, vol. 7, 518–22, Spanish Mexican Land Grants, California State Archives.
109. Antonio to Pío Pico, vol. 7, 518–22.
110. Antonio to Pío Pico, vol. 7, 518–22.
111. Tomás Estenaga to Los Angeles Prefecture, letter, vol. 7, 518–22, Spanish Mexican Land Grants, California State Archives.
112. Manuel Antonio, vol. 5, 234–38, Spanish Mexican Land Grants, California State Archives; Chávez-García, *Negotiating Conquest*, 60–61.
113. Antonio to Pío Pico, vol. 7, 518–22.
114. Haas, *Conquests and Historical Identities*, 38.
115. Argüello was the son of José Darío Argüello, one of the original pobladores de Los Angeles and colonial governor of California. Santiago Argüello's brother, Luis

Antonio Argüello, served as Mexican governor from 1822 to 1825. Argüello was politically very well connected, having served as alcalde (mayor) of San Diego and second district prefecture for Los Angeles. He owned a tremendous amount of land in Alta California, having been awarded grants for the 22,184-acre Rancho Trabuco in present day Orange Country and the 58,875-acre former mission Rancho San Diego.

116. Santiago Argüello to Pío Pico, vol. 7, 518–22, Spanish Mexican Land Grants, California State Archives.

117. María Guirado married Irish American John Downey in 1852; Downey became California's seventh governor after the U. S- Mexico War. Lynn Cook and Janet Ladue, *The First Ladies of California* (Xlibris, 2007), 32–35; Rafael Guirado to Los Angeles Prefect, vol. 6, 156–57, Los Angeles County Prefecture Records, Huntington Library, San Marino, California.

118. Antonio María Lugo was the son of Francisco Salvador Lugo, one of the original pobladores of Los Angeles. Antonio María served as a distinguished soldier at Santa Barbara and in 1816 became alcalde de Los Angeles. In 1810 he received a Spanish land grant for the 29,513-acre Rancho San Antonio and in 1841 a grant for the 22,193-acre Rancho Santa Ana del Chino, part of the former San Gabriel Mission's land. He fathered eight children, five sons and three daughters, all of whom held prominent social positions. Daughter María Antonia married into the wealthy distinguished Yorba Family, supporting a very strong oligarchic bond. María Merced married José Pérez, cousin of Eulalía Pérez and owner of Rancho San Pascual. Six years after Pérez's death, in 1848, María Merced married the first American mayor of Los Angeles, Stephen C. Foster. In 1852, she launched an unsuccessful attempt to obtain title to Rancho San Pascual, land she had lost to Manual Garfías because of his denunciation for abandonment. For more information on Antonio María Lugo, see Roy E. Whitehead, *Lugo: A Chronicle of Early California* (San Bernardino, Calif.: San Bernardino Museum Association, 1978). For more on the marriages of these women, see Casas, *Married to a Daughter of the Land*, and Chávez-García, *Negotiating Conquest*. For Stephen Foster, see H. D. Barrow, "Stephen C. Foster," *Annual Publication of the Historical Society of Southern California and Pioneer Register, Los Angeles*, 4, no. 2 (1898): 179–83.

119. Antonio María Lugo to Los Angeles Prefect, vol. 1, 158–59A, Los Angeles County Prefecture Records, Huntington Library, San Marino, California.

120. Argüello to Pío Pico, vol. 7, 518–22.

121. Manuel Antonio, vol. 5, 234–38, Spanish Mexican Land Grants, California State Archives.

122. Marginal note to vol. 1, 156–57 and 158–59A, 7 August 1842, Los Angeles County Prefecture Records, Huntington Library, San Marino, California.

123. Serafino de Jesús, vol. 6, 1–2, Spanish Mexican Land Grants, California State Archives.

124. Serafino de Jesús, vol. 5, 458–60, Spanish Mexican Land Grants, California State Archives.

125. "Regarding Zerefino de Jesús," vol. 1, 408, Los Angeles, 12 May 1843, Los Angeles County Prefecture Records, Huntington Library, San Marino, California.
126. Files for ex-neophytes: Próspero, vol. 1, 396; Emilio Joaquín, vol. 1, 399; Valencia, vol. 1, 395. Los Angeles County Prefecture Records, Huntington Library, San Marino, California.
127. Emilio Joaquín, vol. 1, 399, Los Angeles County Prefecture Records, Huntington Library, San Marino, California.
128. This idea is informed by the work of theorist Ellie D. Hernández on what she terms postnationalism. Hernández, discussing how twentieth century transnationalism effects minority activism and civil rights, argued that Chicana/os and other minority groups experience a type of "dislocation in which they are caught or suspended between the national order and an emerging transnationalism." She presented postnationalism as a way in which "cultural national identity formation provided means of participation within a segregated society." Ellie D. Hernández, *Postnationalism in Chicana/o Literature and Culture* (Austin: University of Texas Press, 2009), 5–10.
129. The idea of doubling stems from the notion of third space and third space agency. This is an invaluable idea as it interrogates the power dynamics involved in the negotiations between dominant and marginal groups within larger nationalist projects. See Homi K. Bhaba, *The Location of Culture* (New York: Routledge Press, 1994), 86–88; Emma Pérez, *The Decolonial Imaginary*, 32–33.

CHAPTER 4

1. Michael J. González, *This Small City Will Be a Mexican Paradise: Exploring the Origins of Mexican Culture in Los Angeles, 1821–1846* (Albuquerque: University of New Mexico Press, 2005), 65–66.
2. For a discussion of marriage, see Almaguer, *Racial Fault Lines*; Casas, *Married to a Daughter of the Land*; Castañeda, "Engendering the History of Alta California," 230–59; Chávez-García, *Negotiating Conquest*; González, *Refusing the Favor*; and Heidenreich, *This Land Was Mexican Once*, 55–56.
3. Heidenreich, *This Land Was Mexican Once*, 75–76, 81.
4. David Torres-Rouff, *Before L.A.*, 106–7.
5. Miroslava Chávez-García, *Negotiating Conquest*, 67; González, *This Small City Will Be a Mexican Paradise*, 55–59; Monroy, "The Creation and Re-Creation of Californio Society," 178–79.
6. Chávez-García, *Negotiating Conquest*, 67.
7. Weber, *The Mexican Frontier*, 211.
8. Almaguer, *Racial Fault Lines*, 54–55; González, *This Small City Will Be a Mexican Paradise*, 58.
9. Sánchez, *Telling Identities*, 111, 116.
10. Almaguer, *Racial Fault Lines*, 47–48.
11. Monroy, *Thrown Among Strangers*, 115; Weber, *The Mexican Frontier*, 215.

12. Almaguer, *Racial Fault Lines*, 46; González, *This Small City Will be a Mexican Paradise*, 58–59; Haas, *Conquests and Historical Identities*, 31, 37; Heidenreich, *This Land Was Mexican Once*, 59–60.
13. Monroy, *Thrown Among Strangers*, 136–38.
14. Monroy, "The Creation and Re-Creation of Californio Society," 183; Monroy, *Thrown Among Strangers*, 145–46; González, *This Small City Will Be a Mexican Paradise*, 23–24.
15. González, *This Small City Will Be a Mexican Paradise*, 67; Steven W. Hackel, "Land, Labor, and Production: The Colonial Economy of Spanish and Mexican California," in *Contested Eden: California Before the Gold Rush*, ed. Ramón Gutiérrez and Richard J. Orsi, 111–46 (Berkeley: University of California Press, 1998), 134; Almaguer, *Racial Fault Lines*, 48–51.
16. González, This Small City Will Be a Mexican Paradise, 39. See also Weber, *The Mexican Frontier*, 212–13.
17. Almaguer, *Racial Fault Lines*, 51; Weber, *The Mexican Frontier*, 211.
18. Stephen Silliman, *Lost Laborers in Colonial California: Native Americans and the Archaeology of Rancho Petaluma* (Tucson: University of Arizona Press, 2004), 69.
19. Silliman, *Lost Laborers*, 69–70. In his testimonio José del Carmen Lugo detailed the specific jobs and methods used by ranch hands. José del Carmen Lugo, "Vida de un ranchero, 1877," BANC MSS C-D 118, 104–6. From the Collection of the Bancroft Library, Index of the Spanish-Mexican Private Land Records and Cases of California. University of California, Berkeley.
20. Almaguer, *Racial Fault Lines*, 49; Silliman, *Lost Laborers*, 70.
21. Chávez-García, *Negotiating Conquest*, 68–69; Silliman, *Lost Laborers*, 70.
22. Chávez-García, *Negotiating Conquest*, 68; Haas, *Conquests and Historical Identities*, 53; Heidenreich, *This Land Was Mexican Once*, 68; Monroy, "The Creation and Re-Creation of Californio Society," 187; Monroy, *Thrown Among Strangers*, 151; Silliman, *Lost Laborers*, 69.
23. Almaguer, *Racial Fault Lines*, 49; Monroy, *Thrown Among Strangers*, 151; Silliman, *Lost Laborers*, 69.
24. For specific occupation listed in the census, see Padrones 1836, 1844, vol. 3, 666–802, Los Angeles City Archives (Los Angeles, CA); see also Howard J. Nelson, "The Two Pueblos of Los Angeles: Agricultural Village and Embryo Town," *Southern California Quarterly* 59, no. 1 (Spring 1977): 5.
25. The term *sirvientes* refers to people who worked as servants at the homesteads. The padrón distinguishes between two types of labradores; first are general farm laborers and the second are *labradores propietadores*, farmers who own their own lands, and *cigarreros* or cigar makers.
26. Padrón, 1836, Los Angeles City Archives, Spanish Version, 46–47; For an overview of the padrónes see, Howard J. Nelson, "The Two Pueblos of Los Angeles," 1–11.
27. Nelson, "The Two Pueblos of Los Angeles," 6. For a detailed description of the embroidery, see Antonio Franco Coronel, "Cosas de California: Vecino de la Ciudad de Los Angeles, 1877," BANC MSS C-D 61, 236–37, Bancroft Library, University of California, Berkeley.

28. Los Angeles Padrón, 1836, Los Angeles City Archives, 48–49.
29. Los Angeles Padrón, 1836, 49–51.
30. The record lists Juan Mariné and Helena Guillén. See Los Angeles Padrón, 1844, Los Angeles City Archives.
31. Los Angeles Padrón, 1836, 510.
32. These children, ranging in age from eighteen to thirty-four, were the offspring of Mariné's marriage to Maria Antonia Sepúlveda, not Eulalia Pérez. With reference to Fruto Mariné, witnesses in the land investigations for Enrique Sepúlveda's denouncement of San Pascual identified Fruto as a soldier who had often been in trouble with the law. See Sepúlveda to Governor Alvarado, 10 February 1840, vol. 7, 370, California State Archives, Spanish Mexican Land Grants.
33. The 1844 Padrón is not as thorough as the 1836 Padrón. Historian Howard J. Nelson states that the padrón was not carefully done and that the enumerator indiscriminately applied occupational titles and failed to count vagrants and prostitutes The enumerator's carelessness may explain why San Pascual was overlooked as an organized rancho. Also, it should be noted that the prostitutes to which Nelson refers may be women in the pueblo designated as *mala vida* (MV). The MV designation was assigned to women who were defined as living outside socially defined gender and sexual norms. While some may have been prostitutes, not all were. For more on the 1836 and 1844 Padrónes, see Howard J. Nelson, "The Two Pueblos of Los Angeles," 1–11.
34. Robert Cleland, *Cattle on a Thousand Hills: Southern California, 1850–1880* (San Marino, Calif.: Huntington Library, 1963); Pitt, *The Decline of the Californios.*
35. Haas, *Conquests and Historical Identities*, 9.
36. Haas, *Conquests and Historical Identities*, 49.
37. Chávez-García, *Negotiating Conquest*, 67.
38. Monroy, "The Creation and Re-creation of Californio Society," 183.
39. Silliman, *Lost Laborers*, 21–22; Chávez-García, *Negotiating Conquest*, 68.
40. William David Estrada, *The Los Angeles Plaza: Sacred and Contested Space* (Austin: University of Texas Press, 2008), 297–98.
41. Chávez-García, *Negotiating Conquest*, 69; John Kielbasa, *Historic Adobes of Los Angeles County, Southern County, Avila Adobe*, accessed May 15, 2012, http://www.laokay.com/halac.
42. Kielbasa, *Historic Adobes of Los Angeles County.*
43. Kielbasa, *Historic Adobes of Los Angeles County.*
44. Los Angeles Padrón, 1836, 511.
45. Chávez-García, *Negotiating Conquest*, 27–28; Monroy, "The Creation and Re-creation of Californio Society," 186; Monroy, *Thrown Among Strangers*, 140–43.
46. Pubols, *The Father of All*, 58.
47. For a similar argument, see Haas, *Conquests and Historical Identities*, 49.
48. Chávez-García, *Negotiating Conquest*, 27; Monroy, "The Creation and Re-Creation of Californio Society," 186; Pubols, *The Father of All*, 69–70.

49. Pubols, *The Father of All*, 69. For physical descriptions of the adobes in Mexican California, see *Archeology in America: An Encyclopedia*, vol. 5, *The Southwest and Great Basin Plateau*, ed. Francis P. MacManon (Westport, Conn.: Greenwood Publishing, 2009); and Harold Kirker, *California's Architectural Frontier: Style and Tradition in the Nineteenth Century* (Salt Lake City: Peregrine Smith, 1973), 1–22.
50. Chávez-García, *Negotiating Conquest*, 28; Casas, *Married to a Daughter of the Land*, 97; Monroy, "The Creation and Re-Creation of Californio Society," 184.
51. Monroy, *Thrown Among Strangers*, 151; Pubols, *The Father of All*, 70.
52. Casas, *Married to a Daughter of the Land*, 52–53; Heidenreich, *This Land Was Mexican Once*, 99–100; Monroy, *Thrown Among Strangers*, 151–52.
53. Castañeda, "Engendering the History of California, 1769–1848," in *Three Decades of Engendering History*, 244. 244; Heidenreich, *This Land Was Mexican Once*, 101; Sánchez, *Telling Identities*, 190–91; Weber, *The Mexican Frontier*, 218.
54. Castañeda, "Engendering the History of California, 1769–1848," in *Three Decades of Engendering History*, 244; Heidenreich, *This Land Was Mexican Once*, 101.
55. Gutiérrez, *When Jesus Came, the Corn Mothers Went Away*, 177.
56. Pubols, *The Father of All*, 13–14.
57. See chapter 3 for more in detail discussion of Mariné's heirs. Marriage Record Juan Marin and María Antonia Sepúlveda, 6 September 1797, San Gabriel Mission Records, Number 00433, Huntington Library, Early Population Project Database, 2006, http://missions.huntington.org/MarriageDate.aspx?ID=22862.
58. Reference to María Merced Lugo's marriage to José Pérez is contained in the marriage record for Charles "Carlos" Foster to María Merced Lugo, 5 August 1848, San Gabriel Mission Records, No. 02057, Huntington Library, Early Population Project Database, 2006, http://missions.huntington.org/MarriageDate.aspx?ID=3240.
59. Marriage Record for Maria Encarnación Sepúlveda and Francisco Avila, November 8, 1822, San Gabriel Mission Records, No. 01634, Huntington Library, Early Population Project Database, 2006, http://missions.huntington.org/MarriageDate.aspx?ID=3027. See also Manuel Garfias and María Luisa Avila, Matrimonial Investigation, San Gabriel Mission Matrimonial Investigation Records, McPherson Collection, Special Collections, Honnold Mudd Library, Claremont University Consortium (Claremont, CA).
60. In 1825, Enrique Sepúlveda married María Bernarda Alanís, the daughter of wealthy landowner Máximo Alanís. Maxímo Alanís was the grantee of Rancho San José de Buenos Ayres, a 4,438-acre allotment that is the present site of Westwood, the University of California Los Angeles, Holmby Hills, and Bel Air in West Los Angeles. The marriage between Enrique and María Bernarda began a link between the Alanís and Sepúlveda families that continued into future generations. Marriage Record for Sepúlveda and Alanís, 19 January 1825, San Fernando Mission Records, No. 00749, Huntington Library, Early Population Project Database, 2006, http://missions.huntington.org/MarriageDate.aspx?ID=22862.
61. Casas, *Married to a Daughter of the Land*, 52.

62. Almaguer, *Racial Fault Lines*, 50; Hackel, "Land, Labor, and Production," 134; Monroy, *Thrown Among Strangers*, 100–102.
63. Weber, *The Mexican Frontier*, 222–24.
64. Lechos hechas de álamo foradas con cuero. Lugo, "Vida de un ranchero."
65. Hechas con latitas y encima colocado un cuero, mientras los que no tenían otra cosa, se echaban sobre un cuero. Lugo, "Vida de un ranchero," 80.
66. "Las mujeres tenían particular cuidado en el adorno de sus camas, cuyas sábanas y fundas de almohada habían de estar perfiladas, bordadas ó caladas." Coronel, "Cosas de California."
67. Lugo, "Vida de un ranchero," 79–80; Weber, *The Mexican Frontier*, 222–24.
68. Por lo general, en la clase pobre, que era la mayor parte de la población . . . pocos tenían platos, cucharas o tenedores. Lugo, "Vida de un ranchero," 83–84.
69. Lugo, "Vida de un ranchero," 83–84.
70. Coronel, "Cosas de California," 237–38.
71. Monroy, "The Creation and Re-Creation of Californio Society," 187–88.
72. Coronel, "Cosas de California," 237.
73. Coronel, "Cosas de California," 237.
74. Coronel, "Cosas de California," 237.
75. Weber, *The Mexican Frontier*, 218–20.
76. Weber, *The Mexican Frontier*, 218–20.
77. Coronel, "Cosas de California," 232; Monroy, "The Creation and Re-Creation of Californio Society," 188.
78. Coronel, "Cosas de California," 232–33. Jose Lugo provides a similar description in his testimonio; see Lugo, "Vida de un ranchero," 88–90.
79. Coronel, "Cosas de California," 233.
80. Coronel, "Cosas de California," 235.
81. Coronel, "Cosas de California," 235.
82. Weber, *The Mexican Frontier*, 220.
83. Weber, *The Mexican Frontier*, 220.
84. Coronel, "Cosas de California," 235.
85. Coronel, "Cosas de California," 234.
86. Monroy, "The Creation and Re-Creation of Californio Society," 188.
87. Coronel, "Cosas de California," 245.
88. Weber, *The Mexican Frontier*, 220–21.
89. Chávez-García, *Negotiating Conquest*, 27.
90. The words *medio paso* mean half step. Weber, *The Mexican Frontier*, 220.
91. Hayden White, *Metahistory: The Historical Imagination in Nineteenth-Century Europe* (Baltimore: Johns Hopkins University Press, 1973), 4.
92. White argued that historical writing follows three types: emplotment, argument, and ideological implication. The argument tells history according to what the historian thinks it ought to be. There are four argument types: formalist, organicist, mechanistic, and contextualism. See White, *Metahistory*, 6–10, 14.
93. Pubols, *The Father of All*, 90.

94. Pubols, *The Father of All*, 102.
95. Casas, *Married to a Daughter of the Land*, 65–66; Haas, *Conquests and Historical Identities*, 73.
96. Lugo, "Vida de un ranchero," 230.
97. Lugo, "Vida de un ranchero," 122.
98. Monroy, "The Creation and Re-Creation of Californio Society," 188.
99. Coronel, "Cosas de California," 245; Lugo, "Vida de un ranchero," 122.
100. José Arnaz, "Recuerdos," BANC MSS C-D 32, 14–15, Bancroft Library, University of California, Berkeley.
101. Monroy, "The Creation and Re-Creation of Californio Society," 188.
102. Monroy, "The Creation and Re-Creation of Californio Society," 188.
103. Pubols, *The Father of All*, 97–98.
104. Arnaz, "Recuerdos," 15.
105. Arnaz, "Recuerdos," 19; Coronel, "Cosas de California," 248–61; Lugo, "Vida de un ranchero," 123–25.
106. Lugo, "Vida de un Ranchero," 123.
107. Lugo, "Vida de un Ranchero," 123.
108. Although not in contemporary dictionaries, Bancroft referred to the term *tecolero* as a Californianism, a word used by Californios to describe the master of ceremonies at Californios' fandangos. Various Californios such as Coronel and Mariano Vallejo used the term in their testimonios to refer to the man in charge of the dance. See Hubert Howe Bancroft, *Histories of the Pacific States of North America: California Pastoral* (San Francisco: The History Company Publishers, 1888), 532.
109. Coronel, "Cosas de California," 245.
110. Monroy, "The Creation and Re-Creation of Californio Society," 187.
111. Arnaz, "Recuerdos," 17.
112. Arnaz, "Recuerdos," 17–18.
113. Arnaz, "Recuerdos," 32, 24; Coronel, "Cosas de California," 231.
114. Camarillo, *Chicanos in a Changing Society*, 12–13; Pubols, *Father of All*, 83–86.
115. Robert V. Kemper, "The Compadrazgo in Urban Mexico," *Anthropological Quarterly* 55, no.1 (January 1982): 23.
116. Pubols, *The Father of All*, 31.
117. Pubols, *The Father of All*, 31.
118. Coronel, "Cosas de California," 231.
119. José Enrique Sepúlveda, Baptismal Record, April 29, 1791, San Diego Presidio Records, Number 30888, Huntington Library, Early Population Project Database, 2006, http://missions.huntington.org/BaptismalData.aspx?ID=30888.
120. Kemper, "Compadrazgo in Urban Mexico," 20.
121. Pubols, *The Father of All*, 31–31.
122. Arnaz, "Recuerdos," 15.
123. González, *Refusing the Favor*, 113–14.
124. For more detail about foreigners' interactions with Spanish missionaries, refer to chapter 1 in this book.

125. Los Angeles Padrón, 1836.
126. Immigrants into Los Angeles came from a variety of places such as England, France, Spain, Portugal, Germany, Ireland, Italy, and Chile. See Los Angeles Padrón 1836, Los Angeles City Archives, English translation.
127. Casas, *Married to a Daughter of the Land*, 19, 149; Torres-Rouff, *Before L.A.*, 56.
128. Bandini was born in Peru in 1800. His father was a Spanish trader named José Bandini who sailed to California from Peru in 1818 with his son. The elder Bandini made a name for himself through his participation in Mexican independence. Juan Bandini made his reputation through his extensive political involvement during the Mexican Period. He became a wealthy landowner and well respected amongst the Californio elite. For more information on the Bandini Family, see Patricia Baker, "The Bandini Family," *The Journal of San Diego History* 15, no. 1 (Winter 1969): 23–27.
129. Maurice H. Newmark and Marco R. Newmark, *Census of the City and County of Los Angeles, California for the Year 1850* (Los Angeles: The Times-Mirror Press, 1929).
130. Quoted in W.W. Robinson, *Land in California*, 73.

CHAPTER 5

1. Lisbeth Haas, "War in California, 1846–1848," in *Contested Eden* by Anthony Kirk, ed. Ramón A. Gutiérrez and Richard J. Orsi (Berkeley: University of California Press, 1998), 333.
2. Heidenreich, *This Land Was Mexican Once*, 79–81.
3. Heidenreich, *This Land Was Mexican Once*, 81; Haas, "War in California," 336.
4. Heidenreich, *This Land Was Mexican Once*, 81–84; Haas, "War in California," 333–34, 339–41.
5. Haas, "War in California," 342.
6. Haas, "War in California," 342–43.
7. Haas, "War in California," 343.
8. Escondido is about 100 miles south of Los Angeles in San Diego County. This land is not connected to Rancho San Pascual in Los Angeles County. The site of this battle was part of the 13,000-acre Rancho Guejito granted to José María Orozco in 1845. For more information on Rancho Guejito see Bruce Coons, "A Brief History of Ranch Guejito," *Save Our Heritage Organization Magazine* 38, no. 1 (winter 2007), accessed September 1, 2012, http://sohosandiego.org/reflections/2007-1/guejito_history.html.
9. Montebello is located 17 miles east of Los Angeles.
10. The Battle of La Mesa took place in the present-day city of Vernon, located 10 miles southwest of Montebello.
11. David A. Clary, *Eagles and Empires: The United States, Mexico, and the Struggle for a Continent* (New York: Bantam Books, 2009), 255–56.
12. Haas, "War in California," 345.
13. Haas, "War in California," 345.

14. Pitt, *The Decline of the Californios*, 53–55.
15. Pitt, *The Decline of the Californios*, 103.
16. Hackel, "Land, Labor, and Production," 132–33.
17. John Ryan Fischer, *Cattle Colonialism: An Environmental History of California and Hawai'i* (Chapel Hill: University of North Carolina Press, 2015), 176.
18. Hackel, "Land, Labor, and Production," 132; Pitt, *The Decline of the Californios*, 12, 86.
19. Robert Cleland, *The Cattle on a Thousand Hills: Southern California, 1850–1880*, 2nd ed. (San Marino: Huntington Library, 1951), 103; Lawrence James Jelinek, "'Property of Every Kind': Ranching and Farming During the Gold-Rush Era," in *A Golden State: Mining and Economic Development in Gold Rush California*, eds. James Rawls and Richard Orsi (Berkeley: University of California Press, 1999), 233–34.
20. Cleland, *Cattle on a Thousand Hills*, 106–7.
21. Maurice H. Newmark and Marco R. Newmark, *Census of the City and County of Los Angeles, California for the Year 1850* (Los Angeles: Times-Mirror Press, 1929).
22. Later, J. S. Griffin gave land in this region to the Indiana Colony as a way of encouraging the colony to buy San Pascual. Griffin did not consider this area very viable due its location at the base of the San Gabriel Mountains.
23. Manuel Garfias to Carlos Hanewald, 9 March 1850, Heslop Family Papers, 1833–1906, mssHM35490, Huntington Library, San Marino, California.
24. Manuel Garfias to Carlos Hanewald and John Pine, 13 March 1850, Heslop Family Papers, 1833–1906, mssHM35490, Huntington Library, San Marino, California.
25. The only physical evidence of the Garfias adobe are some ruins located at 424 Arroyo Drive, South Pasadena, CA 91030; most of the home was leveled during the 1880s land boom.
26. Benjamin Eaton quoted in Robinson, *Land in California*, 86; Materials relating to Benjamin S. Eaton, BANC MSS C-D 974, Bancroft Library, Berkeley, California.
27. Perry M. Green, "History of Pasadena," in *A Southern Paradise*, ed. R. W. C Farnsworth (Pasadena, Calif.: Farnsworth, 1883), 36.
28. Green, "History of Pasadena," 36.
29. Richard Henry Dana, *Two Years Before the Mast: A Personal Narrative of Life at Sea* (New York: Harper, 1840), 214.
30. Robinson, *Land in California*, 73.
31. "1851, March 3-09 Stat. 631, Act to Settle Private Land Claims in California" (2016). US Government Legislation and Statutes. 7. Accessed April 9, 2018, https://digitalcommons.csumb.edu/cgi/viewcontent.cgi?article=1006&context=hornbeck_usa_2_d.
32. Ivy B. Ross, "The Confirmation of Spanish and Mexican Land Grants in California" (PhD diss., University of California, Berkeley, 1928), 37.
33. W. W. Robinson, *Land in California*, 85.
34. W. W. Robinson, *Land in California*, 85.
35. John Caughey, "Don Benito Wilson: An Average Southern Californian," *Huntington Library Quarterly* 2, no. 3 (April 1939): 286; Charles B. Churchill, *Adventurers*

and Prophets: American Autobiographers in Mexican California, 1828–1847 (Spokane: Clark, 1995); Torres-Rouff, *Before L.A.*, 55–56.

36. The Yorbas were one of Southern California's oldest and wealthiest families. Patriarch José Antonio Yorba was the grantee of Santiago de Santa Ana, totaling 165,000 acres in 1810. Bernardo Yorba was the owner of the 13,000-acre Cañada de Santa Ana granted to him in 1834. For the Wilson and Yorba marriage record, see San Gabriel Mission Records, Number 01966, Huntington Library, Early Population Project Database, 2006, http://missions.huntington.org/MarriageData.aspx?ID=3600; Casas, *Married to a Daughter of the Land*, 149–50; W. W. Robinson, *Land in California*, 87.
37. For more on Benjamin Wilson, see Nat B. Read, *Don Benito: From Mountain Man to Mayor, Los Angeles, 1841–1878* (Los Angeles: Angel City Press, 2008); Torres-Rouff, *Before L.A.*, 55–56.
38. Maurice H. Newmark and Marco R. Newmark, *Census of the City and County of Los Angeles, California for the Year 1850* (Los Angeles: The Times—Mirror Press, 1929).
39. W.W. Robinson, *Land in California*, 85.
40. Manuel Garfias and Luisa Avila to Benjamin Wilson, 15 January 1859, Heslop Family Papers, 1833–1906, mssHM35490, Huntington Library, San Marino, California.
41. Almaguer, *Racial Fault Lines*, 66; Torres-Rouff, *Before L.A.*, 83.
42. Almaguer, *Racial Fault Lines*, 67.
43. Chávez-García, *Negotiating Conquest*, 81–85; Torres-Rouff, *Before L.A.*, 83. For a discussion of the Treaty of Guadalupe's land guarantees, see Richard Griswold del Castillo, *Treaty of Guadalupe Hidalgo.*
44. John O'Sullivan, "Annexation," *United States Magazine and Democratic Review*, 17, no. 1 (July-August 1845): 5–10. For the origin of the phrase Manifest Destiny, see Pitti, *The Devil in Silicon Valley*, 28, and Julius W. Pratt, "The Origin of Manifest Destiny," *The American Historical Review* 32, no. 4 (July 1927): 795–98.
45. Thomas Jefferson to George Rogers Clark, 25 December 1780, in *The Papers of Thomas Jefferson*, ed. Julian Boyd, Charles T. Cullen, and Barbara Oberg (Princeton, NJ: Princeton University Press, 1950), 4: 237; quoted in John M. Murrin, "The Jeffersonian Triumph and American Exceptionalism," *Journal of the Early Republic* 20, no. 1 (Spring 2000): 3. John Adams to John Jay, 8 May 1785, in *The Works of John Adams, Second President of the United State, with a Life of the Author*, ed. Charles Francis Adams (Boston: Little, Brown, 1850), 8: 246; quoted in Murrin, "The Jeffersonian Triumph," 8.
46. Murrin, "The Jeffersonian Triumph," 1–25.
47. Reginald Horsman, *Race and Manifest Destiny: The Origins of American Anglo Saxonism* (Cambridge, Mass.: Harvard University Press, 1981), 229.
48. Almaguer, *Racial Fault Lines*, 13.
49. O'Sullivan and other expansionists believed it their duty to expand American control over the entire continent by removing the obstacles impeding Anglo-Saxon civilization. Removal of racially inferior people allowed for the growth of Amer-

ican Anglo-Saxon civilization, marked through the establishment of Protestant Christianity, growth of democratic institutions, economic prosperity, and progress among racially inferior peoples. Utilizing legal maneuvers and genocide, Americans drove Indigenous peoples from their lands, all the while rationalizing their actions by citing Indians racial weakness and inferiority. Almaguer, *Racial Fault Lines*, 12; Pitti, *The Devil in Silicon Valley*, 34–35.

50. In 1830, the Indian Removal Act confiscated lands in Georgia and Alabama and opened the areas to American settlement. The removal sent the Cherokee, Creek, Chickasaws, Choctaw, and Seminole peoples to Indian Territory in Oklahoma. The act was a central part of westward expansion and exemplifies the contradictory ideals of racialized territorial expansion. This federal order affected Indigenous groups defined by many American as the Five Civilized Tribes because they had most closely assimilated into Anglo-American cultural norms. To differing degrees each group had adopted Christianity, horticulture, centralized government, market trade, and race-based slavery, all reflections of Manifest Destiny. Despite their adaptation of American ideals and culture, American society and the federal government advocated their removal. Their removal to Indian Territory, which bordered Mexican Territory, coincided with American migration into Tejas y Coahuila in the 1830s. It contributed to the problem northern Mexicans faced with Indian raids and violence; presence of more Indians caused Mexicans more worry about their regional security. The historical conflict between northern Mexico and Native Americans, such as the Comanche, created conditions that allowed for Americans armed with the ideas of Manifest Destiny to migrate into the region. American Anglo-Saxons believed that they, not the racially inferior Mexicans, could transform this region and bring civilization. For more on the impact of Native Americans on northern Mexico and how relations with Indians facilitated the American Conquest, see Brian Delay, *War of a Thousand Deserts: Indian Raids and the U.S.–Mexican War* (New Haven, Conn.: Yale University Press, 2008). For California, see Benjamin Madley, *An American Genocide: The United States and the California Indian Catastrophe, 1846–1876* (New Haven, Conn.: Yale University Press, 2016); Jason Pierce, *Making the White Man's West: Whiteness and the Creation of the American West* (Boulder: University of Colorado Press, 2016), 228–32.

51. Horsman, *Race and Manifest Destiny*, 210.

52. See Dana, *Two Years Before the Mast*, 1840; Lansford Hastings, *The Emigrants' Guide to Oregon and California* (Cincinnati: Conclin, 1845).

53. Hastings, *The Emigrants' Guide to Oregon and California*, 113.

54. Pitti, *The Devil in Silicon Valley*, 35.

55. Elizabeth Raymond, "When the Desert Won't Bloom: Environmental Limitation and the Great Basin," in *Many Wests: Place, Culture, and Regional Identity*, ed. David M. Wrobel and Michael S. Steiner (Lawrence: University Press of Kansas, 1997), 75–76.

56. Spanish fantasy heritage refers to a fictionalized narrative and interpretation of California's history that emphasizes the Spanish Colonial and Mission Periods. It

was used by both Californios and Euro-Americans to connect the city's history to its Spanish origins and downplay its Mexican and Indigenous history. Californios used it to maintain power and distinguish themselves from the lower classes by claiming Spanish cultural identity. The lower classes utilized it as a way of superficially accepting landed Californios as their class allies, at least temporarily, by ignoring Californios' presumption of their presumed racial inferiority. See James Sandos, "'Because He Is a Liar and a Thief': Conquering the Residents of 'Old' California, 1850–1880," in *Rooted in Barbarous Soil: People, Culture, and Community in Gold Rush California*, eds. Keven Starr and Robert J. Orsí (Berkeley: University of California Press, 2000), 106–8. For Spanish fantasy heritage, see Carey McWilliams, *North from Mexico: The Spanish Speaking People of the U.S.* (Philadelphia: Lippincott, 1949), 35–40. See also Yolanda Venegas, "The Erotics of Racialization: Gender and Sexuality in the Making of California," *Frontiers: A Journal of Women's Studies* 25, no. 3 (September 2004): 67.

57. Pitti, *The Devil in Silicon Valley*, 35; Venegas, "The Erotics of Racialization," 67.
58. Almaguer, *Racial Fault Lines*, 58; Casas, *Married to a Daughter of the Land*, 148.
59. Pierce, *Making the White Man's West*, 72–73; Venegas, "The Erotics of Racialization," 67.
60. Horsman, *Race and Manifest Destiny*, 9, 15–16.
61. Horsman, *Race and Manifest Destiny*, 14–20.
62. Horsman, *Race and Manifest Destiny*, 191–92; Pierce, *Making the White Man's West*, 72.
63. Matthew Jacobson, *Whiteness of a Different Color: European Immigrants and the Alchemy of Race* (Cambridge, Mass.: Harvard University Press, 1998), 41–43; Pierce, *Making the White Man's West*, 13.
64. Following the war and statehood, Anglos migrated into Northern California and quickly outnumbered Mexicans. In Southern California Mexicans remained the largest minority population until the railroad prompted the land boom of the 1870s. For information about populations, refer to Almaguer, *Racial Fault Lines*, 87–88, and Richard White, *"It's Your Misfortune and None of My Own": A New History of the American West* (Norman: University of Oklahoma Press, 1991), 186.
65. This speaks to the pliability of white racial identity and whiteness. What constitutes white was continuously redefined dependent on the specific social, political, and cultural context. There are limitations in conflating Euro-American ethnic groups into one white Anglo category. Placing them into one category fails to account for the heterogeneity of whiteness. For a discussion of white groups' racial fluidity after 1840, see Jacobson, *Whiteness of a Different Color* (pp. 43–44); for a discussion of the limitations of conflating white people into one category, see Neil Foley, *The White Scourge: Mexicans, Blacks, and Poor Whites in Texas Cotton Culture* (Berkeley: University of California Press, 1997), 7–8.
66. Critical race theorist Ian F. Haney López argues that "races are constructed relationally, against one another, rather than in isolation." See "The Social Construction of Race," in *Critical Race Theory: The Cutting Edge*, ed. Richard Delgado (Philadelphia: Temple University Press, 1995), 196.

67. Kimberlé Williams Crenshaw, "Race, Reform, and Retrenchment: Transformation and Legitimation in Antidiscrimination Law," *Harvard Law Review* 101, no. 7 (May 1988): 1372.
68. In the debate over slavery, the idea of African Americans as subjugated racial others legitimated slavery and social inequality. In the American Southwest, Mexicans became the racial other and were racialized similar to African Americans. For a discussion of bipolar conceptualization in Western thought, see Jacques Derrida, *Dissemination*, trans. Barbara Johnson (London: Continuum International Publishing, 2004), viii. For a discussion of race, skin color, and otherness, see Frantz Fanon, *Black Skins, White Masks*, trans. Richard Philcox (New York: Grove Press, 1952).
69. Griswold del Castillo, *Treaty of Guadalupe Hidalgo*, 189–90.
70. Almaguer, *Racial Fault Lines*, 24; Jacobson, *Whiteness of a Different Color*, 7; Pierce, *Making the White Man's West*, 14.
71. Menchaca, "Chicano Indianism," 587; Pierce, *Making the White Man's West*, 234.
72. Sánchez, *Telling Identities*, 58.
73. Laura Gómez, *Manifest Destinies: The Making of the Mexican Race* (New York: New York University Press, 2008), 3; White, *"It's Your Misfortune and None of My Own,"* 186–87.
74. Almaguer, *Racial Fault Lines*, 46, 55–56; Pierce, *Making the White Man's West*, 233.
75. Almaguer, *Racial Fault Lines*, 56; Camarillo, *Chicanos in a Changing Society*, 109–12; Heidenreich, *This Land Was Mexican Once*, 143.
76. Almaguer, *Racial Fault Lines*, 57–58; Menchaca, "Chicano Indianism," 587–88; Pierce, *Making the White Man's West*, 233.
77. The California state legislature passed the Anti-Vagrancy Law of 1855, also known as the Greaser Act, to ensure the control of the Mexican American population. It required that Mexicans show that they were gainfully employed and were not public charges. See Almaguer, *Racial Fault Lines*, 57; Camarillo, *Chicanos in a Changing Society*, 108.
78. Almaguer, *Racial Fault Lines*, 65; Heidenreich, *This Land Was Mexican Once*, 147–48.
79. Haas, *Conquests and Historical Identities*, 134; Jason E. Pierce, *Making the White Man's West*, 234.
80. George Ward Burton, *Men of Achievement in the Great Southwest* (Los Angeles: Los Angeles Times, 1904), 15. For a list of Californio elected officials from 1850 to 1859, see table 33 in Richard Griswold del Castillo, *The Los Angeles Barrio, 1850–1880: A Social History* (Berkeley: University of California Press, 1979); Charles D. Willard, *The Herald's History of Los Angeles City* (Los Angeles: Kingsley-Barnes & Neuner, 1901), 244.
81. Sánchez, *Telling Identities*, 270.
82. William Estrada, "The Last Latino Mayor of Los Angeles: José Cristóbal Aguilar, 1866–1868, 1871–1872," *The City Project Blog: Equal Justice, Democracy, and Livability for All*, June 30, 2005. Accessed March 21, 2013, http://www.cityprojectca.org/blog/archives/117.

83. Torres-Rouff, *Before L.A.*, 201.
84. In this election, Toberman received 715 votes in comparison to Aguilar's 350. For election results, see Los Angeles City Council Documents, *Common Council Session December 5, 1872*, vol. 8, 132–35. Aguilar was Los Angeles's last Mexican mayor until the 2005 election of Antonio Villaraigosa.
85. Narratives of Californio decline identify the 1870s and 1880s as the decades when Californios lost their political power. Often, these accounts compare the loss in Northern and Southern California. In contending that Californios' decline of status began in the 1850s, the present work is not focusing on the loss of political power but rather the decline of social power and cooperation between Californios and assimilated Euro-Americans and immigrants in the 1840s and 1850s. For discussion of Californios' decline in political power in the 1870s, see Almaguer, *Racial Fault Lines*, 70–71; Camarillo, *Chicanos in a Changing Society*; Cleland, *The Cattle on a Thousand Hills: Southern California, 1850–1880*; Juan Gomez-Quiñones, *Roots of Chicano Politics, 1600–1940* (Albuquerque: University of New Mexico Press, 1994), 234; Monroy, *Thrown Among Strangers*; Pitt, *The Decline of the Californios*; Louise Pubols, "Patriarchy and Power in Mexican California, 1800–1880," in *Continental Crossroads: Re-mapping U.S.-Mexico Borderlands History*, eds. Samuel Truett and Elliott Young (Durham: Duke University Press, 2004), 67–94; and Sandos, "'Because He Is a Liar and a Thief,'" 86–112.
86. For a similar argument specifically examining 1855–1856, see Torres-Rouff, *Before L.A.*, 94–132.
87. Paul Bryan Gray, *A Clamor for Equality: Emergence and Exile of Californio Activist Francisco P. Ramírez* (Lubbock: Texas Tech University Press, 2012), 15.
88. Gray, *A Clamor for Equality*, 10–14.
89. Gray, *A Clamor for Equality*, 15–16.
90. Gray, *A Clamor for Equality*, 16.
91. Gray, *A Clamor for Equality*, 17–18.
92. Camarillo, *Chicanos in a Changing Society*, 110; Gray, *A Clamor for Equality*, 18; Pitt, *The Decline of the Californios*, 186.
93. In her work on the formation of the African American community in Los Angeles, Campbell found that the imposition of American control and the influx of Americans resulted in the import of racialized ideas about Mexicans, African Americans, Chinese, Japanese, and other people of color. These racially based ideas often manifested themselves in violent attacks on these groups. See Marne L. Campbell, *Making of Black Los Angeles: Class, Gender, and Community, 1850–1930* (Chapel Hill: University of North Carolina Press, 2016), 26–30.
94. "Situación de los Hispano-Americanos en California," *El Clamor Público*, 1, no. 9 (October 23, 1855). Accessed August 1, 2012, http://digitallibrary.usc.edu. From El Clamor Público, Huntington Library. Digitally reproduced by the University of Southern California Digital Library, Los Angeles.
95. "Situación de los Hispano-Americanos en California."

96. "Americanos! Californios!" *El Clamor Público*, 2, no. 34 (February 21, 1857). Accessed August 1, 2012. http://digitallibrary.usc.edu. From El Clamor Público, Huntington Library. Digitally reproduced by the University of Southern California Digital Library, Los Angeles.
97. Las doz razas. "Americanos! Californios!" *El Clamor Público*, 2, no. 34.
98. "Americanos! Californios!" *El Clamor Público*, 2, no. 34.
99. Pitt, *The Decline of the Californios*, 127.
100. Camarillo, *Chicanos in a Changing Society*, 14–15.
101. "Lo Que Dicen los Democratas, Los Californios son una raza degrada, negros, distinguirlos de los Indios, poca diferencia, entre ellos y la raza negra," *El Clamor Público*, 5, no. 5, July 30, 1859. Accessed August 1, 2012, http://digitallibrary.usc.edu. From *El Clamor Público*, Huntington Library. Digitally reproduced by the University of Southern California Digital Library, Los Angeles.
102. For more on Californios' control of politics, and economic changes, see Camarillo, *Chicanos in a Changing Society*, 22–31.
103. John S. Griffin to Benjamin Wilson, 1859, incomplete letter, Los Angeles. Correspondence and Business Records 1858, box 12, Benjamin Wilson Collection, Huntington Library, San Marino, California.
104. John S. Griffin to Benjamin Wilson, 15 January 1859, letter, Los Angeles. Correspondence and Business Records 1859, box 13, Benjamin Wilson Collection, Huntington Library, San Marino, California.
105. John S. Griffin to Benjamin Wilson, 15 January 1859.
106. Agreement Between Benjamin and Margaret Wilson and John C. Keever over Water Rights, 1860, Benjamin Davis Wilson Collection, Huntington Library, San Marino, California.
107. See Daniel Worster, *Rivers of Empire: Water, Aridity, and the Growth of the American West* (New York: Pantheon Press, Reprint 1985).
108. In addition to this title, he was commemorated by several other places that bear his name. For instance, one of the most well-known peaks of the San Gabriel Mountains is Mount Wilson. In the 1860s, Wilson explored the mountain in the hope of finding trees to process into wooden casks for wine from his lake vineyard. The trail he took up to the peak was later named the Mount Wilson Trail. Aside from his imprint on Pasadena, Wilson is remembered as the grandfather of World War II general George S. Patton, son of his daughter Ruth. Wilson also owned Ranchos Jurupa and Rubidoux, which now comprise the city of Riverside, California.
109. Raymundo Yorba to Benjamin Wilson, 4 October 1859, Buena Vista, letter, Correspondence and Business Records 1859, box 13, Benjamin Wilson Collection, Huntington Library, San Marino, California.
110. Newspaper clipping, invitations, and cards, box 39, Benjamin Wilson Collection, Huntington Library, San Marino, California.
111. "Aviso Interesante, Se Vende, Twist y Aguilar, Manuel Garfias," *El Clamor Público* 2, no. 42, April 18, 1857. From *El Clamor Publico*, Huntington Library. Accessed

August 1, 2012, http://digitallibrary.usc.edu. Digitally reproduced by the University of Southern California Digital Library, Los Angeles.

112. Barraclough, *Making the San Fernando Valley*, 27; Pitti, *The Devil in Silicon Valley*, 35–40.
113. Horsman, *Race and Manifest Destiny*, 189–207; 208–28; Pierce, *Making the White Man's West*, 30–31.
114. González, *Refusing the Favor*, 108.
115. González, *Refusing the Favor*, 108–9.
116. John S. Griffin to Benjamin Wilson, unknown month and date, 1859, incomplete letter, Los Angeles. Correspondence and Business Records 1858, box 12, Benjamin Wilson Collection, Huntington Library, San Marino, California.
117. Barraclough, *Making the San Fernando Valley*, 27.
118. Barraclough, *Making the San Fernando Valley*, 29–30.
119. Jelinek, "Property of Every Kind," 233–35; Pitt, *The Decline of the Californios*, 247.
120. Charles Nordhoff, *California for Health, Pleasure, and Residence: A Book for Travelers and Settlers* (New York: Harper, 1873), 18.
121. Nordhoff, *California for Health, Pleasure, and Residence*, 18–19.
122. Jelinek, "Property of Every Kind," 243.
123. Ann Lund, *Historic Pasadena: An Illustrated History* (San Antonio, Tex.: Historical Publishing Network, 1991), 22.
124. In 1804 the San Gabriel Mission had one orange orchard with forty-four seedling trees later transplanted into other areas of Los Angeles during the mid-nineteenth century. For more on California's early citrus industry, see Walter Ebeling, *The Fruited Plain: The Story of American Agriculture* (Berkeley: University of California Press, 1980), 352.
125. William Wolfskill was an American fur trapper from Missouri who came to California from Taos, New Mexico. Arriving in Los Angeles in 1831, Wolfskill became a Mexican citizen. In the 1836 and 1844 city padrónes, he is referred to as Guillermo Wolfskill, a laborer. See Padrón de la Ciudad de Los Angeles y Su Jurisdicción, Año de 1836, Los Angeles City Archives, English translation, 465; Padrón de 1844, English translation, 552. For more information on Wolfskill's life, see H. D. Barrow, "William Wolfskill, The Pioneer," *Annual Publication of the Historical Society of Southern California and of the Pioneers of Los Angeles County*, vol. 5–6: *1902–1904* (Oakland: University of California Press), 287–94; David J. Weber, *The Taos Trappers: The Fur Trade in the Far Southwest, 1540–1846* (Norman: University of Oklahoma Press, 1980), 144–45; Iris Wilson, *William Wolfskill 1796–1866: Frontier Trapper to California Rancher* (Glendale, Calif.: Clark, 1965). In 1841, Wilson married María Magdalena Lugo, daughter of prominent Californios Ygnacio and Rafaela Lugo. He became a renowned viticulturist who is credited with being the first American to plant oranges in Los Angeles.
126. Ebeling, *The Fruited Plain*, 353; Jelinek, "Property of Every Kind," 247.
127. Douglas C. Sackman, *Orange Empire: California and the Fruits of Eden* (Berkeley: University of California Press, 2007), 40.

128. Ebeling, *The Fruited Plain*, 353–54.
129. Ebeling stated that in 1866, before his death, William Wolfskill's last crop of oranges sold for $25,000 on the tree (Ebeling, *The Fruited Plain*, 353).
130. For a detailed analysis of these images see chapter 1 in Sackman, *Orange Empire*.
131. Phoebe S. Kropp, *California Vieja: Culture and Memory in a Modern American Place* (Berkeley: University of California Press, 2006), 26.
132. Sackman, *Orange Empire*, 7.
133. Sackman, *Orange Empire*, 7–8.
134. Sackman, *Orange Empire*, 24.
135. Sackman, *Orange Empire*, 9.
136. Henry Markham Page, *Pasadena: Its Early Years* (Los Angeles: Morrison, 1964), 10.
137. General Albert Sidney Johnston had fought in the U.S.-Mexico War in the 1840s. In May 1861, Jefferson Davis appointed him general in the Confederate Army. Johnston died at the Battle of Shiloh in April of 1862. For Johnston's role in the Civil War, see James M. McPherson, *Battle Cry of Freedom: The Civil War Era* (New York: Oxford University Press, 1988). Daniel M. Berry, the land scout for the Indiana Colony, refers to Johnston's passing in his letter to T. B. Elliot. See Daniel M. Berry to Thomas Balch Elliott, September 12, 1873, letter, box 1, Papers of Thomas Balch Elliot, 1873–1874, Huntington Library, San Marino, California.
138. Deed to Portion of Tract of San Pascual, Benjamin D. Wilson and Margaret S. Wilson to Eliza G. Johnston, 11 December 1862. box 9, Papers of James Filmore Crank, 1880–1902, Huntington Library, San Marino, California.
139. Robert H. Peterson, Altadena's *Golden Years* (Alhambra: Sinclair, 1976), 23.
140. Daniel M. Berry to Thomas Balch Elliott, 12 September 1873, letter. box 1, Papers of Thomas Balch Elliot, 1873–1874, Huntington Library, San Marino, California.
141. On April 27, 1863, the steamboat Ada Hancock, owned by well-known businessman Phineas Banning, exploded during a routine trip to transport passengers in the San Pedro Bay. Fifty passengers died, including Sue Wilson, daughter of Benjamin Wilson. For a discussion of this explosion, see William B. Seacrest, *California Disasters 1800–1900* (Fresno, Calif.: Quill Driver Books, 2005), 102–5.
142. Power of Attorney, Eliza Johnston to John S. Griffin, 30 January 1865, box 9, Papers of James F. Crank, 1880–1902, Huntington Library, San Marino, California.
143. Deed to Fair Oaks, Eliza Johnston to John S. Griffin, 12 September 1866, box 9, Papers of James F. Crank, 1880–1902, Huntington Library, San Marino, California.
144. Eaton's wife, Helena Hayes, was the sister of Griffin's wife, Louisa Hayes. See Benjamin Hayes and Marjorie Tisdale Wolcott, *Pioneers: Notes from the Diaries of Judge Benjamin Hayes, 1849–1875* (Wisconsin: Arno Press, 1976), x.
145. Eaton was a long-time resident of Los Angeles and had served in a variety of positions such as associate justice for the circuit court, Los Angeles district attorney, and tax assessor. See Harris Newmark, *Sixty Years in California 1865–1913: Containing the Reminisces of Harris Newmark*, eds. Maurice Newark and Marco Newmark (New York: Knickerbocker Press, 1916), 50.

146. Newmark, *Sixty Years in California*, 50.
147. Deed of Land, Benjamin Wilson to Benjamin Eaton, 19 November 1868, box 9, Papers of James F. Crank, 1880–1902, Huntington Library, San Marino, California.
148. Deed of Land, Eliza Johnston to Benjamin Eaton, 19 December 1868, box 9, Papers of James F. Crank, 1880–1902, Huntington Library, San Marino, California.
149. Barraclough, *Making the San Fernando Valley*, 26.
150. Barraclough, *Making the San Fernando Valley*, 26–27.
151. For a discussion of the process in the San Fernando Valley, see Barraclough, *Making the San Fernando Valley*, 26–27.
152. García, *A World of Its Own*, 21.
153. Barraclough, *Making the San Fernando Valley*, 29.

CHAPTER 6

Epigraph: Thomas Balch Elliot, "History of the San Gabriel Orange Growers Association," 1874, box 1, Papers of the Thomas Balch Elliott Collection, 1873–1874, Huntington Library, San Marino, California.

1. Barraclough, *Making the San Fernando Valley*, 30; Jenny Bourne, *In Essentials, Unity: An Economic History of the Grange* (Athens: Ohio University Press, 2017), 7, 9–10; Steven Hahn and Jonathan Prude, "Introduction," in *The Countryside in the Age of Capitalist Transformation: Essays in the Social History of Rural America*, eds. Steven Hahn and Jonathan Prude (Chapel Hill: University of North Carolina Press, 1985), 3. For a thorough review of the era's economics, see Edward Kirkland, *Industry Comes of Age: Business, Labor, and Public Policy, 1860–1897* (New York: Holt, Rinehart, and Winston, 1961).
2. Barraclough, *Making the San Fernando Valley*, 30; Hal Barron, "Staying Down on the Farm: Social Processes of Settled Rural Life in the Nineteenth-Century North," in *The Countryside in the Age of Capitalist Transformation: Essays in the Social History of Rural America,* eds. Steven Hahn and Jonathan Prude (Chapel Hill: University of North Carolina Press, 1985), 328–29.
3. Barraclough, *Making the San Fernando Valley*, 30.
4. Barraclough, *Making the San Fernando Valley*, 28–32.
5. García, *A World of Its Own*, 25.
6. Glenn S. Dumke, *The Boom of the Eighties in Southern California* (San Marino, Calif.: Huntington Library, 1963), 7.
7. Elliot, "History of the San Gabriel Orange Growers Association."
8. Thomas Balch Elliott, "The Articles of the California Colony of Indiana," box 2, Papers of the Thomas Balch Elliott Collection, 1873–1874, Huntington Library, San Marino, California.
9. This is the amount that the colonists were willing to pay in monthly installments for the entire colony. Berry was authorized to look only for land that was no more than $5.00 per acre.
10. Elliott, "The Articles of the California Colony of Indiana."

11. Barraclough, *Making the San Fernando Valley*, 41.
12. White, *"It's Your Misfortune and None of My Own,"* 143–48.
13. Barraclough, *Making the San Fernando Valley*, 26; García, *A World of Its Own*, 29–30.
14. Elliot, "The Articles of the California Colony of Indiana."
15. Elliott, "The Articles of the California Colony of Indiana."
16. Elliot, "History of the San Gabriel Orange Growers Association."
17. For a discussion on the rise of tourism in connection with the railroad, see J. Valerie Fifer, *American Progress: The Growth of Transport, Tourist, and Information Industries in the Nineteenth-Century West* (Chester, Conn.: Globe Pequot, 1988); Earl Pomeroy, *In Search of the Golden West: The Tourist in Western America* (Lincoln: University of Nebraska, 1990).
18. For examples, see Kropp, *California Vieja*, and Sackman, *Orange Empire.*
19. William McClung, *Landscapes of Desire: Anglo Mythologies of Los Angeles* (Berkeley: University of California Press, 2000), 107–9.
20. Hal Rothman, *Devil's Bargain: Tourism in the Twentieth-Century American West* (Lawrence: University of Kansas, 1998), 12.
21. Horsman, *Race and Manifest Destiny*, 1–2.
22. Stacy Camp, "From Nuisance to Nostalgia: The Historical Anthropology of Nature Tourism in Southern California, 1890–1940," *Historical Archeology* 47, no. 3 (September 2013): 87.
23. Charles Nordhoff, *California for Health, Pleasure, and Residence.*
24. For a contemporary's perspective, see Harris Newmark, *Sixty Years in California*, 445. For discussion of Nordhoff as a booster, see Dumke, *The Boom of the Eighties*, 30; McClung, *Landscapes of Desire*, 107.
25. For a discussion of Los Angeles's place within this health movement, see John E. Baur, "Los Angeles County in the Health Rush, 1870–1900," *California Historical Society Quarterly* 31 (March 1952): 13–31.
26. Nordhoff, *California for Health, Pleasure and Residence*, 19.
27. Dumke, *The Boom of the Eighties*, 200–201.
28. D. M. Berry to Thomas Balch Elliot, 30 August 1873, San Diego, letter, box 1, Papers of the Thomas Balch Elliott Collection, 1873–1874, Huntington Library, San Marino, California.
29. Berry to Thomas Balch Elliot, 30 August 1873.
30. D. M. Berry to Thomas Balch Elliot, 5 September 1873, Los Angeles, letter, box 1, Papers of the Thomas Balch Elliott Collection, 1873–1874, Huntington Library, San Marino, California.
31. Berry to Thomas Balch Elliot, San Diego, 30 August 1873.
32. Berry to Thomas Balch Elliot, 5 September 1873.
33. Dumke, *The Boom in the Eighties*, 216.
34. D. M Berry to Thomas Balch Elliot, 9 September 1873, Los Angeles, letter, box 1, Papers of the Thomas Balch Elliott Collection, 1873–1874, Huntington Library, San Marino, California.
35. Berry to Thomas Balch Elliot, 9 September 1873.

36. D. M Berry to Thomas Balch Elliot, 12 September 1873, Los Angeles, letter, box 1, Papers of the Thomas Balch Elliott Collection, 1873–1874, Huntington Library, San Marino, California.
37. Dumke, *The Boom of the Eighties*, 216.
38. Nordhoff, *California for Health, Pleasure and Residence*, 117.
39. Berry to Thomas Balch Elliot, 12 September 1873.
40. Berry to Thomas Balch Elliot, 12 September 1873.
41. D. M. Berry to Thomas Balch Elliot, 18 September 1873, Los Angeles, box 1, Papers of the Thomas Balch Elliott Collection, 1873–1874, Huntington Library, San Marino, California.
42. Hal Barron, "Staying Down on the Farm: Social Processes of Settled Rural Life in the Nineteenth-Century North," in *The Countryside in the Age of Capitalist Transformation: Essays in the Social History of Rural America*, eds. Steven Hahn and Jonathan Prude (Chapel Hill: University of North Carolina Press, 1985), 328–29.
43. Barraclough, *Making the San Fernando Valley*, 30, 33; Dumke, *The Boom of the Eighties*, 16.
44. For more on this concept, see Frederick Jackson Turner, "The Significance of the Frontier in American History," *Annual Report of the American Historical Association for the Year 1893* (Washington, D.C.: Government Printing Office and American Historical Association, 1894), 199–227; Ray Allen Billington, *America's Frontier Heritage* (Los Angeles: Holt, Rinehart and Winston, 1963).
45. Russell Richardson, "The Drama of the Soil," *Los Angeles Times*, January 2, 1929, G3; quoted in Barraclough, *Making the San Fernando Valley*, 33.
46. Barraclough, *Making the San Fernando Valley*, 40–41.
47. D. M. Berry to Mrs. Helen Elliott, 23 September 1873, Los Angeles, letter, box 1, Papers of the Thomas Balch Elliott Collection, 1873–1874, Huntington Library, San Marino, California.
48. Berry to Mrs. Helen Elliott, 23 September 1873.
49. William Deverell, *Whitewashed Adobe: The Rise of Los Angeles and the Remaking of Its Mexican Past* (Berkeley: University of California Press, 2004), 27.
50. Barraclough, *Making the San Fernando Valley*, 32.
51. D. M. Berry to T. B. Elliott, 21 August 1873, San Francisco, letter, box 1, Papers of the Thomas Balch Elliott Collection, 1873–1874, Huntington Library, San Marino, California. Berry was referring to the German agricultural colony of Anaheim. The city of Anaheim is located on former rancho lands of the Yorba Family. For a discussion of Anaheim's German heritage, see Lucile E. Dickson, "The Founding and Early History of Anaheim, California," *Annual Publication of the Historical Society of Southern California* 11, no. 2 (1919): 26–37; also see Dumke, *The Boom of the Eighties*, 112–13.
52. D. M. Berry to Mrs. Helen Elliott, 19 September 1873, Los Angeles, letter, box 1, Papers of the Thomas Balch Elliott Collection, 1873–1874, Huntington Library, San Marino, California.
53. Berry to Mrs. Helen Elliott, 19 September 1873.
54. Deverell, *Whitewashed Adobe*, 41; Haas, *Conquests and Historical Identities*, 169–73.

55. Richard Griswold del Castillo, "La Raza Hispano Americana: The Emergence of an Urban Culture Among the Spanish Speaking of Los Angeles, 1850–1880" (Ph.D. diss., University of California Los Angeles, 1974), 66; quoted in Camarillo, *Chicanos in a Changing Society*, 116.
56. Barraclough, *Making the San Fernando Valley*, 41; García, *A World of Its Own*, 31.
57. For a discussion of white supremacy and California's racialized labor force and class structure, see Almaguer, *Racial Fault Lines*, 19–26.
58. Howard Lamar, "From Bondage to Contract: Ethnic Labor in the American West, 1600–1890," in *The Countryside in the Age of Capitalist Transformation: Essays in the Social History of Rural America*, eds. Steve Hahn and Jonathan Prude (Chapel Hill: University of North Carolina Press, 1985), 309–10.
59. Despite their presence in the region, the padrónes and census do not list them as Kanakas or Rapanui; this may be a result from their classification as Indians or landless Mexicans.
60. Sucheng Chen, "A People of Exceptional Character: Ethnic Diversity, Nativism, and Racism in the California Gold Rush," in *Rooted in Barbarous Soil: People, Culture, and Community in Gold Rush California*, eds. Kevin Starr and Richard Orsi (Berkeley: University of California Press, 2000), 74.
61. Andrew Gyory, *Closing the Gate: Race, Politics, and the Chinese Exclusion Act* (Chapel Hill: University of North Carolina Press, 1998), 18.
62. Sucheng Chen, *Bittersweet Soil: The Chinese in California Agriculture, 1860–1910* (Berkeley: University of California Press, 1986), 2, 56. In Pasadena, Chinese laborers worked in the orange packing houses and on construction projects. For example, most of more than 250 workers who built the Raymond Hotel were Chinese. See Alexander Saxton, *The Indispensable Enemy: Labor and the Anti-Chinese Movement in California* (Berkeley: University of California, 1971).
63. Almaguer, *Racial Fault Lines*, 166–67.
64. Almaguer, *Racial Fault Lines*, 168.
65. Berry to T. B. Elliott, 21 August 1873.
66. Berry to Mrs. Helen Elliott, 23 September 23, 1873.
67. Nordhoff, *California for Health, Pleasure, and Residence*, 85.
68. Nordhoff, *California for Health, Pleasure, and Residence*, 89–90.
69. Carey McWilliams, *Southern California: An Island on Land* (Salt Lake City: Gibbs Smith, 1946), 23–24, 47–48; Menchaca, "Chicano Indianism," 592–94.
70. Nordhoff, *California for Health, Pleasure, and Residence*, 155.
71. Nordhoff, *California for Health, Pleasure, and Residence*, 157.
72. McClung, *Landscapes of Desire*, 107.
73. Kropp, *California Vieja*, 9–10, 19.
74. Nordhoff, *California for Health, Pleasure, and Residence*, 156.
75. Nordhoff, *California for Health, Pleasure, and Residence*, 158.
76. Nordhoff, *California for Health, Pleasure, and Residence*, 159.
77. John Forster married Isadora Pico, Pío Pico's sister. Through this marriage he acquired portions of the former Mission San Juan Capistrano lands. Later, because

of his loans to the Pico family, he was able to acquire other Pico land holdings. Upon his arrival in Southern California, Berry met with Forster to discuss the possibility of purchasing land around San Diego. Berry described him as "rich as a pirate." For Forster's assimilation into Californio society, see Monroy, *Thrown Among Strangers*, 160. For Berry's statement, see D. M. Berry to T. B. Elliott, 21 August 1873.

78. One of the primary causes for the Panic of 1873 was overspeculation on railroad profits after the Civil War. In the attempt to establish the most profitable routes, railroads sold billions of dollars' worth of bonds and stocks. It soon became clear that the profit estimates had been too high. Railroads could not pay their debts, leading to the financial panic. For more on the Panic of 1873, see Elmus Wicker, *Banking Panics of the Gilded Age* (New York: Cambridge University Press, 2000), 16–33.
79. D. M. Berry to T. B. Elliott, 20 September 1873, Los Angeles, letter, box 1, Papers of the Thomas Balch Elliott Collection, 1873–1874, Huntington Library, San Marino, California.
80. D. M. Berry to T. B. Elliott, 8 October 1873, Los Angeles, letter, box 1, Papers of the Thomas Balch Elliott Collection, 1873–1874, Huntington Library, San Marino, California.
81. D. M. Berry to T. B. Elliott, 14 October 1873, Los Angeles, letter, box 1, Papers of the Thomas Balch Elliott Collection, 1873–1874, Huntington Library, San Marino, California; Dumke, *The Boom of the Eighties*, 215–16.
82. D. M. Berry to T. B. Elliott, 19 October 1873, Los Angeles, box 1, Papers of the Thomas Balch Elliott Collection, 1873–1874, Huntington Library, San Marino, California.
83. The link between land and self-sufficiency originated in the Jeffersonian concept of the yeoman farmer. Westward expansion renewed the sense of rugged masculinity that was perceived as lost because of industrialization. For discussion of Manifest Destiny, agrarianism, and masculinity, see Amy Greenberg, *Manifest Manhood and the Antebellum American Empire* (New York: Cambridge University Press, 2005), and David Chang, *The Color of the Land: Race, Nation, and the Politics of Land Ownership in Oklahoma, 1832–1929* (Chapel Hill: University of North Carolina). For a discussion of industrialization and masculinity, see David Roediger, *Wages of Whiteness: Race and the Making of the American Working Class* (London: Verso, 1991).
84. D. M. Berry to T. B. Elliott, 8 November 1873, Los Angeles, letter, box 1, Papers of the Thomas Balch Elliott Collection, 1873–1874, Huntington Library, San Marino, California.
85. D. M. Berry to T. B. Elliott, 12 November 1873, Los Angeles, letter, box 1, Papers of the Thomas Balch Elliott Collection, 1873–1874, Huntington Library, San Marino, California; Dumke, *The Boom of the Eighties*, 85–86.
86. Berry and the SGOGA wanted only the 2,516 acres at the center of San Pascual. Griffin, wanting to secure the deal, added the additional 1,386 acres of land that

ran at the base of the San Gabriel Mountains. This land later became the city of Altadena. For details on the arrangement, see D. M. Berry to T. B. Elliott, 18 December 1873, Los Angeles, letter, box 1, Papers of the Thomas Balch Elliott Collection, 1873–1874, Huntington Library, San Marino, California.

87. D. M. Berry to T. B. Elliott, 26 December 1873, Los Angeles, letter, box 1, Papers of the Thomas Balch Elliott Collection, 1873–1874, Huntington Library, San Marino, California.
88. John S. Griffin to Thomas Croft, deed to San Pascual, 26 December 1873, box 1, Papers of Thomas Balch Elliott Collection, 1873–1874, Huntington Library, San Marino, California.
89. Thomas Balch Elliot, "History of the San Gabriel Orange Growers Association."
90. Page, *Pasadena: Its Early Years*, 28.
91. Page, *Pasadena: Its Early Years*, 29.
92. Hiram Reid, *History of Pasadena*, 125–26.
93. Page, *Pasadena: Its Early Years*, 35.
94. Berry to T. B. Elliott, 9 September, 1873; D. M. Berry to T. B. Elliott, 26 September 1873, Los Angeles, letter, box 1, Papers of the Thomas Balch Elliott Collection, 1873–1874, Huntington Library, San Marino, California.
95. D. M. Berry to Mrs. Helen Elliott, 28 September 1873, Los Angeles, letter, box 1, Papers of the Thomas Balch Elliott Collection, 1873–1874, Huntington Library, San Marino, California.
96. Berry to Mrs. Helen Elliott, 28 September 1873; Dumke, *The Boom of the Eighties*, 76–77.
97. D. M. Berry to Mrs. Helen Elliott, 18 October 1873, Los Angeles, letter, box 1, Papers of the Thomas Balch Elliott Collection, 1873–1874, Huntington Library, San Marino, California.
98. Harris Newmark, *Sixty Years in California*, 336–37; Benjamin C. Truman, *Semi-Tropical California: Its Climate, Healthfulness, Productiveness, and Scenery* (San Francisco: Bancroft, 1874), 180.
99. Newmark, *Sixty Years in Southern California*, 50.
100. Ann Erdman, "PIO Mystery History," *Pasadena PIO Blog*, October 15, 2009, accessed March 21, 2013, http://pasadenapio.blogspot.com/2009/10/mystery-history-solved_15.html; Newmark, *Sixty Years in Southern California*, 445.
101. Page, *Pasadena: Its Early Years*, 36.
102. Page, *Pasadena: Its Early Years*, 37.
103. Page, *Pasadena: Its Early Years*, 37.
104. Reid, *History of Pasadena*, 411–13.
105. Berry to T. B. Elliott, 30 August 1873.
106. Berry to T. B. Elliott, 8 October 1873.
107. D. M. Berry to T. B. Elliott, Los Angeles, January 1874 (date unknown), letter, box 1, Papers of the Thomas Balch Elliott Collection, 1873–1874, Huntington Library, San Marino, California.

108. James Guinn, *A History of California and An Extended History of Los Angeles Environs* (Los Angeles: Historical Record Company, 1915), 1:463; Newmark, *Sixty Years in Southern California*, 448; Page, *Pasadena: Its Early Years*, 38.
109. T. B. Elliott, "Possible Names for City," unknown date and year, box 2, Papers of the Thomas Balch Elliott Collection, 1873–1874, Huntington Library, San Marino, California.
110. Reid, *History of Pasadena*, 338.
111. Reid, *History of Pasadena*, 338.
112. Reid, *History of Pasadena*, 339.
113. Renato Rosaldo, "Imperialist Nostalgia," *Representations*, no. 26 (Spring 1989): 107.
114. Rosaldo, "Imperialist Nostalgia," 108.
115. Page, *Pasadena: Its Early Years*, 43.
116. Dumke, *The Boom of the Eighties*, 86–87; Newmark, *Sixty Years in Southern California*, 412; 445.
117. Dumke, *The Boom of the Eighties*, 88.
118. Page, *Pasadena: Its Early Years*, 43.
119. J. W. Wood, *Pasadena, California, Historical and Personal: A Complete History of the Indiana Colony* (Boston: Harvard University Press, 1917), 137.
120. Dolland M. Graham, quoted in Page, *Pasadena: Its Early Years*, 48.
121. García, *A World of Its Own*, 21.
122. García, *A World of Its Own*, 22–23.
123. Dumke, *The Boom of the Eighties*, 20.
124. Torres-Rouff, *Before L.A.*, 199–202. For a discussion on California's relationship with the railroad, see William Deverell, *Railroad Crossing: Californians and the Railroad, 1850–1910* (Berkeley: University of California Press, 1996).
125. Torres-Rouff, *Before L.A.*, 220.
126. Margaret Wilson, Diaries, Letter Book, and School Notebooks, 22 January 1868, box 38, Papers of the Benjamin Davis Wilson Collection, 1836–1894, Huntington Library, San Marino California.
127. Margaret Wilson, Diaries, Letter Book, and School Notebooks, 24 July 1872, box 38, Papers of the Benjamin Davis Wilson Collection, 1836–1894, Huntington Library, San Marino California.
128. Page, *Pasadena: Its Early Years*, 57.
129. Page, *Pasadena: Its Early Years*, 57.
130. Dumke, *The Boom of the Eighties*, 88; Newmark, *Sixty Years in Southern California*, 586; Wood, *History of Pasadena*, 467–68.
131. The billiard hall and saloon were a major source of conflict among residents. Many wanted Pasadena to be a community free of alcohol. After months of disagreement, Pasadena kept its saloon, and residents who opposed the idea left the town and established the city of South Pasadena. See Dumke, *The Boom of the Eighties*, 89; Page, *History of Pasadena*, 59–61.
132. Page, *Pasadena: Its Early Years*, 57.

133. Page, *Pasadena: Its Early Years*, 70–71.
134. Page, *Pasadena: Its Early Years*, 70–71.
135. Wood, *Pasadena, California*, 144–45.
136. Wood, *Pasadena, California*, 146.
137. U.S. Department of the Interior, *Population of the United States at the Tenth Census: 1880* (Washington D.C.: Government Printing Office, 1882); *Population of the United States at the Eleventh Census: 1890* (Washington D.C.: Government Printing Office, 1895).
138. Wood, *Pasadena, California*, 145.
139. Page, *Pasadena: Its Early Years*, 108.
140. Page, *Pasadena: Its Early Years*, 109.
141. Page, *Pasadena: Its Early Years*, 146.
142. Newmark, *Sixty Years in Southern California*, 592.

CONCLUSION

Epigraph: Eulalia Pérez, "Una vieja y sus recuerdos dictados," 128.

1. Tournament of Roses, "History of the Rose Parade," accessed, August 1, 2017, https://www.tournamentofroses.com/history/rose-parade.
2. City of Pasadena, "Heritage: A Short History of Pasadena's Native American, Spanish, and Mexican Heritage," accessed August 1, 2017, http://www.cityofpasadena.net/History.
3. I use the term *dynamic continuity* to refer to the shared commonalities among missionaries, rancheros, and gentlemen farmers across each period and how they used their power to create their respective landscapes and sociocultural identities.
4. Because the San Gabriel Mission followed the larger trends within Alta California, this discussion reflects the general history of Alta California's mission system.
5. Located in Mexico City, El Ángel de la Independencia, or the Angel of Independence, is the official monument commemorating the War for Mexican Independence in 1810.
6. This symbol was the Aztec deity Huitzilopochtli's indication to the Mexica people that they should settle at Tenochititlan, the site of present-day Mexico City. For a detailed discussion of Huitzilopochtli and the foundation of Tenochtitlan, see Manuel Aguilar Moreno, *Handbook to Life in the Aztec World* (New York: Oxford University Press, 2006), 142–46.
7. Anna Gorman, "Rose Parade Float Will Pay Tribute to Mexico," *Los Angeles Times*, December 16, 2009.
8. Anonymous ALIPAC Reactions quoted in Immigration Clearinghouse, "Mexico to Have Entry in Rose Parade- First in 40 Years," December 26, 2009, Immigration Clearinghouse, accessed March 18, 2018, http://web.archive.org/web/20100019092131/http://immigrationclearinghouse.org:80/mexico-to-have-entry-in-rose-parade-first-in-40-years.

9. Barbara Coe, quoted in Cindy Carcamo, "Rose Parade Float to Celebrate Mexico's Bicentennial," *Orange County Register*, December 29, 2009, accessed March 1, 2013, http://www.ocregister.com/articles/float-226168-parade-mexico.html.
10. Art Pedroza, December 31, 2009, "Racists Rush to Condemn Mexican Entry in the 2010 Rose Parade," *The Orange Juice Blog*, accessed March 1, 2013, http://www.orangejuiceblog.com/2009/12/racists-rush-to-condemn-mexican-entry-in-the-2010-rose-parade.
11. Anonymous ALIPAC Reactions quoted in Immigration Clearinghouse, "Mexico to Have Entry in Rose Parade- First in 40 Years," December 26, 2009 31, 2009, Immigration Clearinghouse, accessed March 18, 2018, http://web.archive.org/web/20100109092131/http://immigrationclearinghouse.org:80/mexico-to-have-entry-in-rose-parade-first-in-40-years.

BIBLIOGRAPHY

ARCHIVES AND MANUSCRIPTS COLLECTIONS

BANCROFT LIBRARY, BERKELEY, CALIFORNIA

Antonio Franco Coronel, "Cosas de California: Vecino de la ciudad de Los Angeles," 1877
Documents Pertaining to the Adjudication of Private Land Claims in California, circa 1852–1892
Documentos Relativos a las Misiones de California [Documents Related to the California Missions], 1769–1802, vol. 1 and 2
Eulalia Pérez, "Una vieja y sus recuerdos dictados . . . a la edad avanzada de 139 años, 1877," Index of the Spanish-Mexican Private Land Records and Cases of California, vol. 1–3
J. N. Bowman Papers Regarding California History, 1890–1965
"Recuerdos de José Arnaz," 1878
"María Teresa de la Guerra Hartnell, narrativa de la distinguida matron Californiana," 1875
Materials Relating to Benjamin S. Eaton
Pío Pico, Narración Histórica, 1877
Spanish Archives, Archivos de las Misiones, 1769–1856
William Petty Hartnell Papers, 1815–1852

CALIFORNIA STATE ARCHIVES, SACRAMENTO

Spanish Mexican Land Grants California State Archives, vol. 1–7

HENRY E. HUNTINGTON LIBRARY, SAN MARINO, CALIFORNIA

Benjamin Wilson Collection, 1836–1894
Heslop Family Papers, 1833–1906
Los Angeles County Prefecture Records, vol. 1 and A
Papers of Thomas Balch Elliot, 1873–1874
Papers of James F. Crank, 1880–1902

HONNOLD MUDD LIBRARY, CLAREMONT, CALIFORNIA

San Gabriel Mission Matrimonial Investigation Records, McPherson Collection

SANTA BARBARA MISSION ARCHIVE LIBRARY, SANTA BARBARA, CALIFORNIA

Annual Mission Report, San Gabriel Mission, 1824
California Mission Documents
Junípero Serra Collection

LOS ANGELES CITY ARCHIVES

Los Angeles City Council Documents
Padrón, 1836
Padrón, 1844

NEWSPAPERS

El Clamor Público
Examiner
Los Angeles Times
Orange County Register

WEBSITES

City of Pasadena Website, Office of the City Manager, http://cityofpasadena.net
City of Pasadena, "Heritage: A Short History of Pasadena's Native American, Spanish, and Mexican Heritage," accessed August 1, 2017, http://www.cityofpasadena.net/History
Huntington Library, Early Population Project Database, http://missions.huntington.org
Immigration Clearinghouse, http://immigrationclearinghouse.org (site discontinued)
Keepers of Our Indigenous Ways, Inc., Tongva Language, http://www.keepersofindigenousways.org

Pío Pico Genealogy, Pío Pico Inc., http://www.piopico.org/The_Family_Genealogy_of_Pio_Pico.htm

The Orange Juice Blog, http://www.orangejuiceblog.com

Tournament of Roses, "History of the Rose Parade," accessed August 1, 2017, https://www.tournamentofroses.com/history/rose-parade

PUBLISHED PRIMARY SOURCES

Bandini, Juan. "A Statistical Description of Alta California." In *Lands of Promise and Despair: Chronicles of Early California, 1535–1846*, edited by Rose Marie Beebe and Robert M. Senkewicz. Santa Clara: Santa Clara University, 2001, 375–85.

Dana, Richard Henry. *Two Years Before the Mast: A Personal Narrative of a Sailor's Life at Sea*. New York: Harper and Brothers, 1840.

Echeveste Reglamento, May 19, 1773. In Francisco Palou, *Historical Memoirs of New California*, edited and translated by Herbert E. Bolton, vol. 1, 58–77. Berkeley: University of California Press, 1926.

Evertsen, John R., Maurice Harris Newmark, Marco Ross Newmark, and Hector Alliot. *Census of the City and County of Los Angeles, California, for the Year 1850; Together with an Analysis and an Appendix*. Los Angeles: Times-Mirror Press, 1929.

Hastings, Lansford W. *The Emigrants' Guide to Oregon and California Containing Scenes and Incidents of a Party of Oregon Emigrants: A Description of California, with a Description of the Different Routes to Those Countries, and All Necessary Information Relative to the Equipment, Supplies, and the Method of Traveling*. Cincinnati: George Conclin, 1845.

Hayes, Benjamin Ignatius, and Marjorie Tisdale Wolcott. *Pioneer Notes from the Diaries of Judge Benjamin Hayes, 1849–1875*. New York: Arno Press, 1976.

Hoffman, Ogden. *Reports of Land Cases Determined in the United States District Court for the Northern District of California*. San Francisco: Numa Hubert, 1862.

Jones, William Carey, and William M. Eddy. *Report of the Secretary of the Interior, Communicating a Copy of the Report of William Carey Jones Special Agent to Examine the Subject of Land Titles in California*. Washington, D.C.: Gideon, 1850.

Lasuén, Fermín Francisco de, and Finbar Kenneally. *Writings of Fermín Francisco de Lasuén*. Washington, D.C.: Academy of American Franciscan History, 1965.

Nordhoff, Charles. *California: For Health, Pleasure, and Residence: A Book for Travellers and Settlers*. New York: Harper, 1873.

O'Sullivan, John. "Annexation," *United States Magazine and Democratic Review*, 17, no. 1 (July-August 1845): 5–10.

Recopilación de leyes de los reynos de las Indias. Madrid: Cultura Hispánica, 1973.

Robinson, Alfred, and Gerónimo Boscana. *Life in California: During A Residence of Several Years in That Territory: Comprising a Description of the Country and the Missionary Establishments, with Incidents, Observations, etc.: Illustrated with Numerous Engravings by an American*. New York: Wiley and Putnam, 1846.

Señan, José Francisco de Paula. *The Letters of José Señan, O.F.M., Mission San Buenaventura, 1796–1823*. San Francisco: Howell-Books, 1962.

Tac, Pablo. "Indian Life and Customs at Mission San Luis Rey: A Record of California Mission Life Written by Pablo Tac, An Indian Neophyte," edited and translated by Minna and Gordon Hewes. *The Americas* 9, no. 1 (July 1952): 87–106.

Truman, Benjamin Cummings. *Semi-tropical California: Its Climate, Healthfulness, Productiveness, and Scenery*. San Francisco: Bancroft, 1874.

U.S. Department of the Interior, *Population of the United States at the Seventh Census: 1850* Washington D.C.: Government Printing Office, 1853.

———. *Population of the United States at the Eight Census: 1860*. Washington D.C.: Government Printing Office, 1864.

———. *Population of the United States at the Ninth Census: 1870*. Washington D.C.: Government Printing Office, 1872.

———. *Population of the United States at the Tenth Census: 1880*. Washington D.C.: Government Printing Office, 1882.

———. *Population of the United States at the Eleventh Census: 1890*. Washington D.C.: Government Printing Office, 1895.

United States Land Commission. *Acts and Regulations of the United States Land Commission for Settling Private Land Claims in California*. San Francisco, 1852.

SECONDARY SOURCES

Adorno, Rolena. "Discourses on Colonialism: Bernal Díaz, Las Casas, and the Twentieth-Century Reader." *Modern Language Notes* 103 (March 1988): 239–58.

Almaguer, Tomás. *Racial Fault Lines: The Historical Origins of White Supremacy in California*. Berkeley: University of California Press, 1994.

Alonzo, Armando C. *Tejano Legacy: Rancheros and Settlers in South Texas, 1734–1900*. Albuquerque: University of New Mexico Press, 1998.

Archibald, Robert. *The Economic Aspects of the California Missions*. Washington, D.C.: Academy of American Franciscan History, 1978.

Baker, Patricia. "The Bandini Family." *Journal of San Diego History* 15, no. 1 (Winter 1969): 23–27.

Bancroft, Hubert Howe. *Histories of the Pacific States of North America: California Pastoral*. San Francisco: History Company, 1888.

———. *History of California*, vol. 1. San Francisco: Bancroft, 1884.

———. *The Works of Hubert Howe Bancroft*. San Francisco: History Company, 1888.

Barr, Juliana. *Peace Came in the Form of a Woman: Indians and Spaniards in the Texas Borderlands*. Chapel Hill: University of North Carolina Press, 2007.

Barraclough, Laura R. *Making the San Fernando Valley: Rural Landscapes, Urban Development, and White Privilege*. Athens: University of Georgia Press, 2011.

Barron, Hal. "Staying Down on the Farm: Social Processes of Settled Rural Life in the Nineteenth-Century North." In *The Countryside in the Age of Capitalist Transforma-*

tion: Essays in the Social History of Rural America, edited by Steven Hahn and Jonathan Prude, 327–43. Chapel Hill: University of North Carolina Press, 1985.

Barrow, H. D. "Stephen C. Foster," *The Quarterly* 3–4. (1883): 179–83.

———. "William Wolfskill, The Pioneer." *Annual Publication of the Historical Society of Southern California and of the Pioneers of Los Angeles County* 5–6 (1902–1904): 287–94.

Baur, John E. "Los Angeles County in the Health Rush, 1870–1900." *California Historical Society Quarterly* 31 (March 1952): 13–31.

Bean, Lowell. *Mukatâ People: The Cahuilla Indians of Southern California*. Berkeley: University of California Press, 1972.

Bean, Lowell, and Charles R. Smith. "Gabrielino." In *Handbook of North American Indians*. Vol 8, *California*, edited by William Sturtevant, 538–49. Washington D.C.: Smithsonian Institution, 1978.

Beebee, Richard. "Judge Benjamin Eaton: Father of Pasadena, South Pasadena, and Altadena." *The Quarterly Magazine* (Spring 2007). Accessed September 10, 2012. http://www.thequarterly.com/spr07content/pdf/p37.pdf (site discontinued).

Beebe, Rose Marie, and Robert M. Senkewicz. *Junípero Serra: California, Indians, and the Transformation of a Missionary*. Norman: University of Oklahoma, 2015.

Beebe, Rose Marie, and Robert M. Senkewicz, eds. *Land of Promise and Despair: Chronicles of Alta California, 1535–1846*. Santa Clara, Calif.: Santa Clara University, 2001.

Bhaba, Homi K. *The Location of Culture*. New York: Routledge Press, 1994.

Billington, Ray Allen. *America's Frontier Heritage*. Los Angeles: Holt, Rinehart and Winston, 1963.

Billington, Ray Allen, and Martin Ridge. *Westward Expansion: A History of the American Frontier*. 6th ed. Albuquerque: University of New Mexico Press, 2001.

Blake, Kevin S., and Jeffery S. Smith. "Pueblo Mission Churches as Symbols of Permanence and Identity." *Geographical Review* 90, no. 3 (July 2000): 359–80.

Bolton, Herbert E. "The Mission as a Frontier Institution in the Spanish-American Colonies." *American Historical Review* 23, no. 1 (October 1917): 42–61.

Boscana, Gerónimo, Alfred Robinson, Phil Townsend Hanna, and John Peabody Harrington. *Chinigchinich*. Santa Ana, Calif.: Fine Arts Press, 1933.

Bourne, Jenny. *In Essentials, Unity: An Economic History of the Grange*. Athens: Ohio University Press, 2017.

Bouvier, Virginia Marie. *Women and the Conquest of California, 1542–1840: Codes of Silence*. Tucson: University of Arizona Press, 2001.

Bowman, J. N. "Weights and Measurements of Provincial California." *California Historical Quarterly*, 30, no. 4 (December 1951): 315–38.

Burton, George Ward. *Men of Achievement in the Great Southwest: A Story of Pioneer Struggles During Early Days in Los Angeles and Southern California. With Biographies, Heretofore Unpublished Facts, Anecdotes, and Incidents in the Lives of the Builders*. Los Angeles: Los Angeles Times, 1904.

Camarillo, Albert. *Chicanos in a Changing Society: From Mexican Pueblos to American Barrios in Santa Barbara and Southern California, 1848–1930*. Cambridge, Mass.: Harvard University Press, 1979.

Camp, Stacy. "From Nuisance to Nostalgia: The Historical Anthropology of Nature Tourism in Southern California, 1890–1940." *Historical Archeology* 47, no. 3 (September 2013): 81–96.

Campbell, Marne L. *Making Black Los Angeles: Class, Gender, and Community, 1850–1917*. Chapel Hill: University of North Carolina, 2016.

Carpio, Genevieve Carpio. "From Citrus Belt to Inland Empire: Race, Place, and Mobility in Southern California 1880–2000." PhD diss., University of Southern California, 2013. http://digitallibrary.usc.edu/cdm/ref/collection/p15799coll3/id/323141.

Carrera Stampa, Manuel. "Evolution of Weights and Measurements in New Spain." *Hispanic American Historical Review*, 29, no. 1 (February 1949): 2–24.

Carrillo, Carlos. "Speech of Carlos Antonio Carrillo in the Mexican Chamber of Deputies, Requesting Adequate Courts for the Administration of Justice in Alta California, 1831." In *The Coming of Justice to California: Three Documents*. Edited by John Galvin. Translated by Adelaide Smithers. San Francisco: John Howell Books, 1963.

———. "The California Delegate Argues for Rule of Law." In *Lands of Promise and Despair: Chronicles of Early California, 1535–1846*. Edited by Rose Marie Beebe and Robert M. Senkewicz. Santa Clara, Calif.: Santa Clara University, 2001, 386–89.

Casas, María Raquel. "María Feliciana Araballo." In *Latinas in the United States, Volume 1*, edited by Vicki L. Ruiz and Virginia Sánchez Korrol, 55–56. Bloomington: Indiana University Press, 2006.

———. *Married to a Daughter of the Land: Spanish-Mexican Women and Interethnic Marriage in California, 1820–1880*. Reno: University of Nevada Press, 2007.

Castañeda, Antonia I. "Engendering the History of Alta California, 1769–1848: Gender, Sexuality and the Family." In *Contested Eden: California Before the Gold Rush*, edited by Ramón A. Gutiérrez and Richard J. Orsi, 230–59. Berkeley: University of California Press, 1998.

———. "Malinche, Calafia, y Toypurina." In *Three Decades of Engendering History: Selected Works of Antonia I. Castañeda*, edited by Linda Heidenreich and Antonia Castañeda, 65–88. Denton: University of North Texas Press, 2014.

———. "Presidarias y Pobladoras: Spanish Mexican Women in Frontier Monterey, Alta California, 1770–1821." PhD diss., Stanford University, 1990.

———. "Sexual Violence in the Policies and Politics of Conquest: Amerindian Women and the Spanish Conquest of Alta California." In *Building with Our Hands: New Directions in Chicana Studies*, edited by Adela de la Torre and Beatríz Pesquera, 15–33. Berkeley: University of California Press, 1993.

Castillo, Edward D. "Gender Status Decline, Resistance, and Accommodation Among Female Neophytes in the Missions of California: A San Gabriel Case Study." *American Indian Cultures and Research Journal* 18, no. 1 (1994): 67–93.

Caughey, John. "Don Benito Wilson: An Average Southern Californian." *Huntington Library Quarterly* 2, no. 3 (April 1939): 285–300.

Chang, David. *The Color of the Land: Race, Nation, and the Politics of Land Ownership in Oklahoma, 1832–1929*. Chapel Hill: University of North Carolina Press, 2010.

Chávez-García, Miroslava. *Negotiating Conquest: Gender and Power in California, 1770s to 1880s*. Tucson: University of Arizona Press, 2004.

Chen, Sucheng. "A People of Exceptional Character: Ethnic Diversity, Nativism, and Racism in the California Gold Rush." In *Rooted in Barbarous Soil: People, Culture, and Community in Gold Rush California*, edited by Kevin Starr and Richard Orsi, 44–85. Berkeley: University of California Press, 2000.

———. *Bittersweet Soil: The Chinese in California Agriculture, 1860–1910*. Berkeley: University of California Press, 1986.

Churchill, Charles B. *Adventurers and Prophets: American Autobiographers in Mexican California, 1828–1847*. Spokane: Clark, 1995.

Clary, David A. *Eagles and Empire: The United States, Mexico, and the Struggle for a Continent*. New York: Bantam Dell, 2009.

Cleland, Robert. *The Cattle on a Thousand Hills: Southern California, 1850–1880*. San Marino: Huntington Library, 1963.

Connaughton, Brian. "The Enemy Within: Catholics and Liberalism in Independent Mexico, 1821–1860." in *The Divine Charter: Constitutionalism and Liberalism in Nineteenth-Century Mexico*, edited by Jaime E. Rodríguez, 183–202. Lanham: Rowman and Littlefield, 2005.

Cook, Lynn, and Janet Ladue. *The First Ladies of California*. Bloomington, Ind.: Xlibris, 2007.

Cook, Sherburne Friend. *The Conflict Between the California Indian and White Civilization*. Berkeley: University of California Press, 1976.

Coons, Bruce. "A Brief History of Ranch Guejito." *Save Our Heritage Organization Magazine* 38 no.1 (2007). Accessed September 1, 2012. http://sohosandiego.org/reflections/2007-1/guejito_history.html.

Cope, R. Douglas. *The Limits of Racial Domination: Plebian Society in Colonial Mexico City*. Madison: University of Wisconsin Press, 1994.

Cosgrove, Denis. *Social Formation and Symbolic Landscape*. Madison: University of Wisconsin Press, 1984.

Costello, Julia G. "Purchasing Patterns of the California Missions in Ca. 1805." *Historical Archaeology* 26, no. 1 (1992): 59–66.

Crenshaw, Kimberlé Williams. "Race, Reform, and Retrenchment: Transformation and Legitimation in Antidiscrimination Law." *Harvard Law Review* 101, no. 7 (May 1988): 1331–87.

de la Guerra, Angustias. "Occurrences in Hispanic California." In *Nineteenth Century Californio Testimonials*, edited by Rosaura Sánchez, Beatrice Pita, and Bárbara Reyes, 193–200. La Jolla: University of California San Diego/Third World Studies, 1994.

de la Teja, Jesús F. "Discovering the Tejano Community in 'Early' Texas." *Journal of the Early Republic* 18, no. 1 (Spring 1998): 73–98.

———. *Tejano Leadership in Mexican and Revolutionary Texas*. College Station: Texas A&M Press, 2010.

DeLay, Brian. *War of a Thousand Deserts: Indian Raids and the U.S.-Mexican War*. New Haven: Yale University Press; 2008.

Dear, Michael, and Jennifer Wolch. "How Territory Shapes Social Life." In *The Power of Geography: How Territory Shapes Social Life*, edited by Jennifer Wolch and Michael Dear, 1–18. Boston: Unwin Hyman, 1989.

Derrida, Jacques. *Dissemination*. Translated by Barbara Johnson. London: Continuum International Publishing, 2004.

Deusen, Nancy Elena. *Between the Sacred and the Worldly: Institutional and Cultural Practice of Recogimiento in Colonial Lima*. Stanford, Calif.: Stanford University Press, 2001.

Deverell, William Francis. *Whitewashed Adobe: The Rise of Los Angeles and the Remaking of Its Mexican Past*. Berkeley: University of California Press, 2004.

Dickson, Lucile E. "The Founding and Early History of Anaheim, California." *Annual Publication of the Historical Society of Southern California* 11, no. 2 (1919): 26–37.

Dumke, Glenn S. *The Boom of the Eighties in Southern California*. San Marino, Calif.: Huntington Library, 1963.

Ebeling, Walter. *The Fruited Plain: The Story of American Agriculture*. Berkeley: University of California Press, 1979.

Engelhardt, Zephyrin. *San Fernando Rey: The Mission of the Valley*. Chicago: Franciscan Herald Press, 1927.

———. *San Gabriel Mission and the Beginnings of Los Angeles*. San Gabriel, Calif.: Mission San Gabriel, 1927.

Erdman, Ann. "PIO Mystery History," *Pasadena Public Information Office Blog*, October 15, 2009. Accessed March 21, 2012. http://pasadenapio.blogspot.com/2009/10/mystery-history-solved_15.html.

Estrada, William D. "The Last Latino Mayor of Los Angeles: José Cristóbal Aguilar, 1866–1868, 1871–1872." *The City Project Blog: Equal Justice, Democracy, and Livability for All*, June 30, 2005. Accessed March 21, 2013. http://www.cityprojectca.org/blog/archives/117.

———. *The Los Angeles Plaza: Sacred and Contested Space*. Austin: University of Texas Press, 2008.

Fanon, Frantz. *Black Skins, White Masks*. Translated by Richard Philcox. New York: Grove Press, 1952.

Farnsworth, Paul, and Robert H. Jackson. "Cultural, Economic, and Demographic Change in the Missions of Alta California: The Case of Nuestra Señora de la Soledad." In *The New Latin American Mission History*, edited by Erick Langer and Robert H. Jackson, 109–29. Lincoln: University of Nebraska Press, 1995.

Fifer, Valerie. *American Progress: The Growth of Transport, Tourist, and Information Industries in the Nineteenth-Century West*. Chester, Conn.: Globe Pequot, 1988.

Fischer, John Ryan. *Cattle Colonialism: An Environmental History of California and Hawai'i*. Chapel Hill: University of North Carolina Press, 2015.

Fogleson, Robert. *The Fragmented Metropolis: Los Angeles, 1850–1930*. Cambridge, Mass.: MIT Press, 1967.

Foley, Neil. *The White Scourge: Mexicans, Blacks, and Poor Whites in Texas Cotton* Culture. Berkeley: University of California Press, 1997.

Foucault, Michel. *The History of Sexuality*. New York: Pantheon, 1978.

Frank, Ross. *From Settler to Citizen: New Mexico Development and the Creation of the Vecino Society*. Berkeley: University of California Press, 2001.

García, Israel Arroyo. "Lucas Alamán." in *The Concise Encyclopedia of Mexico*, edited by Michael Werner, 5–7. Chicago: Fitzroy Dearborn Press, 2001.

García, Matt. *A World of Its Own: Race, Labor, and Citrus in the Making of Greater Los Angeles, 1900–1970*. Chapel Hill: University of North Carolina Press, 2001.

Gates, Paul W. *Land and Law in California: Essays on Land Policies*. Ames: Iowa State University Press, 1991.

Geertz, Clifford. *The Interpretation of Cultures: Selected Essays*. New York: Basic Books, 1973.

Geiger, Maynard, and José Ma. De Zalvidea. "Reply of Mission San Gabriel to the Questionnaire of the Spanish Government in 1812 Concerning the Native Culture of the California Mission Indians." *The Americas* 12, no. 1 (July 1959): 77–84.

Gentilcore, R. Louise. "Missions and Mission Lands of Alta California." *Annals of the Association of American Geographers* 51, no. 1 (March 1961): 46–72.

Giddens, Anthony. *Central Problems in Social Theory: Action, Structure, and Contradiction in Social Analysis*. Berkeley: University of California Press, 1979.

Giorgio, Perissinotto, ed. *Documenting Everyday Life in Early Spanish California: The Santa Barbara Presidio: Memorias y Facturas, 1779–1810*. Santa Barbara, Calif.: Santa Barbara Trust for Historic Preservation, 1998.

Gómez, Laura E. *Manifest Destinies: The Making of the Mexican American Race*. New York: New York University, 2007.

Gomez-Quiñones, Juan. *Roots of Chicano Politics, 1600–1940*. Albuquerque: University of New Mexico Press, 1994.

González, Deena J. *Refusing the Favor: The Spanish-Mexican Women of Santa Fe, 1820–1880*. New York: Oxford University Press, 1999.

González, Michael J. "Searching for the Feathered Serpent: Exploring the Origins of Mexican Culture in Los Angeles, 1830–1850." PhD diss., University of California, Berkeley, 1993.

Green, Perry M. "History of Pasadena." In *A Southern Paradise*, edited by R. W. C Farnsworth. Pasadena: Farnsworth, 1883.

Greenberg, Amy. *Manifest Manhood and the Antebellum American Empire*. New York: Cambridge University Press, 2005.

Greenfield, Amy Butler. *A Perfect Red: Empire, Espionage, and the Quest for the Color of Desire*. New York: HarperCollins, 2005.

Griswold del Castillo, Richard. *Treaty of Guadalupe Hidalgo: A Legacy of Conquest*. Norman: University of Oklahoma Press, 1990.

———. "La Raza Hispano Americana: The Emergence of an Urban Culture Among the Spanish Speaking of Los Angeles, 1850–1880." Ph.D. diss., University of California Los Angeles, 1974.

Guinn, J. M. *A History of California and an Extended History of Its Southern Coast Counties, Also Containing Biographies of Well-Known Citizens of the Past and Present.* Los Angeles: Historic Record Co., 1907.

Gunn Allen, Paula. *The Sacred Hoop: Recovering the Feminine in the American Indian Tradition.* Boston: Beacon Press, 1985.

Gutiérrez, Ramón. *When Jesus Came, the Corn Mothers Went Away: Marriage, Sexuality, and Power in New Mexico, 1500–1848.* Stanford, Calif.: Stanford University Press, 1991.

Guy, Donna, and Thomas Sheridan, *Contested Ground: Comparative Frontiers on the Northern and Southern Edges of the Spanish Empire.* Tucson: University of Arizona Press, 1998.

Gyory, Andrew, *Closing the Gate: Race Politics and the Chinese Exclusion Act.* Chapel Hill: University of North California Press, 1998.

Haas, Lisbeth. *Conquests and Historical Identities in California, 1769–1936.* Berkeley: University of California Press, 1995.

Hackel, Steven W. *Children of Coyote, Missionaries of Saint Francis: Indian-Spanish Relations in Colonial California, 1769–1850.* Chapel Hill: University of North Carolina Press, 2005.

———. "Land, Labor, and Production: The Colonial Economy of Spanish and Mexican California." In *Contested Eden: California Before the Gold Rush*, edited by Ramón Gutiérrez and Richard J. Orsi, 111–46. Berkeley: University of California Press, 1998.

———. "Sources of Rebellion: Indian Testimony and the Mission San Gabriel Uprising of 1785," *Ethnohistory* 50, no. 4 (Fall 2003): 643–69.

Hahn, Steven, and Jonathan Prude, "Introduction." In *The Countryside in the Age of Capitalist Transformation: Essays in The Social History of Rural America*, edited by Steven Hahn and Jonathan Prude. Chapel Hill: University of North Carolina Press, 1985.

Hale, Charles A. *Mexican Liberalism in the Age of Mora, 1821–1853.* New Haven, Conn.: Yale University Press, 1968.

Hall, Stuart. "Cultural Identity and Diaspora." In *Identity: Community, Culture, Difference*, edited by Jonathan Rutherford, 222–37. London: Lawrence and Wishart, 1990.

Hämäläinem, Pekka. "The Shapes of Power: Indians, Europeans, and North American Worlds from Seventeenth to Nineteenth Centuries." In *Contested Spaces of Early America*, edited by Juliana Barr and Edward Countryman, 31–68. Philadelphia: University of Pennsylvania, 2014.

Heidenreich, Linda. *"This Land Was Mexican Once": Histories of Resistance from Northern California.* Austin: University of Texas Press, 2007.

Hernández, Ellie D. *Postnationalism in Chicana/o Literature and Culture.* Austin: University of Texas Press, 2009.

Hornbeck, David. "Land Tenure and Rancho Expansion in Alta California, 1784–1846." *Journal of Historical Geography* 4, no. 4 (October 1978): 371–90.

Horsman, Reginald. *Race and Manifest Destiny: The Origins of American Racial Anglo-Saxonism.* Cambridge, Mass.: Harvard University Press, 1981.

Hurtado, Albert. *John Sutter: A Life on the North American Frontier.* Norman: University of Oklahoma Press, 2006.

Hutchinson, C. Alan. *Frontier Settlement in Mexican California: The Híjar-Padrés Colony and Its Origins, 1769–1835*. New Haven, Conn.: Yale University Press, 1969.

Jackson, Robert H. "Northwestern New Spain: The Pimería Alta and the Californias." In *New Views of Borderlands History*, edited by Robert H. Jackson, 73–106. Albuquerque: University of New Mexico Press, 1998.

———. "The Changing Economic Structure of the Alta California Missions: A Reinterpretation." *Pacific Historical Review* 61, no. 4 (May 1992): 387–415.

———. "The Formation of Frontier Indigenous Communities: Missions in California and Texas." In *New Views of Borderlands History*, edited by Robert H. Jackson, 131–56. Albuquerque: University of New Mexico Press, 1998.

Jackson, Robert H., and Edward D. Castillo. *Indians, Franciscans, and Spanish Colonization: The Impact of the Mission System on California Indians*. Albuquerque: University of New Mexico Press, 1995.

Jacobson, Matthew. *Whiteness of a Different Color: European Immigrants and the Alchemy of Race*. Cambridge, Mass.: Harvard University Press, 1998.

Jelinek, Lawrence James. "'Property of Every Kind': Ranching and Farming During the Gold-Rush Era." In *A Golden State: Mining and Economic Development in Gold Rush California*, edited by James Rawls and Richard Orsi, 233–49. Berkeley: University of California Press, 1999.

Johnston, Bernice. *California's Gabrielino Indians*. Los Angeles: Southwest Museum, 1962.

Jones, Oakah L. *Los Paisanos: Spanish Settlers on the Northern Frontier of New Spain*. Norman: University of Oklahoma Press, 1979.

Kellogg, Susan. "From Parallel and Equivalent to Separate but Unequal: Tenocha Mexica Women, 1500–1700." In *Indian Women of Colonial Mexico*, edited by Susan Schroeder, Stephanie Wood, and Robert Haskett, 123–43. Norman: University of Oklahoma Press, 1999.

Kemper, Robert V. "The Compadrazgo in Urban Mexico." *Anthropological Quarterly* 55 no. 1 (January 1982): 17–30.

Kessell, John L. *Pueblos, Spaniards, and the Kingdom of New Mexico*. Norman: University of Oklahoma Press, 2008.

Kielbasa, John. "Historic Adobes of Los Angeles County, Southern County, Avila Adobe." Accessed May 15, 2012. http://www.laokay.com/halac.

Kirker, Harold. *California's Architectural Frontier: Style and Tradition in the Nineteenth Century*. Santa Barbara, Calif.: Peregrine Smith, 1973.

Knaut, Andrew L. *The Pueblo Revolt of 1680: Conquest and Resistance in Seventeenth Century New Mexico*. Norman: University of Oklahoma Press, 1995.

Knobloch, Frieda. *Culture of Wilderness: Agriculture as Colonization in the American West*. Chapel Hill: University of North Carolina, 1996.

Kroeber, A. L. *Handbook of the Indians of California*. New York: Dover, 1976.

Kropp, Phoebe S. *California Vieja: Culture and Memory in a Modern American Place*. Berkeley: University of California Press, 2006.

Lake, Alison. *Colonial Rosary: The Spanish and Indian Missions of California*. Athens: Ohio University Press, 2014.

Lamar, Howard. "From Bondage to Contract: Ethnic Labor in the American West, 1600–1890." In *The Countryside in the Age of Capitalist Transformation: Essays in the Social History of Rural America*, ed. Steve Hahn and Jonathan Prude, 293–324. Chapel Hill: University of North Carolina Press, 1985.

Langer, Erick and Robert Langer, eds. *The New Latin American Mission History*. Lincoln: University of Nebraska Press, 1995.

Lerner, Gerda Lerner. *The Creation of Patriarchy*. New York: Oxford University Press, 1986.

Lightfoot, Kent G. *Indians, Missionaries, and Merchants: The Legacy of Colonial Encounters on the California Frontiers*. Berkeley: University of California Press, 2005.

Livingston, M. M. "The Earliest Spanish Land Grants in California." *Annual Publication of the Historical Society of Southern California* 9, no. 3 (1914): 195–96.

López, Ian F. "The Social Construction of Race." In *Critical Race Theory: The Cutting Edge*, edited by Richard Delgado, 191–203. Philadelphia: Temple University Press, 1995.

Martin, Cheryl, and Mark Wasserman, *Latin America and Its People*. New York: Pearson Longman, 2005.

Martin, Cheryl English. *Governance and Society in Colonial Mexico: Chihuahua in the Eighteenth Century*. Stanford, Calif.: Stanford University Press, 1996.

Mason, William. *The Census of 1790: A Demographic History of Colonial California*. Novato, Calif.: Ballena Press, 1998.

McCawley, William. *The First Angelinos: The Gabrielino Indians of Los Angeles*. Novato, Calif.: Ballena Press, 1996.

McClung, William. *Landscapes of Desire: Anglo Mythologies of Los Angeles*. Berkeley: University of California Press, 2000.

McPherson, James M. *Battle Cry of Freedom: The Civil War Era*. New York: Oxford University Press, 1988.

McWilliams, Carey. *North From Mexico: The Spanish Speaking People of the U.S.* Philadelphia: Lippincott, 1949.

Menchaca, Martha. "Chicano Indianism: A Historical Account of Racial Repression in the United States." *American Ethnologist* 20, no. 3 (August 1993): 583–603.

———. *Recovering History, Constructing Race the Indian, Black, and White Roots of Mexican Americans*. Austin: University of Texas Press, 2001.

Meyer, Michael C., William L. Sherman, and Susan M. Deeds. "The First Mexican Empire." In *The Course of Mexican History*, 6th edition. New York: Oxford University Press, 1999, 288–97.

Miller, Bruce W. *The Gabrielino*. Los Osos, Calif.: Sand River Press, 1991.

Milliken, Randall. *A Time of Little Choice: The Disintegration of Tribal Culture in the San Francisco Bay Area, 1769–1810*. Banning, Calif.: Ballena Press, 1995.

Moehring, Eugene P. *Urbanism and Empire in the Far West, 1840–1890*. Reno: University of Nevada Press, 2004.

Monroy, Douglas. "The Creation and Re-Creation of Californio Society." In *Contested Eden: California before the Gold Rush*, edited by Ramón A. Gutiérrez and Richard J. Orsi, 173–95. Berkeley: University of California Press, 1998.

———. *Thrown Among Strangers: The Making of Mexican American Culture in California.* Berkeley: University of California Press, 1993.

Montgomery, Charles. *The Spanish Redemption: Heritage, Power, and Loss on New Mexico's Upper Rio Grande.* Berkeley: University of California Press, 2002.

Moorhead, Max L. *The Presidio: Bastion of the Spanish Borderlands.* Norman: University of Oklahoma Press, 1975.

Moreno, Manuel Aguilar. *Handbook to Life in the Aztec World.* New York: Oxford University Press, 2006, 142–46.

Murrin, John M. "The Jeffersonian Triumph and American Exceptionalism." *Journal of the Early Republic* 20, no. 1 (Spring 2000): 1–25.

Nelson, Howard J. "The Two Pueblos of Los Angeles: Agricultural Village and Embryo Town." *Southern California Quarterly* 59, no. 1 (Spring 1977): 1–11.

Newmark, Harris. *Sixty Years in California 1865–1913: Containing the Reminisces of Harris Newmark*, edited by Maurice Newark and Marco Newmark. New York: Knickerbocker Press, 1916.

Newmark, Maurice H., and Marco R. Newmark. *Census of the City and County of Los Angeles, California for the Year 1850.* Los Angeles: The Times-Mirror Press, 1929.

Noel, Charles C. "Missionary Preachers in Spain: Teaching Social Virtue in the Eighteenth Century." *American Historical Review* 90, no. 4 (October 1985): 813–36.

Ogden, Adele. *The California Sea Otter Trade, 1784–1848.* Berkeley: University of California Press, 1941.

Omi, Michael, and Howard Winant. *Racial Formation in the United States: From the 1960s to the 1990s.* 2nd ed. New York: Routledge, 1994.

Ortíz, Fernando. *Contrapunteo Cubano del tabaco y el azúcar* [Cuban counterpoint tobacco and sugar]. Havana: Jésus Montero, 1940.

Page, Henry Markham. *Pasadena: Its Early Years.* Los Angeles: Morrison, 1964.

Pérez, Emma. *The Decolonial Imaginary: Writing Chicanas Into History.* Bloomington: Indiana University Press, 1999.

Peterson, Robert H. *Altadena's Golden Years: More than 250 Photographs of the Community's Early Landmarks, Events, and People.* Alhambra, Calif.: Sinclair, 1976.

Pierce, Jason. *Making the White Man's West: Whiteness and the Creation of the American West.* Boulder: University of Colorado Press, 2016.

Pitt, Leonard. *The Decline of the Californios: A Social History of the Spanish-Speaking Californians, 1846–1890.* Berkeley: University of California Press, 1966.

Pitti, Stephen. *The Devil in Silicon Valley: Northern California, Race, and Mexican Americans.* Princeton, N.J.: Princeton University Press, 2003.

Pomeroy, Earl. *In Search of the Golden West: The Tourist in Western America.* Lincoln: University of Nebraska, 1990.

Pratt, Julius W. "The Origin of Manifest Destiny." *The American Historical Review* 32, no. 4 (July 1927): 795–98.

Prieto, Covadonga Lamar. "Land Ownership as a Resources for Constructing Otherness in 19th Century California." In *Otherness in Hispanic Culture*, edited by Teresa

Fernández Ulloa, 288–310. New Castle upon Tyne, UK: Cambridge Scholars Publishing, 2014.

Pubols, Louise. "Patriarchy and Power in Mexican California, 1800–1880." In *Continental Crossroads: Re-mapping U.S.-Mexico Borderlands History*, edited by Samuel Truett and Elliott Young, 67–94. Durham, N.C.: Duke University Press, 2004.

———. *The Father of All: The de la Guerra Family, Power, and Patriarchy in Mexican California*. Western Histories 1. Berkeley, Calif.: University of California Press and Huntington Library, 2009.

Radding, Cynthia. *Wandering Peoples: Colonialism, Ethnic Spaces, and Ecological Frontiers in Northwestern Mexico, 1700–1850*. Durham, N.C.: Duke University Press, 1997.

Rawls, James J. *Indians of California: The Changing Image*. Norman: University of Oklahoma Press, 1984.

Raymond, Elizabeth. "When the Desert Won't Bloom: Environmental Limitation and the Great Basin." In *Many Wests: Place, Culture, and Regional Identity*, edited by David M. Wrobel and David S. Steiner, 71–92. Lawrence: University Press of Kansas, 1997.

Read, Nat B. *Don Benito: From Mountain Man to Mayor, Los Angeles, 1841–1878*. Los Angeles: Angel City Press, 2008.

Reid, Hiram A., and Alfred James McClatchie. *History of Pasadena, Comprising An Account of the Native Indian, the Early Spanish, the Mexican, the American, the Colony, and the Incorporated City, Occupancies of the Rancho San Pasqual, and Its Adjacent Mountains, Canyons, Waterfalls and Other Objects*. Pasadena, Calif.: Pasadena History Co., 1895.

Reid, Hugo, and Robert F. Heizer. *The Indians of Los Angeles County: Hugo Reid's Letters of 1852*. Los Angeles: Southwest Museum, 1968.

Reyes, Bárbara. *Private Women, Public Lives: Gender and the Missions of the Californias*. Austin: University of Texas Press, 2009.

Ríos-Bustamante, Antonio. "Los Angeles, Pueblo and Region, 1781–1850: Continuation and Adaptation on the North Mexican Periphery." Ph.D. diss., University of California, Los Angeles, 1985.

———. *Mexican Los Angeles*. Moorpark, Calif.: Floricanto Press, 1992.

Robinson, W. W. *Land in California, The Story of Mission Lands, Ranchos, Squatters, Mining Claims, Railroad Grants, Land Scrip and Homesteads*. Berkeley: University of California Press, 1948.

Roediger, David. *Wages of Whiteness: Race and the Making of the American Working Class*. London: Verso, 1991.

Romo, Ricardo. *East Los Angeles: History of a Barrio*. Austin: University of Texas Press, 1983.

Rosaldo, Renato. "Imperialist Nostalgia." Special issue, *Representations: Memory and Counter-Memory*, no. 26 (Spring 1989): 107–22.

Ross, Ivy B. "The Confirmation of Spanish and Mexican Land Grants in California." Ph.D. diss., University of California, Berkeley, 1928.

Rothman, Hal. *Devil's Bargain: Tourism in the Twentieth-Century American West*. Lawrence: University of Kansas, 1998.

Sackman, Douglas Cazaux. *Orange Empire: California and the Fruits of Eden*. Berkeley: University of California Press, 2005.

Sánchez, Rosaura. *Telling Identities: The Californio Testimonios*. Minneapolis: University of Minnesota Press, 1995.

Sánchez, Rosaura, Beatrice Pita, and Bárbara Reyes, eds. *Nineteenth Century Californio Testimonials*. La Jolla, Calif.: University of California San Diego/Third World Studies, 1994.

Sandos, James A. "'Because He Is a Liar and a Thief': Conquering the Residents of 'Old' California, 1850–1880." In *Rooted in Barbarous Soil: People, Culture, and Community in Gold Rush California*, edited by Keven Starr and Robert J. Orsí, 86–112. Berkley: University of California Press, 2000.

———. *Converting California: Indians and Franciscans in the Missions*. New Haven: Yale University Press, 2004.

Santiago, Mark. *Massacre at the Yuma Crossing: Spanish Relations with the Quechans, 1789–1782*. Tucson: University of Arizona Press, 2010.

Saxton, Alexander. *The Indispensable Enemy: Labor and the Anti-Chinese Movement in California*. Berkeley: University of California, 1971.

Schaff, Philip. *The Creeds of Christendom: With A History and Critical Notes*. New York: Harper, 1877.

Scott, Joan Wallach. *Gender and the Politics of History*. New York: Columbia University Press, 1988.

Seacrest, William B. *California Disasters, 1812–1899: Firsthand Accounts of Fires, Shipwrecks, Floods, Epidemics, Earthquakes and Other California Tragedies*. Sanger, Ca: Quill Driver Books/Word Dancer Press, 2005.

Seed, Patricia. "Social Dimensions of Race: Mexico City, 1753." *Hispanic American Historical Review*, 62(4), 1982: 569–606.

———. *To Love, Honor, and Obey in Colonial Mexico: Conflicts Over Marriage Choice, 1574–1821*. Stanford, Calif.: Stanford University Press, 1988.

Sheridan, Thomas E. *Los Tucsonenses: The Mexican Community in Tucson, 1854–1941*. Tucson: University of Arizona, 1986.

Silliman, Stephen. *Lost Laborers in Colonial California: Native Americans and the Archaeology of Rancho Petaluma*. Tucson: University of Arizona Press, 2004.

———. "Theoretical Perspectives on Labor and Colonialism: Reconsidering the California Missions." *Journal of Anthropological Archaeology* 20, no. 4 (December 2001): 379–407.

Silverblatt, Irene. *Moon, Sun and Witches: Gender Ideologies and Class in Inca and Colonial Peru*. Princeton, N.J.: Princeton University Press, 1987.

Soja, Edward. *Postmodern Geographies: The Reassertion of Space in Critical Social Theory*. London: Verso, 1989.

Spitzzeri, Paul R. *The Workman and Temple Families of Southern California, 1830–1930*. Dallas: Seligson, 2008.

Starr, Kevin. *California: A History*. New York: Modern Library, 2005.

Stern, Steve J. *The Secret History of Gender: Women, Men, and Power in Late Colonial Mexico*. Chapel Hill: University of North Carolina Press, 1995.

Sweet, David. "The Ibero-American Frontier Mission in Native American History." In *The New Latin American Mission History*, edited by Erick Langer and Robert H. Jackson, 1–46. Lincoln: University of Nebraska Press, 1995.

Thompson, Joseph A. *El Gran Capitán: José De la Guerra*. Los Angeles: Franciscan Fathers of California, 1961.

Tinker-Salas, Miguel. *In the Shadow of the Eagle: Sonora and the Transformation of the Border During the Porfiriato*. Berkeley: University of California Press, 1997.

Torres-Rouff, David. *Before L.A.: Race, Space, and Municipal Power in Los Angeles, 1781–1894*. New Haven, Conn.: Yale University Press, 2013.

Trexler, Richard C. *Sex and Conquest: Gendered Violence, Political Order, and the European Conquest of the Americas*. Ithaca, N.Y.: Cornell University Press, 1995.

Truman, Benjamin C. *Semi-tropical California: Its Climate, Healthfulness, Productiveness, and Scenery*. San Francisco: Bancroft, 1874.

Turner, Frederick Jackson. "The Significance of the Frontier in American History." *Annual Report of the American Historical Association for the Year 1893* (pp. 199–227). Washington, D.C.: Government Printing Office and American Historical Association, 1894.

Valerio-Jimenez, Omar. *River of Hope: Forging Identity and Nation in the Rio Grande Borderlands*. Durham: Duke University Press, 2013.

Van Deusen, Nancy. *Between the Sacred and the Worldly: The Institutional and Cultural Practice of Recogimiento in Colonial Lima*. Stanford, Calif.: Stanford University Press, 2001.

Venegas, Yolanda. "The Erotics of Racialization: Gender and Sexuality in the Making of California," *Frontiers: A Journal of Women's Studies* 25, no. 3 (2004): 63–89.

Veyna, Angelina. "'It Is My Last Wish That . . .': A Look at Colonial Nuevo Mexicanas Through their Testaments." In *Building with Our Hands: New Directions in Chicana History*, edited by Adela de la Torre and Beatríz Pesquera, 91–108. Berkeley: University of California Press, 1990.

Voss, Barbara L. "A Land of Ethnogenesis: Material Culture, Power, and Identity." In *Contemporary Issues in California Archaeology*, edited by Terry L. Jones and Jennifer E. Perry, 303–18. Walnut Creek, Calif.: Left Coast Press, 2012.

———. "From Casta to Californio: Social Identity and the Archaeology of Culture Contact." *American Anthropologist* 107, no. 3 (2005): 461–74.

Wallace, Edith. "Sexual Status and Role Differences." In *Handbook of North American Indians*, edited by William Sturtevant, vol. 8, *California*, edited by Robert F. Heizer, 683–89. Washington, D.C.: Smithsonian Press, 1978.

Weber, David J. *Bárbaros: Spaniards and Their Savages in the Age of Enlightenment*. New Haven, Conn.: Yale University Press, 2005.

———. *The Mexican Frontier, 1821–1846: The American Southwest Under Mexico*. Albuquerque: University of New Mexico Press, 1982.

———. *The Spanish Frontier in North America*. New Haven, Conn.: Yale University Press, 1992.

———. *The Taos Trappers: The Fur Trade in the Far Southwest, 1540–1846*. Norman: University of Oklahoma Press, 1971.

Welch, Rosanna. *A Brief History of the Tongva Tribe: The Native Inhabitants of the Lands of the Puente Hills Reserve*. Claremont, Calif.: Claremont Graduate University, 2006.

White, Hayden V. *Metahistory. The Historical Imagination in Nineteenth-Century Europe*. Baltimore: Johns Hopkins University Press, 1973.

White, Richard. *"It's Your Misfortune and None of My Own": A History of the American West*. Norman: University of Oklahoma Press, 1991.

Whitehead, Roy E. *Lugo: A Chronicle of Early California*. San Bernardino, Calif.: San Bernardino Museum Association, 1978.

Wicker, Elmus. *Banking Panics of the Gilded Age*. Cambridge, UK: Cambridge University Press, 2000.

Wilson, Iris. *William Wolfskill 1796–1866: Frontier Trapper to California Rancher*. Glendale, Calif.: Clark,1965.

Wood, John Windell. *Pasadena, California, Historical and Personal; A Complete History of the Organization of the Indiana Colony, Its Establishment on the Rancho San Pascual and Its Evolution into the City of Pasadena. Including a Brief Story of San Gabriel Mission*. Pasadena, Calif.: Wood, 1917.

Wood, William. "The Trajectory of Indian Country in California: Rancherias, Villages, Pueblos, Missions, Ranchos, Reservations, Colonies, and Rancherias." *Tulsa Law Review* 44, no. 317 (2013): 321–22.

Worster, Donald. *Rivers of Empire: Water, Aridity, and the Growth of the American West*. New York: Pantheon Books, 1985.

Wright, Doris M. *A Yankee in Mexican California: Abel Stearns, 1798–1848*. Santa Barbara, Calif.: Hebberd, 1977.

INDEX

ABOUT THE AUTHOR

Yvette J. Saavedra is an assistant professor of history at California State University San Bernardino.